The Treatment of Schizophrenia – Status and Emerging Trends

Hans D. Brenner
Wolfgang Böker
Ruth Genner
(Editors)

# The Treatment of Schizophrenia –
# Status and Emerging Trends

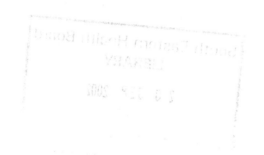

Hogrefe & Huber Publishers
Seattle · Toronto · Göttingen · Bern

**Library of Congress Cataloging-in-Publication Data**

The treatment of schizophrenia : status and emerging trends / Hans Dieter Brenner, Wolfgang Böker, and Ruth Genner.
  p. cm.
  Includes bibliographical references and index.
  ISBN 0-88937-195-4
  1. Schizophrenia – Treatment. I. Brenner, H. D. (Hans D.). II. Böker, W. (Wolfgang). III. Genner, Ruth, 1951–
  RC514.T6935 2001      616.89'8206–dc21      00-039544

**Canadian Cataloging in Publication Data**

Main entry under title:
The treatment of schizophrenia : status and emerging trends
Papers presented at the Vth International Schizophrenia Symposium held in Bern, Switzerland, June 5–7, 1997.
Includes bibliographical references and index.
ISBN 0-88937-195-4

  1. Schizophrenia – Treatment – Congresses. I. Brenner, H. D. 1943–  . II. Böker, Wolfgang, 1933–  .
  III. Genner, Ruth, 1951–  . IV. International Schizophrenia Symposium (5th : 1997 : Bern, Switzerland.
  RC514.T734 2001      616.89'8206      C00-930956-X

Cover illustration "Stadtplan von Bern : Nidek-Bruk" by Adolf Wölfli (1864–1930) © Adolf-Wölfli-Stiftung, Art Museum, Bern, Switzerland

Copyright © 2001 by Hogrefe & Huber Publishers d, Kilkenny
Lacken,

USA:              P.O. Box 2487, Kirkland, WA 98083-2487
                  Phone (425) 820-1500, Fax (425) 823-8324
CANADA:           12 Bruce Park Avenue, Toronto, Ontario M4P 2S3
                  Phone (416) 482-6339
SWITZERLAND:      Länggass-Strasse 76, CH-3000 Bern 9
                  Phone (031) 300-4500, Fax (031) 300 4590
GERMANY:          Rohnsweg 25, D-37085 Göttingen
                  Phone (0551) 496090, Fax (0551) 4960988

Printed in Germany
ISBN 0-88937-195-4
Hogrefe & Huber Publishers, Seattle · Toronto · Bern · Göttingen

# Contents

# Psychological and Psychosocial Therapies

# Community Mental Health Services

# Preface

The present reader – a compendium of contributions to the V International Schizophrenia Symposium Bern held in 1997 – has been produced in traditional collaboration with Hogrefe & Huber Publishers. This edition of the reader enlarges upon integrative therapy approaches in schizophrenia, which was the topic of the reader for the IV Symposium published in 1997 (H.D. Brenner, W. Böker, R. Genner (Eds.), *Towards a Comprehensive Therapy for Schizophrenia*, Hogrefe & Huber Publishers 1997). The contributions are structured into four thematic sections focusing on the state-of-the-art in research and current trends in the development of innovative therapy approaches in schizophrenia. First, findings from the field of neurobiological research and the effectiveness of a new generation of antipsychotic drugs are presented; this section is followed by several outlines of psychological and psychosocial therapy formats, and finally by progress reports on recent developments from the fields of both community psychiatry and mental health care research.

We extend our sincere thanks to the authors, not least for their acceding to the publisher's constructive revisions. The English translations were organized by the individual contributors.

Ruth Genner was in charge of compiling and editing the reader. In this, she was able to call upon the expert knowledge of Professor Hugh Freeman in regard to quality of the translations. Christine Haas transcribed the manuscripts with skill and commitment. We are grateful to all those who, in one form or other, contributed to the publication of this reader.

Bern, Spring 2000

W. Böker                                                                    H.D. Brenner

# Contributors

Andres, Karl, PhD, *University Psychiatric Services Bern, UPD, Bolligenstrasse 111, CH-3000 Bern 60, Switzerland*

Blair, Karen E., MS, *Community & Rehabilitative Psychiatry (116AR), West Los Angeles VA Medical Center, 11301 Wilshire Blvd, Los Angeles, CA 90073, USA*

Brenner, Hans Dieter, MD, PhD, *University Psychiatric Services Bern, UPD, Laupenstrasse 49, CH-3010 Bern, Switzerland*

Chisholm, Daniel, PhD, *Center for the Economics of Mental Health, Institute of Psychiatry, 7, Windsor Walk, London SE5 8BB, UK*

Drake, Robert E., PhD, *New Hampshire-Dartmouth Psychiatric Research Center, 2 Whipple Place, Lebanon, NH 03755, USA*

Eggers, Christian, MD, *Rheinische Kliniken Essen, Postfach 103043, D-45030 Essen, Germany*

Fleming, Shelley, PhD, *University of Nebraska, Lincoln, 209 Burnett Hall, Lincoln, NB 68588-0308, USA*

Freeman, Hugh, MD, *21, Montagu Square, London W1H 1RE, UK*

Glynn, Shirley M., PhD, *Community & Rehabilitative Psychiatry (116AR), West Los Angeles VA Medical Center, 11301 Wilshire Blvd, Los Angeles, CA 90073, USA*

Hallam, Angela, PhD, *Center for the Economics of Mental Health, Institute of Psychiatry, 7, Windsor Walk, London SE5 8BB, UK*

Henn, Fritz A., MD, *Zentralinstitut für Seelische Gesundheit, J5, D-68159 Mannheim, Germany*

Hodel, Bettina, PhD, *University Psychiatric Services Bern, UPD, Laupenstrasse 49, CH-3010 Bern, Switzerland*

Hoffmann, Holger, *University Psychiatric Services Bern, UPD, Laupenstrasse 49, CH-3010 Bern, Switzerland*

Kunz, Barbara, MA, *University Psychiatric Services Bern, UPD, Laupenstrasse 49, CH-3010 Bern, Switzerland*

Kupper, Zeno, PhD, *University Psychiatric Services Bern, UPD, Laupenstrasse 49, CH-3010 Bern, Switzerland*

Liberman, Robert Paul, MD, *Community & Rehabilitative Psychiatry (116AR), West Los Angeles VA Medical Center, 11301 Wilshire Blvd, Los Angeles, CA 90073, USA*

Lockwood, Austin, RMN, *University of Manchester, Academic Unit, Royal Preston Hospital, Sharoe Green Lane, Fulwood, Preston, PR2 4HAT, UK*

Marder, Stephen R., MD, *Community & Rehabilitative Psychiatry (116AR), West Los Angeles VA Medical Center, 11301 Wilshire Blvd, Los Angeles, CA 90073, USA*

Marshall, Max, MD, *University of Manchester, Academic Unit, Royal Preston Hospital, Sharoe Green Lane, Fulwood, Preston, PR24HAT, UK*

McGurk, Susan R., PhD, *Vanderbilt University Medical Center, Department of Psychiatry, 1601 23rd Avenue South, Suite 306, Nashville, TN 37212, USA*

McHugo, Gregory J., PhD, *New Hampshire-Dartmouth Psychiatric Research Center, 2 Whipple Place, Lebanon, NH 03755, USA*

Meltzer, Herbert Y., MD, *Vanderbilt University Medical Center, Department of Psychiatry, 1601 23rd Avenue South, Suite 306, Nashville, TN 37212, USA*

Merlo, Marco C. G., MD, *HUG Département de psychiatrie, Belle-Idée, Clinique de psychiatrie adulte I, Chemin du Petit-Bel 2, CH-1225 Chêne-Bourg, Switzerland*

Möller, Hans-Jürgen, MD, *Psychiatric Hospital of the Ludwig-Maximilian-University Munich, Nussbaumstrasse 7, D-80336 Munich, Germany*

Mueser, Kim T., PhD, *New Hampshire-Dartmouth Psychiatric Research Center, 2 Whipple Place, Lebanon, NH 03755, USA*

Nil, Rico, PhD, *Lundbeck (Switzerland) AG, Postfach, CH-8152 Opfikon, Switzerland*

Pfammatter, Mario, MA, *University Psychiatric Services Bern, UPD, Laupenstrasse 49, CH-3010 Bern, Switzerland*

Reed, Dorie, PhD, *University of Nebraska, Lincoln, 209 Burnett Hall, Lincoln, NB 68588-0308, USA*

Riecher-Rössler, Anita, MD, *Psychiatric University Hospital, Sector West and Central Socialpsychiatric Services, Militärstrasse 8, P.O. Box 1930, CH-8021 Zürich, Switzerland*

Roder, V., PhD, *University Psychiatric Services Bern, UPD, Bolligenstrasse 111, CH-3000 Bern 60, Switzerland*

Rössler, Wulf, MD, PhD, *Psychiatric University Hospital, Sector West and Central Socialpsychiatric Services, Militärstrasse 8, P.O. Box 1930, CH-8021 Zürich, Switzerland*

Schöttke, H., PhD, *University of Osnabrück, FB8, D-49069 Osnabrück, Germany*

Sheitman, Brian, MD, *The University of North Carolina, Clinical Research Unit, Dorothea Dix Hospital, CB#7160, School of Medicine, Chapel Hill, NC 27599-7168, USA*

Spaulding, William D., PhD, *University of Nebraska, Lincoln, 209 Burnett Hall, Lincoln, NB 68588-0308, USA*

Sullivan, Mary, PhD, *University of Nebraska, Lincoln, 209 Burnett Hall, Lincoln, NB 68588-0308, USA*

Wehnert, A., PhD, *Lundbeck (Switzerland) AG, Postfach, CH-8152 Opfikon, Switzerland*

Wiedl, Karl Heinz, PhD, *University of Osnabrück, FB8, D-49069 Osnabrück, Germany*

Wienöbst, J., PhD, *University of Osnabrück, FB8, D-49069 Osnabrück, Germany*

Wirshing, Donna Ames, MD, *Community & Rehabilitative Psychiatry (116AR), West Los Angeles VA Medical Center, 11301 Wilshire Blvd, Los Angeles, CA 90073, USA*

Wirshing, William, MD, *Community & Rehabilitative Psychiatry (116AR), West Los Angeles VA Medical Center, 11301 Wilshire Blvd, Los Angeles, CA 90073, USA*

# Neurobiological Basis for the Treatment of Schizophrenia

# Possible Neurochemical Causes for Structural Changes in Schizophrenia

Fritz A. Henn

To begin to put together a comprehensive neurobiology of schizophrenia, we need to know, first, what precisely is schizophrenia? What are the boundaries of the disorder; is it a family of disorders or a single illness, and are we looking for general etiological principles or a common pathophysiology for a symptom complex? Second, what are the anatomical bases for the symptoms; in other words, where do we look to find the biological basis of this problem? Third, how is the neurobiology altered at a cellular and molecular level to produce this disease picture? When the problem is outlined in this fashion, it becomes clear that a complete statement about the neurobiology of schizophrenia is not yet possible. However, the last 30 years have led to an increasingly more focused understanding of this problem.

## What is Schizophrenia?

There is still no consensus, even 85 years after Eugen Bleuler (1911) first coined the term, as to what schizophrenia is. Using the Kraepelinian systematic classification of psychosis, Bleuler redefined the disorder as "schizophrenia" from the Greek words referring to splitting of the mind. He described the four fundamental symptoms as – ambivalence, disturbed association of thoughts, inappropriate affect, and a preference of fantasy over reality. These symptoms suggested a splitting of the normally integrated functions that co-ordinate thought and affect. In this formulation, psychotic symptoms such as hallucination and delusions were not distinguishing features of the disorder, since they were felt to be more widely seen in psychiatric conditions. Bleuler clearly felt that this was a group of disorders rather than a single disease state, and this view is consistent with that held by a majority of researchers in the field today. This paper will describe the elements of a common pathophysiological mechanism, including a mechanism for the production of psychotic symptoms. It will also aim to describe conditions which result in thought disorder, asocial or socially isolated behavior, ambivalence, and blunted or inappropriate affect. It is unlikely that such a mechanism will be present in all cases currently classified as schizophrenia, but it may play a role in three more chronic cases in which continual cell loss appears to play a role. This description cannot yet lead to the etiological roots of the disorder, it will aim to highlight those brain areas and functions which are disrupted to produce the symptom picture long felt to be characteristic of schizophrenia.

## Anatomical Basis

The first approach to the attempt to build a neurobiology of schizophrenia is to ask: "Where is the anatomical basis of the symptom complex seen in schizophrenia?" Initially, since classic neuropathological studies revealed little, the term *functional psychosis* was coined and psychological explanations were given a central role in explaining symptom formation. However, the advent of modern high-resolution imaging of the brain through CAT scans, a renewed interest in the anatomy of schizophrenia took place. Beginning with the landmark study of Johnstone, Crow et al. in 1976 which reported enlarged cerebral ventricles in schizophrenic patients, a great deal of work has been done using this technique. In addition, modern neuropathological studies of post mortem samples of schizophrenic brain have been carried out, as well as a variety of functional imaging techniques, which have recently taken advantage of the selective activation of specific brain regions. These studies have led to a possible anatomical circuit underlying schizophrenic symptoms.

The studies show that on average schizophrenic patients have a larger ventricular volume than normal control populations; this involves about 30% of schizophrenic patients having ventricles outside the range seen in normal controls. Though the question is raised whether this finding is due to treatment, studies of unmedicated first break patients suggest that it is not. Another question is whether the patients with enlarged ventricles represent a subgroup with a structural defect? This also appears not to be so, since an analysis of over 1000 cases reveals a clear unimodal distribution, with no tendency toward a bimodal distribution (Zigun et al. 1992). In addition, a study of discordant monozygotic twins by Goldberg et al. (1994), using very accurate MRI measurements of ventricular size, revealed that in every case, the sick twins have larger ventricles, i.e., less brain mass, than the well twins. In this case, both genetics and the environmental stimulation were totally controlled, and the likely conclusion is that the illness is in some way associated with a reduced brain mass.

Subsequent imaging studies using MRI techniques, which provide much higher resolution, then CAT scans confirmed their data and in addition, have led to the following suggestions: First, that the brain mass appears to be reduced principally in the mesial termporal cortex and rostral hippocampal areas, and second, that there is a tendency in some studies for greater loss to be seen on the left side of the brain.

Post mortem studies have also tended to confirm the impression of cell loss in schizophrenia. In a variety of studies following work by Bogarts (1989) and his co-workers, volumetric assessments of the temporal cortex, hippocampal region, and various periventricular nuclei have found smaller structures in schizophrenic brains, compared to normal controls. To see if cells changed size in schizophrenic brains or if there are fewer cells, several groups have undertaken cell counts. In particular, Beckman (1995) and his group have reported cell counts of the basal ganglia which reveal fewer cells in the brains of schizophrenics, and Pakkenberg (1987), in a study of the thalamus, found a surprisingly large reduction in the number of cells in the medialdorsal thalamic nucleus. This nucleus serves as a relay station between the limbic system, frontal cortex and triato-pallido system, suggesting a connection between the basal ganglion findings and the thalamic findings in one circuit.

In attempting to go beyond cell counts and volumetric measurements, cytoarchitectural studies have been carried out. Recent studies, using functional MRI have confirmed functional loss in frontal dorsolateral cortex and thalamus in unmedicated schizophrenics (Braus et al., 1998). In an important series of studies Andreasen et al. (1994) have convincingly documented that thalamic volumes are reduced in schizophrenic patients. This suggests that in addition to the cortical and limbic regions, the thalamus may be the site of functional problems in schizophrenia. Two sets of cytoarchitectural studies are of particular interest. The first, by Benes et al. (1991) showed consistently fewer small interneurons in specific cortical layers of the frontal cortex. These interneurons are presumably GABAergic and their reduction again suggests cortical disorganization, as well as perhaps pointing to developmental errors leading to pathological alterations underlying schizophrenic symptoms. Akbarian et al. (1993) have reported analogous defects among NADPH-diaphorase containing neurons. They found fewer in specific cortical layers of post mortem brain, but increased numbers in deeper white matter layers. This also suggests a neurodevelopmental defect, with incomplete cell migration.

One type of study that has become possible recently has allowed a sharper focus to develop concerning the possible anatomical areas involved in schizophrenia. This involves functional imaging. Using either positron emission tomography, SPECT, or functional MRI, it is possible to visualize those brain areas which are activated by specific tasks, as well as in a resting state. Initial

5

studies suggested that in a resting state, there was less activity in the frontal portion of the brain (Bartlett et al. 1991). However, this finding was not always reproduced, and an advance was made by using specific tasks to activate brain regions. In particular Weinberger et al. (1986) reported that using the Wisconsin Card Sorting Test, schizophrenic patients showed less activation of the dorsofrontal cortex, using SPECT to assess regional blood flow. The central problems of schizophrenia, as initially defined by Bleuler, included inappropriate affect, thought disorder characterized by an inability to carry out tasks involving executive memory. It is now known from a variety of basic studies that limbic structures in the temporal lobe are involved in regulating affective tone, rendering it appropriate to sensory input, and that the frontal neocortex is involved in handling executive memory function and in associating elements of a sensory experience. The data reviewed suggest that both of these broad anatomical areas are disturbed in schizophrenia. In addition, it is clear that information is relayed from one area to another through the thalamus, which is clearly another site of altered anatomy and disturbed function in schizophrenia. These data suggest that there may not be a discrete lesion in schizophrenia, but that there might be widespread functional disorganization.

In a recent study our group decided to look at a simple activation task using PET, but not to focus on a region of interest but to analyze activity throughout the whole brain during the task. The reason was to see if there might be a generalized defect in processing information which would help to understand both symptom formation in schizophrenia and where major functional defects originate. The task we chose was very simple and easily reproduced, tapping the thumb of the right hand against the index finger. The circuit for this movement is well established and at a cortical level one expects to see activation in the left motor strip laterally in the hand region. Indeed we found this, and schizophrenic patients showed less activation of this region. However, when we analyzed the whole brain to our surprise schizophrenic patients had higher levels of total activation and did not lateralize the response, they also activated the right side of the brain (Guenther, 1994). This result appears to be general as Liddle (1987) reports similar results using auditory input as opposed to a motor task. This suggests that a basic defect could be the gating of information presumably at the level of the thalamus.

In summary then, current information suggests that there could be widespread deficits in schizophrenic brains, possibly due to a developmental defect which involves a circuit between cortex – striato pallidum – thalamus and limbic system. Functional neuroanatomical studies suggest that there are connections between these structures, with the thalamic nuclei playing a mediating role. Recent data suggest that the filtering or gating processes normally thought to take place at a thalamic level are not functioning and that cortical

regions are becoming inappropriately stimulated, leading to schizophrenic symptoms.

The idea that schizophrenia could result from a developmental defect which normally does not become evident until after puberty has been proposed repeatedly in recent years. Feinberg (1982) hypothesized that symptoms developed due to a defect in programmed synaptic elimination after puberty. There have also been many responds of potential developmental problems seen in children at risk for schizophrenia. In a novel study, Walker and Lewine (1990) used home movies to view children who subsequently developed schizophrenia. Using blinded rates, they were able to pick out children with problems in dexterity, gait, and gross motor functions, which allowed identification of the child who would develop schizophrenia before the age of six in every case. This suggests that pathology is already present in the motor system at the earliest stages, but that it is more subtle than the more florid later signs. Longitudinal studies by Häfner et al. (1992, 1995) suggest that in most cases a diagnosis is not made until the first psychotic break, and that a long prodromal period precedes this event.


## Neurochemical Effects

Considering what type of neurochemical effects mediate these anatomically dispersed functions, initial ideas came primarily from pharmacology, and gave rise to the dopamine (DA) hypothesis of schizophrenia. This heuristic proposal arose from the action of neuroleptics in blocking DA receptors together with the effects of overstimulating DA receptors with toxins such as amphetamine. In general, it is now appreciated that dopamine may play a central role in psychotic symptom formation, but that it may not be directly involved in symptoms such as inappropriate affect, asocial behavior, or ambivalence. Therefore, the theory may be reformulated as "the dopamine theory of psychosis" which, while playing a role in schizophrenia, is not the core of the problem (Henn, 1982). This becomes clear when we consider either psychotic depression or psychotic symptoms in mania. In both cases the symptoms respond to neuroleptics with dopamine blocking ability suggesting psychosis per se is vulnerable to dopamine blockade. On the other hand, chronic schizophrenic patients with poverty of speech, anhedonia and lack of motivation show essentially no improvement in these symptoms when treated with classic $D_2$ dopamine blocking medications such as haloperidol.

Subsequent to the formulation of the DA hypothesis, it was discovered that there are multiple DA receptors. Cloning technology has revealed six forms to date, from D to $D_5$, with the central $D_2$ receptor having two forms $D_{2A}$ and $D_{2B}$. The $D_2$, $D_3$, and $D_4$ receptor types constitute one family, and it is not yet clear what role each component plays in the production of psychotic symptoms (Civelli, 1994). In general, it is currently felt that the low-level DA seen in the prefrontal cortex plays a role in regulating subcortical or striatal DA. It is also suggested that prefrontal DA may play a role in reacting to stress, modulating working memory, and in modulating negative symptoms, whilst subcortical DA appears to play a role in positive symptom formation, perhaps directly through its inhibitory effect on thalamic circuits. However, the evidence that DA hyperactivity in subcortical systems is directly responsible for hallucinations and delusions is far from clear. Some, but not all imaging studies suggest increased DA receptor density, and studies of dopamine metabolites are also inconsistent (Kim et al., 1980).

The action of the atypical antipsychotic clozapine on DA systems is relatively specific for the A10 region, suggesting that this area may be particularly involved in symptom formation. This compound, because of its increased efficacy and relatively low antagonism at the $D_2$ site, has provoked studies of other transmitter systems in schizophrenia. Since clozapine interacts with 5HT receptors, increasing interest has been devoted to the role of 5HT in schizophrenia. What is clear is that DA and 5HT are inter-related and that in many ways, 5HT modulates DA activity. It is also clear that many atypical antipsychotics have a high affinity for the 5HT2A receptor — one of 14 5HT receptors identified to date (Meltzer & Lowy, 1987). While it is established that 5HT systems are involved in DA regulation and are altered in a variety of CNS conditions, no compelling evidence suggests a primary role for 5HT in either schizophrenia or psychosis.

A new candidate has emerged in the last few years for the role of major transmitter in the production of schizophrenic symptoms. This is glutamate, first proposed by Kim et al. (1980) in a study of glutamate levels, which was not replicated in two subsequent studies (Gattaz et al., 1982; Perry, 1982). However, the role of glutamate in schizophrenia emerged in the last few years due to two developments. First, the role of NMDA receptor antagonists such as PCP in causing psychosis (Heresco-Levy et al., 1993) and second, a long series of studies begun by Olney et al. (1995) describing the excito-toxic effects of excess glutaminergic activity. These workers have demonstrated that excess glutamate can kill neurons, without significant gliotic reactions. They have gone on to show that in animals, the cerebrocortical neurotoxicity of NMDA antagonists results, due to a shutdown of inhibitory GABA input to posterior cingulate and retrosplenial neurons, leading to excessive excitatory input and then cell injury and death. This phenomenon only occurs in the early adult stage in animals; at younger ages, the neurons appear not to be damaged by

increased excitatory activity. Thus, this hypothesis accounts for the age of onset of psychosis, since destruction of these cells results in hypoactive NMDA activity, while low NMDA activity results in psychosis, as seen in the effects of toxins such as PCP. This scheme can also involve DA overactivity, which can inhibit the glutamate input to the GABA interneurons, which control the excitatory input to the posterior cingulate neurons. Thus, these schemes incorporate the DA hypothesis, as well as the finding of Benes et al. (1991) that GABA cells are lost, and suggest that treatment-responsive patients could have a primary DA problem. On the other hand, causes of excessive excitatory input to the posterior cingulate neurons would result in symptoms not responsive to DA antagonists.

This view of schizophrenia suggests that a toxic reaction which takes place in early adulthood triggers the schizophrenic process; it predicts that cells actually die during this process, establishing the chronicity of the disease state. This hypothesis fits into the anatomical circuit that was hypothesized involving the striato-pallido-thalamic-cortical loop, since glutamate from cortical afference is known to act on GABA interneurons in this circuit. It also provides some testable hypotheses, which should result in future advances in our understanding of schizophrenia.

# References

Akbarian, S., Vinuela, A., Kim, J. J., et al. (1993) Distorted distribution of nicotinamide-adenine dinucleotide phosphate-diaphorase neurons in temporal lobe of schizophrenics implies anomalous cortical development. *Archives of General Psychiatry,* **50**, 178–187.
Andreasen, N. C., Arndt, S., Swayze, V., et al. (1994) Thalamic abnormalities in schizophrenia visualized through magnetic resonance image averaging. *Science,* **266**, 294–298.
Bartlett, E. J., Barouche, F., Brodie, J. D., et al. (1991) Stability of resting deoxiglucose metaolic values in PET studies of schizophrenia. *Psychiatry Research,* **40**, 11–20.
Benes, F. M., McSparren, J., San-Giovanni, J. P. & Vincent, S. L. (1991) Deficits in small interneurons in cingulate cortex of schizophrenic and schizoaffective patients. *Archives of General Psychiatry,* **48**, 996–1001.
Bleuler, E. (1911) Dementia praecox oder die Gruppe der Schizophrenien. In *Handbuch der Psychiatrie. Spezieller Teil, 4. Abt., 1. Hälfte.* (Ed. Aschaffenburg, G.). Leipzig: Deuticke.
Bogerts, B. (1989) Limbic and paralimbic pathology in schizophrenia: Interaction with age and stress related factors. In *Schizophrenia: Scientific Progress.* (Eds. Schulz, S. C. & Tammiga, C.A.), pp. 216–226 New York: Oxford University Press.
Braus, D. F., Ende, G., Weber-Fahr, W., et al. (1998) *Altered Prefrontal Function in Medication-naive First Episode Schizophrenic Patients; an MRI study.* Proc. ISMRM, p. 501.
Civelli, O. (1994) Molecular biology of dopamine receptor subtypes. In *Psychopharmacology – the Fourth Generation of Progress.* (Eds. Bloom, F. E. & Kupfer, D. J.), pp. 155–162. New York: Raven Press.

DeLisi, L. E., Hoff, A. L., Schwartz, J. E., et al. (1991) Brain morphology in first episode schizophrenic-like psychotic patients: A quantitative MRI study. *Biological Psychiatry,* **29**, 159–175.

Feinberg, I. (1982) Schizophrenia: Caused by a fault in programmed synaptic elimination during adolescence. *Journal of Psychiatric Research,* **17**, 319–334.

Gattaz, W. F., Gattaz, D. & Beckmann, H. (1982) Glutamate in schizophrenics and healthy controls. *Arch. Psychiatr. Nervenkr.,* **231**, 221–225.

Goldberg, T. E., Torrey, E. F., Berman, K. B. & Weinberger, D. R. (1994) Relations between neurophysiological performance and brain morphological and physiological measures in monozygotic twins discordant for schizophrenia: Use of an interpair method. *Psych. Res. Neuroimaging,* **55**, 51–61.

Guenther, W., Brodie, J. D., Bartlett, E. J., et al. (1994) Diminished cerebral metabolic response to motor stimulation in schizophrenics: A PET study. *European Archives of Psychiatry & Clinical Neurosciences,* **244**, 115–125.

Häfner, H. & Nowotny, B. (1995) Epidemiology of early-onset schizophrenia. *European Archives of Psychiatry & Clinical Neurosciences,* **245**, 80–92.

Häfner. H., Riecher-Rössler, A., Maurer, K., et al. (1992) First onset and early symptomatology of schizophrenia. A chapter of epidemiological and neurobiological research into age and sex differences. *European Archives of Psychiatry & Clinical Neurosciences,* **242**, 109–118.

Henn, F. A. (1982) Dopamine: A role in psychosis or schizophrenia. In *Schizophrenia as a Brain Disease.* (Eds. Henn, F. A. & Nasrallah, H. A.), pp. 176–195. New York: Oxford University Press.

Heresco-Levy, U., Javitt, D. C. & Zukin, S. R. (1993) The PCP/NMDA model of schizophrenia: Theoretical and clinical implications. *Psychiatric Annals,* **23**, 135–143.

Johnstone, E. C., Crow, T. J., Frith, C. D., et al. (1976) Cerebral ventricular size and cognitive impairment in chronic schizophrenia. *Lancet,* **2**, 924–926.

Kim, J. S., Kornhuber, H. H., Schmid-Burgk, H. & Holzmuller, B. (1980) Low cerebrospinal fluid glutamate in schizophrenic patients and a new hypothesis of schizophrenia. *Neuroscience Letters,* **20**, 379–382.

Liddle, P. F. (1987) Schizophrenic syndromes, cognitive performance and neurological dysfunction. *Psychological Medicine,* **17**, 49–57.

Meltzer, H. Y. & Lowy, M. T. (1987) The serotonin hypothesis of depression. In *The Third Generation of Progress.* (Ed. Meltzer, H. Y.), pp. 513–526. New York: Raven Press.

Olney, J. W. & Farber, N. B. (1995) Glutamate receptor dysfunction and schizophrenia. *Archives of General Psychiatry* (in press).

Pakkenberg, B. (1987) Post-mortem study of chronic schizophrenic brains. *British Journal of Psychiatry,* **151**, 744–752.

Perry, T. L. (1982) Normal CSF and brain glutamate levels in schizophrenia do not support the hypothesis of glutaminergic neuronal dysfunction. *Neuroscience Letters,* **28**, 81–85.

Walker, E. & Lewine, R. J. (1990) Prediction of adult-onset schizophrenia from childhood home movies of the patients. *American Journal of Psychiatry,* **147**, 1052–1056.

Weinberger, D. R., Berman, K. F. & Zec, R. F. (1986) Physiologic dysfunction of dorsolateralprefrontal cortex in schizophrenia: I. Regional cerebral blood flow evidence. *Archives of General Psychiatry,* **43**, 114–125.

Zigun, J. R., Daniel, D. G., Kleinman, J. E. & Weinberger, D. R. (1992) Ventricular enlargement in schizophrenia: Is there really a gender effect? *Archives of General Psychiatry,* **49**, 995–997.

# A Stimulus Barrier Model of Early Onset Schizophrenia: An Integrative Etiological and Therapeutic Approach

Christian Eggers

## Introduction

What can research on the childhood-onset of schizophrenia contribute to the generation of hypotheses on the etiology of schizophrenia in general? Studies of children with schizophrenia are particularly valuable, as the findings are not confounded by factors such as chronic hospitalization or long-term neuroleptic treatment. Indeed high-risk studies of children with a schizophrenic first-degree relative and of the nature and prevalence of premorbid neurobehavioral anomalies have raised new questions about the maturation of cognitive function in those subjects who eventually later develop schizophrenia (Erlenmeyer-Kimling et al., 1997). Nonetheless, it has to be admitted that we are surprisingly ignorant of the comparative data, of many of the normal stages of psychobiological development, and of the interdependence of factors that give rise to a balanced and mature personality capable of adaptive interactions with the environment (Oades et al., 1996; 1997).

Various authors have suggested that an early age of onset for schizophrenia occurs more often in males and that it is associated with an insidious onset, a preponderance of negative symptoms, and poor premorbid adjustment (Castle & Murray, 1991; O'Connell et al., 1997). Patients with an early onset often show neurodevelopmental disorders and related neuroanatomical impairments (e.g., Walker & DiForio, 1997). However, in our two long-term follow-up studies, we have only been able to confirm these reports in part (Eggers, 1973; Eggers & Bunk 1997; Eggers & Klapal, 1997). A bias towards male subjects was not found in our sample with a very early age of onset (≤ 10 years of age), nor in those with an onset between the ages of 10 and 14 years. Indeed, the

11

number of female subjects in our sample exceeded the number of males and the age of onset of positive psychotic symptoms occurred at an earlier age in the female than in the male patients (see Figure 1).

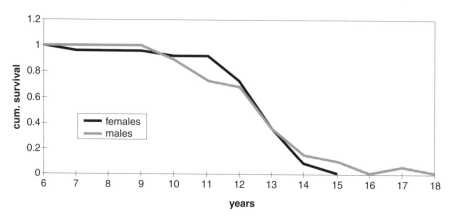

*Figure 1.* Cumulative survival for age at first psychotic symptoms in females (n=25) and males (n=19).

Figure 1 shows a cumulative survival curve for the age at which the first positive psychotic symptoms were noted in 19 male and 25 female patients. The curve illustrates that while males manifested positive psychotic symptoms between the ages of 10 and 18 years, in females they first occurred between the ages of 7 and 15 years. This effect may be attributable to, among several possible factors, the fact that the protective antipsychotic effect of the estrogens does not set in until puberty approaches its peak. This antipsychotic effect may be explained by a neuroleptic-like or neurotrophic effect of the estrogens (Oades & Schepker, 1994) that contributes to the widespread finding of a male predominance for the onset of psychosis in adolescence after puberty has reached its peak. Indeed in contrast to some recent statements (Jablensky & Cole, 1997), it seems quite feasible that the age-related and gender-specific differences in psychosis onset in adolescence can be explained by the opposite neurotrophic effects of the estrogens and androgens on neural pathway development and synaptic pruning (Oades & Schepker, 1994).

Thus, in our sample (loc.cit.), a significant developmental difference emerged for the type of onset. An acute onset predominated in those who developed schizophrenia after the age of 12 years, whereas in those with a very early age of onset the illness developed insidiously. Early symptoms were predominantly negative among those with an insidious course, but positive symptoms prevailed in those with an acute onset of psychosis. Further, the degree of post-psychotic deficit

12

symptoms correlated positively with the age of onset: For example, social disability was much more evident in those with an onset before the age of 12 years than in those with a later onset between 12 and 14 years of age.

More than half the patients in our sample exhibited non-specific behavioral abnormalities that preceded the onset of overt psychotic symptoms. These included: Social withdrawal, increased anxiety, depression, shyness, introversion, suspiciousness, hostility, temper tantrums, aggression, odd beliefs, and magical thinking. Some of these features are consistent with those noted in other longitudinal studies (Fish, 1987). Cognitive and perceptual dysfunctions such as impaired sustained and selective attention, discriminative ability, and an impaired ability to maintain contextual set have also been reported as markers of vulnerability for schizophrenia (McGlashan & Johannessen, 1996).

In a retrospective study, Asarnow et al. (1995) found that during early childhood, most children with schizophrenia showed delays in the acquisition of language as well as impaired or delayed development of visuomotor co-ordination, before the onset of the first psychotic symptoms. It was argued that the developmental delays they recorded in these children represent the comparatively long time required for them to automate certain motor skills. Such a delay in automation may in fact reflect a limited capacity for processing information (Asarnow et al., 1995). A delay in the acquisition of language has also been reported to be a more common feature of patients who became ill before the age of 12 years than in those with a later onset (Alaghband-Rand et al., 1997). This, too, corresponds to one of the preliminary findings from a cohort of 5000 subjects described by Jones et al. (1996).

As yet, there have been few neurobiological studies of early-onset schizophrenia. Nonetheless, there are indications that such patients may have smaller cerebral volumes and reductions in the thalamus, but enlarged parts of the basal ganglia (Frazier, 1996; Alaghband-Rad et al., 1997; Rapoport et al., 1997). A reasonable hypothesis suggests that there could be an association between the severity of the premorbid developmental delay and the degree of insult to or dysfunction in the central nervous system in children with a very early onset of schizophrenia.

## Cognitive Dysfunction

Premorbid cognitive and perceptual dysfunction is also evident in patients who had a very early onset of psychotic symptoms. Consistent with reports from high-risk studies in the literature, Eggers (1991) reported the following dysfunctions of early information processing:

- A difficulty in the structuring of sensory input,
- An over-emphasis on processing irrelevant details, accompanied by a non-hierarchical conceptual organization,
- A poor differentiation between figure and ground, and a tendency to perceive both simultaneously and to rank them equivalently,
- An impaired ability to discriminate between the more and the less important features in a situation.

Adaptive cognitive abilities depend on the ability to prioritize and allocate appropriately the resources for processing significant external and internal stimuli. A precondition for this is the co-ordination and integration of new and unfamiliar sensory input within the existing framework of past experience. The necessary match and mismatch functions involve complex neural interactions both horizontally, for example between neurons in the CA3 part of the hippocampus (Vinogradova, 1975), and vertically in the hierarchical interactions between subcortical and cortical regions. This hierarchy extends initially to the hippocampal-amygdaloid neuronal circuit and further to the integrative interaction between the dorsolateral prefrontal cortex with the striatal-thalamic circuit on the one hand and with the mesolimbic system on the other (Swerdlow & Koob, 1987; Gray et al., 1991; Oades, 1995).

Dysfunction in these brain systems, recognizable in patients' clinical manifestations, is recorded and described neuropsychologically by Magaro (1984) and Hemsley (1987), thus,

- "Schizophrenics are less able to make use of the redundancy and patterning of sensory input to reduce information processing demands" (Hemsley, 1987).
- "Schizophrenics do not maintain a strong conceptual organization of a serial processing strategy ... nor do they organize stimuli extensively relative to others" (Magaro, 1984).

# Gating

The retention of information sets important constraints on how new material is processed. Indeed, even with very rapid information processing, the registration of stimuli in the central nervous system regulates and modifies the processing of the succeeding stimuli. Both longer- and the shorter-term processes are impaired in patients with schizophrenia and in children at high risk for the

illness. A well-documented electrophysiological example of the latter "short-term" effects is provided by the P50 event-related potential. The arrival of stimulus information in the cortices is marked by this inhibitory potential – i.e., processing of potentially irrelevant information is inhibited to allow processing of the new stimulus. The amplitude of the P50, component elicited by this stimulus, can itself be reduced by a stimulus that preceded it by about a tenth of a second. This inhibition of the P50 elicited by the second stimulus may be seen in 85% of presentations for healthy subjects but such "sensory gating" is seen perhaps on only 15% of trials in patients with schizophrenia (e.g., Flach et al., 1996).

Deficits in sensory gating have been experimentally demonstrated from electrical recordings from CA3 neurons in the hippocampus of rats treated with amphetamine – a psychostimulant well-known to be capable of eliciting psychosis in humans (Bickford-Wimer et al., 1990). Early evoked potentials elicited by the second stimulus (e.g., P30) were suppressed by the pre-stimulus but this effect was reduced after the administration of amphetamine. This impairment of sensory gating could be prevented by pre-administration of the antipsychotic dopamine antagonist haloperidol. This provides an elegant confirmation of the earlier results of Vinogradova (1975), whose recording from CA3 neurons pointed to the particular significance of their activity to the generation of orienting and gating responses. The impairment of sensory gating measured by event-related potentials in healthy human subjects under the influence of amphetamine has been the subject of collaborative work from our own laboratory (Kröner et al., 1999).

Data collated by the research team of Freedman and Bickford (e.g., 1994) point to the involvement of cholinergic projections in mediating sensory gating and in particular to the reduced input from the medial septum to the hippocampus. They argue that nicotinic receptors may play an important part, as nicotinic agonists both activate hippocampal receptors and improve sensory gating. Their observation that sensory gating can be transiently improved in patients with schizophrenia after smoking a cigarette or using nicotine chewing gum may underlie the observation that these patients smoke as a form of self-medication, resulting in the administration of less neuroleptic medication (Rodewald et al., 1998).

Following numerous demonstrations in animal studies that agonists of dopamine activity can impair (e.g., apomorphine, amphetamine) and that dopamine antagonists can restore sensory gating (e.g., haloperidol, clozapine), we have been studying the impairment of a form of sensory gating known as prepulse inhibition (PPI) during the treatment course of patients with schizophrenia. Figure 2 illustrates both the impairment of PPI of the P50 response in 15 young patients shortly after admission for their first or second episode and the restoration of this response to near control levels after 2–4 months of neuroleptic treatment. Indeed, there was a close and significant correlation between the improvement of PPI of the P50 response with the decrease of negative symptoms (Bender et al., 1998).

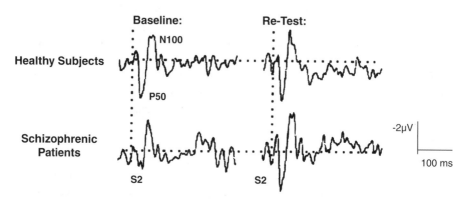

*Figure 2:* Prepulse Inhibition (PPI). ERP difference waves (Cz): no prepulse minus 100 ms prepulse condition.

In this context research findings have to be mentioned which provide strong evidence that stressful life events like maternal deprivation may lead to a severe impairment of propels inhibition which is very similar to PPI deficit seen in schizophrenic patients, and it is interesting that the PPI deficit elicited by a stressful life event can as well be reversed by classical and atypical antipsychotic (Ellenbroek et al. 1998). These important observations supply our psychoneurodevelopmental hypothesis of schizophrenia (see paragraph "stimulus barrier" at the end of this paper).

There is little doubt that children and adults who suffer from schizophrenic psychoses show cognitive deficits that are comparable. Both children and adults with schizophrenia demonstrate the same sorts of difficulties with continuous performance tasks. Such a conclusion is also reflected, for example, by similar changes in both groups of patients of measures of event-related potentials in both early (e.g., N1) and late components (e.g., P3) in situations that are demanding of attentional resources (Strandburg et al., 1990). Furthermore, processing negativity that reflects the facilitation of the attentional trace elicited by a target is: (1) reduced in patients from both age-groups (Strandburg et al., 1994); (2) is lateralized to the right or left depending on whether the patients exhibit active paranoid symptoms and hallucinations or not, respectively (Oades

16

et al., 1994), and; (3) is only weakly expressed in children with a genetic risk for developing schizophrenia (Schreiber et al., 1996). These findings show that in adolescent and adult patients with schizophrenia and in children at risk there are deficiencies in the control and strategic allocation of information processing resources. At the neuropsychological level, children at risk as well as those who manifest schizophrenia, like their adult counterparts, exhibit impairment in blocking out irrelevant information and registering the task-relevant stimulus configurations for adaptive response. Such deficiencies can be regarded as integral to the information-processing disorder of children and adults with schizophrenia or at risk for schizophrenia alike.

## Neocortical-Subcortical Imbalance

It is conceivable – and there are a host of behavioral-biological and neuroanatomical findings in support of this (e.g., lesion and electrical stimulation studies in the area of the hippocampus and the amygdala in primates) – that structural or functional damage in the subcortical area, especially the mesolimbic, striatal and hypothalamic-thalamic structures, can be considered responsible for the perception and cognitive processing dysfunction mentioned here at the beginning (e.g., the poor differentiation between figure and background, where the hippocampus and the amygdala represent the neural substrate). By means of the neural connections of these subcortical structures and the mesolimbic system, in particular with the different areas of the heteromodal association neocortex, their influence on neocortical executive function is explained. This includes their influence on the active short-term memory ("working memory"), which is linked to the normal activity of the dopaminergic memory field neurons in the dorsolateral prefrontal cortex (DLPFC). Thus, the influence of emotions like fear (limbic system) on neocortically controlled executive functions, for example, can be understood.

The extent to which the inter-fronto-thalamo-temporal function disturbance forms a basis for prenatal structural changes, remains an open question. Akbarian et al. (1993 a, b) described an abnormal distribution of NADPH-containing neurons in the gray and white matter, in the temporal as well as in the frontal regions, possibly as a consequence of aberrant migration of neurons during the prenatal period. On the whole, this supports the hypothesis of a disturbance of neural development. Other cytoarchitectural studies have also hinted at a reduction in neurons in the mediodorsal thalamus, as well as some neuronal disorganization in the hippocampus and a reduction of GABAergic corticocortical interneurons (Henn, 1995). In addition to this, the neuropathological studies of Benes et al. (1986, 1994) have demonstrated in schizophrenics a neuronal loss in the area of the prefrontal cortex, which supports the hypothesis of an anatomical and functional limitation of corticofugal and especially cortico-limbic pathways.

The important regions for schizophrenia in the heteromodal association neocortex are the *dorsolateral prefrontal cortex* (DLPFC), the superior temporal gyrus, the inferior parietal lobe, the planum temporale, and Broca's area. In patients with schizophrenia, structural or functional changes have been found in these areas. (For details see Ross & Pearlson 1996).

Dysfunctions in the different parts of the heteromodal association neocortex, in particular the DLPFC, are evident in the impairment of hypothesis development and in the establishment as well as maintenance of hierarchical structured stimulus response configurations. These problems are illustrated by the performance of both schizophrenic children and adults with schizophrenia in the Wisconsin card sorting test, Tower of London test or the CPT.

In schizophrenia, particular etiological significance is ascribed to the neuroanatomical connection between limbic structures and the DLPFC, in which myelination continues to develop through the second and third decades of life (Yakovlev & Le Cours, 1964). Post-mortem examinations have also shown that mesolimbic dopaminergic receptor activity is highest during these decades (McGeer & McGeer, 1981; Bzowej & Seeman, 1985). It is therefore understandable that damage to this region in early childhood remains more or less latent, but later could lead to clinically manifest symptoms, such as first-rank and second-order symptoms, as defined by K. Schneider. The detection of early childhood lesions could contribute to a better understanding of anomalies of premorbid behavior, particularly in the domains of communication, social competence, and prodromal cognitive dysfunction which precede a full-blown schizophrenic psychosis in the second or third decade of life. Just such a functional anatomical explanation for the importance of developmental age for the emergence of psychopathological symptoms is to be found in behavioral-physiological experiments on primates with lesions in the area of the DLPFC. The animals demonstrated unremarkable behavior up until puberty and adolescence, and were able to master delayed response tasks – accomplishments which proved impossible in adulthood (Goldman & Alexander, 1977; Tucker & King, 1967; Goldman, 1967). These observations are in line with the findings supported by Ellenbroek et al. (1998) cited above, i.e., that the effects on prepulse inhibition seen in rats after maternal deprivation did not occur until after puberty.

# Stimulus Barrier

MRI findings in monozygotic twins provide an important neurobiological argument for a dysfunction in cortico-subcortical interactions, implicating impaired mesolimbic as well as frontal function (Weinberger et al., 1992). Further, a PET study by Okubo et al. (1997) showed evidence that a reduction in prefrontal $D_1$ receptors in schizophrenic patients – a finding which correlated with the severity of the negative symptoms and decreased performance in the Wisconsin card sorting test – was in accordance with the hypothesis of diminished mesocortical dopaminergic activity.

Eggers (1991) proposed that the functional consequence of the interaction between the neocortices and the mesolimbic system is the phenomenon that Freud called "Reizschutz" (literally, "sensory protection"). Crucial to a normal balanced development of the brain and, in particular, the corticolimbic interactions are the early childhood experiences gained from personal interactions, and especially those with care-givers. Detailed anatomical investigation of early postnatal development has shown that there are specific phases in the various cortical regions, where the synapse density at first increases, then later decreases (e.g., Braun, 1996). These phases in the reorganization of the synaptic contacts between neurons may account for the several critical phases in the learning process, as well as the high degree of stability of certain childhood experiences over time. Of course, children require adequate stimulus input so that they may acquire behavioral strategies appropriate to both the sensory experience of events as well as those with significant emotional content (Bickerdike et al., 1993; Bock et al., 1996; Cooper, 1985; Gruss & Braun, 1996). This learning process depends on the precise and efficient processing of environmental stimuli that can only occur if the process of synapse selection (pruning) proceeds in an orderly fashion producing an appropriate and conducive substrate.

Modern attachment-behavior research and detailed video analysis of the development of behavior recorded in infants have established how important it is that the "adequate stimulus input" is predicated on "an adequate stimulus barrier" for healthy childhood development. Thus, parents apportion stimulation in accordance with their child's momentary state, its attentiveness, its receptiveness, its coping abilities, and needs (Papousek & Papousek, 1981). In so doing, they normally regulate the impressions and stimulus input from the environment naturally, and indeed personify a "stimulus barrier," in Freud's sense of the term, for the child. This function is pivotal for the child's socio-cognitive development and its integrative abilities.

Indeed, such analyses (Papousek, 1996) have shown that there are universal patterns of non-verbal communication intuitively shown by the parents in response to the infant or child's interest in an interaction, that are exactly contingent on the content of the infant's signal. This parental response is highly sensitive to the infant or child's stage of development and its abilities in the various fields of self-control, perception, and the integration of sensory information into communicative abilities.

The establishment of a secure and solid attachment definitely depends on the quality of the maternal stimulus barrier function, i.e., "whether and to what extent the mother has the right timing and does what is appropriate for the child" (Köhler, 1992, p. 269).

Ainsworth et al. (1978) have brought out the following criteria for the appropriateness of the mother's reaction during early childhood:

- She must take in the signals coming from the neonate and her attention threshold should not be too high.
- She must interpret the signals from the baby's point of view and not project from her own state.
- She must react promptly so that the neonate can develop a relationship between its behavior and her tension-relieving care. Thereby, the neonate experiences its effectiveness and ability to not feel helpless.
- The reaction to the signal of the neonate must be appropriate. The mother should give it no more and no less than it needs for its respective stage of development. She should neither over- nor under-stimulate, spoil, nor deny.

The findings of Jones et al. (1994) are important in this context: the mothers of children who later developed schizophrenia demonstrated impaired maternal functions and abilities, and were particularly limited in their ability to perceive the needs of their children.

Neonates and young infants already possess a far more differentiated and more mature neurocognitive potential on the basis of prenatal brain development, than was previously recognized. Thus, they are able to determine each actual interaction with their reference person, not only subjectively but also objectively (e.g., to establish the beginning and end of an action to which the sufficiently good mother reacts with empathy and tact). The quality of this interactive relatedness determines not only the level of the self-development, but also the infants' relationship to reality. Children lacking the possibility of gradually "creating" their own reality, also lack a feeling for their own personal self and a relationship to reality.

The development of self-esteem in a child and the ability for self-regulation is on the other hand determined by the extent to which the mother is aware of her child's attempts to normalize a briefly disturbed interaction and to build up a dialogue with the mother.

If the infant or toddler finds a lack of success in these attempts, it perceives itself as helpless and shifts its attention away from the mother, comforts itself with the thumb or dummy, starts to rock, becomes expressionless ("glass-eyed"), or develops distracted behavior as the expression of a partial confusion. If there are no compensatory experiences with another reference person, the anxious-avoidant behavior and its withdrawal tendencies become chronic and stabilized as lasting behavioral tendencies, typical of the premorbid features of children who later develop a schizophrenic disorder (Foerster et al., 1991; Jones et al., 1994; Olin & Mednick, 1996). Longitudinal studies of attachment behavior in young infants from 3 to 6 months of age up to puberty have shown that flexible behavioral patterns finally become ingrained and show a lasting constancy (Grossmann & Grossmann, 1991; Tronick et al., 1986).

Psychoanalytical concepts about the self-development and elaboration of an adequate relationship to reality complement the findings of developmental psychological and behavioral biological investigations (Newman, 1996). Psychoanalytical research in children (Winnicott, 1956) has shown that the development of child's self depends not only on the differentiated co-ordination of the mother's interpretation of the child's needs, signals, and behavioral readiness, but also very much on the mother's capacity to identify the mental state of the child. Thus, the development of an adequate relationship to reality is to a large extent dependent on whether the mother or the important reference person is in a position "to show the child that she sees it as a being with intentions whose behavior is determined by thoughts, feelings, opinions and wishes" (Fonagy, 1996, p. 12). It is thus not only dependent on the adequacy of the maternal or paternal perceptions and reactions, but also particularly on their ability to reflect on and imagine the respective psychological conditions of their child.

From the therapeutic point of view, it is important that the therapist takes over this function and that the patient is able "to experience the continuous mental concern for the other person without the threat of overwhelming mental pain or destruction" (Fonagy, 1996, p. 36). It follows from the concepts of the stimulus barrier model that the therapy of schizophrenic patients must be integrative and that individual psychotherapeutic, family dynamic psychoeducative and psychopharmacological methods must be matched to each other.

Psychoeducation ultimately has the aim of gradually enabling the patients and relatives to develop better problem solving abilities and to handle interrelational conflicts more adequately. On the individual level, it is important that the therapist is available to the patient as an emotionally authentic person and to enable the patient to integrate gradually and reconcile internal and external reality with each other. In such an understanding and empathic

21

therapeutic relationship, the patient experiences the therapist's respect and acceptance an feels the therapist treating him as an independent being, with own emotions and reactions. Through this therapeutic demeanour, the patient is able to acknowledge the therapist's effect to understand the dilusional-metaphoric nature of the patient's verbal and non-verbal behavior. In this way, the therapist helps the patient to gain new experiences, and step by step to become able to establish an adequate relationship to reality and to improve communications with the personal surroundings (see also Eggers, 1995).

# References

Ainsworth, M., Blehar, M., Waters, E. & Wall, S. (1978) *Patterns of Attachment: A Psychological Study of Strange Situation.* Hillsdale, NJ: Erlbaum.

Akbarian, S., Bunney, W. E., Potkin, S. G., et al. (1993a) Altered distribution of nicotinamide-adenine dinucleotide phosphate-diaphorase cells in frontal lobe of schizophrenics implies disturbances of cortical development. *Archives of General Psychiatry, 50,* 169–177.

Akbarian, S., Vinuela, A., Kim, J. J., et al. (1993b) Distorted distribution of nicotinamide-adenine dinucleotide phosphate-diaphorase neurons in temporal lobe of schizophrenics implies anomalous cortical development. *Archives of General Psychiatry, 50,*178–187.

Alaghband-Rand, J., McKenna, K., Gordon, C. T., et al. (1995) Childhood onset schizophrenia: The severity of premorbid course. *Journal of American Academic Child & Adolescence Psychiatry, 34,* 1273–1283.

Alaghband-Rand, J., Hamburger, S. D., Giedd, J. N., et al. (1997) Childhood-onset schizophrenia: Biological markers in relation to clinical characteristics. *American Journal of Psychiatry, 154,* 64–68.

Asarnow, R. B., Brown, W. & Strandburg, R. (1995) Children with a schizophrenic disorder: Neurobehavioral studies. *European Archives of Psychiatry & Clinical Neuroscience, 245,* 70–79.

Bender, S., Schall, U., Wolstein, et al. (1998) A topographic ERP follow-up study on 'prepulse inhibition' in first and second episode patients with schizophrenia. *Psychiat. Res. Neuroimaging,* in submission

Benes, F. M., Davidson, J. & Bird, E. D. (1986) Quantitative cytoarchitectural studies of the cerebral cortex of schizophrenics. *Archives of General Psychiatry, 43,* 31–35.

Benes, F. M., Turtle, M., Khan, Y. & Farol, P. (1994) Myelination of a key relay zone in the hippocampal formation occurs in the human brain during childhood, adolescence, and adulthood. *Archives of General Psychiatry, 51,* 477–484.

Bickerdike, M. J., Wright, I. K., Marsden, C. A. (1993) Social isolation attenuates rat forebrain 5-HT release induced by KCI stimulation and exposure to novel environment. *Behavioral Pharmacology, 4,* 231–236.

Bickford-Wimer, P. C., Nagamoto, H., Johnson, R., et al. (1990) Auditory sensory gating in hippocampal neurons: A model system in the rat. *Biological Psychiatry, 27,* 183–192.

Bock, J., Wolf, A. & Braun, K. (1996) Influence of the N-methyl-D-aspartate receptor antagonist DL-2-amino-5-phosphono valeric acid on auditory filial imprinting in the domestic chick. *Neurobiol Learn Mem, 65,* 177–188.

Braun, K. (1996) Synaptische Reorganisation bei frühkindlichen Erfahrungs- und Lern-prozessen: Relevanz für die Entstehung psychischer Erkrankungen. *Zeitschrift für Klinische Psychiatrieund Psychotherapie*, **44**, 253–266.

Bzowej, N. H. & Seeman, P. (1985) Age and dopamine D$_2$ receptors in human brain. *Social Neuroscience Abstracts*, **11**, 889.

Castle, D. J. & Murray, R. M. (1991) The neurodevelopmental basis of sex differences in schizophrenia. *Psychological Medicine*, **21**, 565–575.

Cooper, A. M. (1985) Will neurobiology influence psychoanalysis? *American Journal of Psychiatry*, **142**, 1395–1402.

Eggers, C. H. (1973) *Verlaufweisen kindlicher und präpuberaler Schizophrenien.* Monographien aus dem Gesamtgebiete der Psychiatrie. Bd. 4. Berlin, Heidelberg, New York: Springer.

Eggers, C. H. (1975) Die akute optische Halluzinose im Kindesalter. Klinische, differential-diagnostische, neurophysiologische und entwicklungs-psychologische Aspekte. *Fortschritte in Neurologie und Psychiatrie*, **43**, 441–470.

Eggers, C. H. (1991) Stimulus barrier model of schizophrenia: Convergence of neurobio-logical and developmental-psychological factors. In *Schizophrenia and Youth. Etiology and Therapeutic Consequences.* (Ed. Eggers, C. H.), pp. 29–40. Berlin, Heidelberg, New York: Springer.

Eggers, C. H. (1995) Das Dilemma der Macht – zur Psychotherapie jugendlicher Psychosen. *Jahrbuch der Psychoanalyse*, **34**, 206–238.

Eggers, C. H. & Bunk, D. (1997) The long-term course of childhood onset schizophrenia. *Schizophrenia Bulletin*, **23**, 105–117.

Eggers, C. H. & Klapal, M. (1997) Diagnostische und verlaufstypologische Besonderheiten der Frühschizophrenie. *Fortschritte in Neurologie und Psychiatrie*, **65**, 154–170.

Ellenbroek, B. A., van den Kroonenberg, P. T. J. M. & Cools, A. R. (1998) The effects of an early stressfull life event on sensorimotor gating in adult rats. *Schizophrenia Research*, **30**, 251–260.

Erlenmeyer-Kimling, L., Adamo, U. H., Rock, D., et al. (1997) The New York high-risk project: Prevalence and comorbidity of axis 1 disorders in offspring of schizophrenic parents at 25-year follow-up. *Archives of General Psychiatry*, **54**, 1096–1102.

Fish, B. (1987). Infant predictors of the longitudinal course of schizophrenic development. *Schizophrenia Bulletin*, **13**, 395–410.

Flach, K. A., Adler, L. E., Gerhardt, G. A., et al. (1996) Sensory gating in a computer model of the CA3 neural network of the hippocampus. *Biological Psychiatry*, **40**, 1230–1245.

Foerster, A., Lewis, S., Owen, M. & Murray, R. (1991) Pre-morbid adjustment and person-ality in psychosis. Effects of sex and diagnosis. *British Journal of Psychiatry*, **158**, 171–176.

Fonagy, P. (1996) Fortschritte in der Psychoanalytischen Technik mit jugendlichen Border-line-Patienten. *Zeitschrift der Wiener psychoanalytischen Vereinigung*, **7**, 11–37.

Frazier, J. A., Giedd, J. N, Hamburger, S. D., et al. (1996) Brain anatomic magnetic reso-nance imaging in childhood-onset schizophrenia. *Archives of General Psychiatry*, **53**, 617–624.

Freedman, R., Adler, L. E., Bickford, P., et al. (1994) Schizophrenia and nicotinic recep-tors. *Harvard Review of Psychiatry*, **2**, 179–192.

Goldman, P. S., Alexander, G. E. (1977) Maturation of prefrontal cortex in the monkey revealed by Local Reversible Cryogenic Depression. *Nature*, **267**, 613–615.

Goldman, P. S. (1967) Functional development of the prefrontal cortex in early life and the problem of neronal plasticity. *Exp Neurol*, **32**, 366–387.

Goldman-Rakic, P. S. (1997) Functional and anatomical aspects of prefrontal pathology in schizophrenia. *Schizophrenia Bulletin, 32*, 437–458.

Gray, J. A., Feldon J., Rawlins, J. N. P., et al. (1991) The neuropsychology of schizophrenia. Behav Brain Sci, **14**, 1–(20)–56.

Grossmann, K. E. & Grossmann, K. (1991) Attachment quality as an organizer of emotional and behavioral responses in a longitudinal perspective. In *Attachment across the life cycle*. (Eds. Parkes, C. M., Stevenson-Hinde, J. & Marris P.), pp. 93–114. London: Routledge.

Gruss, M. & Braun, K. (1996) Stimulus evoked glutamate in the medio-rostral neostriatum/hyperstriatum ventrale of domestic chick after auditory filial imprinting: An in vivo microdialysis study. *Journal of Neurochemistry, 66*, 1167–1173.

Hemsley, D. R. (1987) An experimental psychological Model for Schizophrenia. In *Search for Causes of Schizophrenia*. (Eds. Häfner, H., Gattaz, W. F. & Janzarik, W.), pp. 179–188. Berlin, Heidelberg, New York: Springer.

Hemsley, D. R. (1994) Cognitive disturbance as the link between schizophrenic symptoms and their biological bases. *Neurol Psychiatr Brain Res, 2*, 63–170.

Henn, F. A. (1995) Neurobiologie der Schizophrenie. *Schweizer Archiv für Neurologie und Psychiatrie, 146*, 224–229.

Jones, P., Rodgers, B., Murray, R. & Marmot, M. (1994) Child developmental risk factors for adult schizophrenia in the British 1946 birth cohort. *Lancet, 344*, 1398–402.

Köhler, L. (1992) Formen und Folgen früher Bindungserfahrungen. *Forum Psychoanal, 8*, 263–280.

Kröner, S., Schall, U., Ward, P. B., et al. (1999) Effects of prepulses and d-amphetamine on performance and event-related potential measures on an auditory discrimination task. *Psychopharmacology, 145*, 123-132.

Magaro, P. A. (1984) Psychosis and schizophrenia. In *Theories of Schizophrenia and Psychosis*. (Eds. Spaulding, W. D. & Cole, J. K.), pp. 157–230. London: University of Nebraska Press.

McGeer, P.L. & McGeer, E.G. (1981) Neurotransmitters in the aging brain. In *The Molecular Basis of Neuropathology*. (Eds. Darrison, A. M. & Thompson, R. H.), pp. 631–648. London: Edward Arnold, Ltd.

McGlashan, T. H. & Johannessen, J. O. (1996) Early detection and intervention with schizophrenia: Rationale. *Schizophrenia Bulletin, 22*, 201–222.

Newman, K. M. (1996) Winnicott goes to the movies: The false self in ordinary people. *Psychoanal Q, 65*, 787–807.

Oades, R. D. (1995) Connections between studies of the neurobiology of attention, psychotic processes and event-related potentials. *Electroenceph Clin Neurophysiol*, suppl. **44**, 428–438.

Oades, R. D. & Schepker, R. (1994) Serum gonadal hormones in young schizophrenic patients. *Psychoneuroendocrinology, 19*, 373–385.

Oades, R. D., Zerbin, D. & Eggers, CH. (1994) Negative difference (Nd), an ERP marker of stimulus relevance: Different lateral asymmetries for paranoid and nonparanoid schizophrenics. *Pharmacopsychiatry, 27*, 65–67.

Oades, R. D. Roepcke, B. & Schepker, R. (1996) A test of conditioned blocking and its development in childhood and adolescence: Relationship to personality and monoamine metabolism. *Dev Neuropsychol, 12*, 207–230.

Oades, R. D., Dittmann-Balcar, A. & Zerbin, D. (1997) Development and topography of auditory event-related potentials (ERPs): Mismatch and processing negativity in individuals 8-22 years of age. *Psychophysiology, 34*, 677–693.

O'Connell, P., Woodruf P. W. R., Wright, I., et al. (1997) Developmental insanity or dementia praecox: Was the wrong concept adopted? *Schizophrenia Research,* **23**, 97–106.

Okubo,Y., Suhara, T., Suzuki, K., et al. (1997) Decreased prefrontal dopamine D₁.receptors in schizophrenia revealed by PET. *Nature,* **385**, 634–636.

Olin, S.S. & Mednick, S.A. (1996) Risk factors of psychosis: Identifying vulnerable populations premorbidly. *Schizophrenia Bulletin,* **22**, 223–240.

Papoušek, M., Papoušek, H. (1981) Neue Wege der Verhaltensbeobachtung und Verhaltensmikroanalyse. *Sozialpädiatrie,* **3**, 20–22.

Papoušek, M. (1995) *Vom ersten Schrei zum ersten Wort. Anfänge der Sprachentwicklung in der vorsprachlichen Kommunikation.* Bern, Huber

Rapoport, J. L., Giedd, J., Kumra, S., et al. (1997) Childhood-onset schizophrenia: Progressive ventricular change during adolescence. *Archives of General Psychiatry,* **54**, 897–903.

Rodewald, S., Müller, B., Oades, R. D., et al. (1998) Plasma indicators of monoamine metabolism and nicotine consumption: A factor and correlational analysis with schizophrenic symptom clusters. *Schizophrenia Research,* **29** (suppl.), 95.

Ross, C. A. & Pearlson, G. D. (1996) Schizophrenia, the heteromodal association neocortex and development: Potential for a neurogenetic approach. *Trends Neuroscience,* **19**, 171–176.

Schreiber, H., Stolz-Born, G., Kornhuber, H. H. & Born, J. (1996) Elektrophysiologische Korrelate selektiver Aufmerksamkeit bei Kindern und Jugendlichen mit erhöhtem Schizophrenie-Risiko. *Zeitschrift für Kinder- und Jugendpsychiatrie,* **24**, 282–292.

Spitzer, M. (1997) Neuronale Netzwerke und Psychopathologie. *Nervenarzt,* **68**, 21–37.

Strandburg, R. J., Marsh, J. T., Brown, W. S., et al. (1990) Event-related potential correlates of impaired attention in schizophrenic children. *Biological Psychiatry,* **27**, 1103–1115.

Strandburg, R. J., Marsh, J. T., Brown, W. S., et al. (1994) Continuous-Processing related ERPS in Schizophrenic and Normal Children. *Biological Psychiatry,* **35**, 525–538.

Swerdlow, N. R. & Koob, G. F. (1987) Dopamine, schizophrenia, mania, and depression: Toward a unified hypothesis of cortico-striato-pallido-thalamic function. *Behav Brain Sci.* **10**, 197–(208)–245.

Tronick, E., Cohn, J. & Shea, E. (1986) The transfer of affect between mothers and infants. In *Affective Development in Infancy.* (Eds. Brazelton, B. T. & Yogman, M.), pp. 11–26. NJ: Ablex, Norwood.

Tucker, T. J. & Kling, A. (1967) Differential effects of early and late lesions of frontal granular cortex in the monkey. *Brain Research,* **5**, 377–389.

Vinogradova, O. S. (1975) Functional organization of the limbic system in the process of registration of information: Facts and hypotheses. In *The Hippocampus, vol 2: Neuro-Physiology and Behavior.* (Eds. Isaacson, R. L. & Pribram K. H.) New York: Plenum.

Walker, E. F. and DiForio, D. (1997) Schizophrenia: A neural diathesis-stress model. *Psychological Review,* **104**, 667–685.

Weinberger, D. R., Berkman, K. F., Suddath, R. & Torrey, E. F. (1992) Evidence of dysfunction of a prefrontal-limbic network in schizophrenia: A magnetic resonance and regional cerebral blood flow study of discordant monozygotic twins. *American Journal of Psychiatry,* **149**, 890–897.

Winnicot, D. W. (1956) Primary maternal preoccupation. In *Collected Papers: Through Paediatrics to Psycho-Analysis,* pp. 300–305. New York: Basic Books, 1958.

Yakovlev, P. I. & LeCours, A. R. (1964) The myelogenetic cycles of regional maturation of the brain. In *Regional Development of the Brain in Early Life.* (Ed. Minkowski, A.), pp. 3–70. Boston: Blackwell Scientific Publications Inc.

# Pharmacotherapy

# The State of Evaluation and Clinical Benefits of Atypical Neuroleptics

Hans Jürgen Möller

## The Term "Atypical Neuroleptics"

"Atypical neuroleptics" refers to antipsychotic drugs which, compared to typical neuroleptics, have a better balance of antipsychotic efficacy compared with extrapyramidal side-effects. Furthermore, a greater efficacy, compared to conventional neuroleptics in the treatment of negative symptoms in schizophrenia is also often implied in this definition (Möller, 1995). Nevertheless, the term "atypical neuroleptics" is not clearly defined and may give rise to confusion. Some authors prefer a more rigorous definition, which completely excludes the risk of extrapyramidal side-effects. In that case, clozapine, the prototype of atypical neuroleptics, would probably be the only substance which can fulfil these criteria. On the one hand, such a restrictive definition would increase clarity, but on the other hand, it would ignore the specific characteristics of several new neuroleptics.

However, such a clear-cut categorization dividing atypical from typical, conventional neuroleptics does not appear helpful, and furthermore, conventional neuroleptics are themselves a heterogeneous group of drugs. Some conventional neuroleptics show a better balance of benefit to risk, expressed as the relationship of antipsychotic efficacy to extrapyramidal side-effects, compared to other drugs of the same class.

Furthermore, a clear-cut definition becomes even more complicated by the fact that most of the conventional neuroleptics have never been tested according to current methodological standards for their benefits in improving negative symptoms. The same is also true for more elaborated studies on conventional neuroleptics regarding their differences in extrapyramidal side-effects. However, the new generation of atypical neuroleptics has been carefully examined, according to recently updated methodological standards. Thus, their clinical benefits in treating both positive and negative symptoms, as well as any extrapyramidal side-effects, are more rigorously assessed and can contribute to defining the term "atypical neuroleptic." This implies that some conventional neuroleptics might also turn out to have an atypical profile, if they were examined according to current methodological standards for assessing those special clinical characteristics.

Altogether, it is probably not the right approach to classify new drugs more or less automatically as atypical neuroleptics (although most of them have been developed to fulfil this criteria) and to label their precursors as "conventional neuroleptics." This has the negative implication that they show a high incidence of extrapyramidal side-effects and confer no benefit in treating negative symptoms. Some of the older neuroleptics might have an atypical profile, if they were examined more carefully.

In addition to the criteria already mentioned, some authors include efficacy in relieving positive symptoms of schizophrenia, which were previously unresponsive to conventional neuroleptics, in this definition. This makes the categorization even more complicated, presumably not allowing any substance to be labeled as an atypical neuroleptic according to all three criteria of definition. To give practical examples for these theoretical implications, some atypical neuroleptics in clinically use will be considered here. Within the group of older substances, clozapine may be the best example, but also zotepine, based on new results from methodologically rigorous studies from England (Petit et al., 1996). Within the group of substances developed lately, risperidone, olanzapine, sentindole, and amisulpride will also fall under this definition. Remoxipride, which also fulfilled these criteria, had to be withdrawn from the market due to causing severe side-effects after some years of clinical use. Moving on to the next generation of drugs, which are not yet available for clinical use, quetiapine and ziprasidone also claim to be atypical neuroleptics.

## Basic Pharmacology of Atypical Neuroleptics

Pharmacological screening shows that there are some characteristics in atypical neuroleptics, compared to conventional neuroleptics, which may be found in the atypical neuroleptics under consideration, alone or in different combinations. This field is too extensive to be described completely within this chapter, but is reviewed elsewhere (Möller, 1998). Here only the most prominent features which are implied as being part of an atypical profile are mentioned.

1. Characteristics of binding to dopamine-receptors.
   – E.g., balanced relation between $D_2$- and $D_1$-blockade

– Preferential binding to D$_4$-receptors
– Preferential binding to D$_3$-receptors

2. Preferential action on dopamine-receptors of the limbic system

3. Combined dopamine D$_2$- and serotonin-5-HT$_2$-antagonism

Many of these mechanisms apply to clozapine, e.g., a highly preferential binding to D$_4$-receptors, a balanced relation between D$_2$- and D$_1$-receptor occupation, a slightly selective mesolimbic action, and a combination of D$_2$- and 5HT-

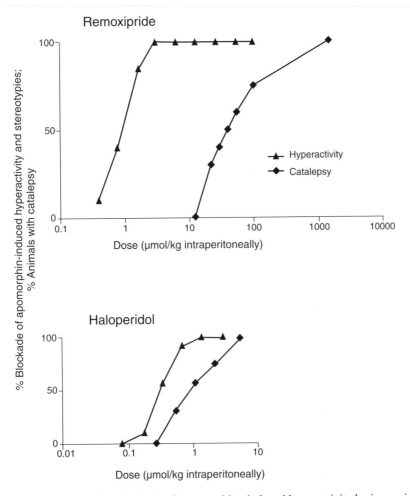

*Figure 1.* Comparison of the blockade of apomorphine-induced hyperactivity by increasing doses of the atypical neuroleptic remoxipride and the traditional neuroleptic haloperidol with the dose-dependent induction of catalepsy (adapted from Ögren et al., 1990).

mechanisms of action. As another example, sertindole combines $D_2$- and 5-$HT_2$-antagonism with a high selectivity for the mesolimbic system, while risperidone is a combined $D_2$-$5HT_2$-antagonist without a preferential mesolimbic action.

There is one common characteristic of all atypical neuroleptics. The dose-response curves for antipsychotic efficacy and extrapyramidal side-effects are widely separated from each other in animal tests. This means that low doses of the drug are able to exert antipsychotic efficacy, and only much higher doses will provoke extrapyramidal symptoms (see Figure 1). This characteristic was first described for clozapine in animal screening tests, with the consequence that investigating its use as a neuroleptic was almost stopped. At that time, it seemed to be common sense that only substances with extrapyramidal side-effects are also capable of exerting neuroleptic action, as had long been known for typical neuroleptics. Inversely, nowadays only substances are further investigated which show this dissociation of the dose-response curves for antipsychotic potency and extrapyramidal side-effects.

## Results of Phase-III-Studies

Many of the drugs mentioned above showed sufficient efficacy in treating negative symptoms, combined with a low incidence of extrapyramidal side-effects, in phase-III-studies which were carried out according to current methodological standards. It goes without saying that these substances also showed good efficacy in treating positive symptoms. As this chapter will concentrate on the "atypical clinical profile," not much space will be given to that aspect. Compared to haloperidol, all new neuroleptics have equal or better efficacy in treating positive symptoms, when administered in their assumed equivalent dosages (Möller, 1998).

Despite the overall high standard of current clinical phase-III-studies for new neuroleptics, there are design differences which have to be carefully considered in the interpretation of results. For example, in both the large phase-III-studies on risperidone (Peuskens, 1995; Marder & Meibach, 1994), only one standard dose of haloperidol was used, whereas risperidone was tested in different doses. It is possible that this might result in wrong conclusions, so far as the advantages of the new substance are concerned. Any advantages with the new substance might occur only with a special dose, compared to an undifferentiated dose of the standard neuroleptic. This is also true for most other new neuroleptics (Beasley et al., 1996a; Tran et al., 1996; Petit et al., 1996). Some studies even test only one hypothetically equivalent dosage of the new substance against one dosage of haloperidol, which is assumed to be a clinically used average dose; many studies either use 10 or 20 mg haloperidol/d. Some critics consider the 20 mg/d dosage of haloperidol as being too high and no longer a clinical standard. Furthermore, some critics point to the fact that such high dosages of these standard substances were given on the assumption of optimal clinical efficacy, without keeping the higher rate of extrapyramidal side-effects in mind. In principle, these arguments may be true, but 20 mg/d of haloperidol was common clinical practice at the time of planning most of these studies, and the assumption of linearity of dosage against extrapyramidal side-effects has not been verified satisfactorily. For example, the 7-arm-study of sertindole vs. haloperiodol (see below) – a design which compares different dosages of the new substance with different dosages of the standard one – should certainly be preferred. However, this methodological advantage has to be paid off with extremely high costs and a large increase in the number of patients.

The large 7-arm-study on sertindole, which tasted three different dosages of sertindole against three dosages of haloperidol and against placebo (Zimbroff et al., 1997). has created a new methodological standard which serve as a model for the future, although it may be harder to carry out studies, due to the high number of patients and extremely high costs, as mentioned above. This study proved the advantage of sertindole, compared to haloperidol at all dosages, in

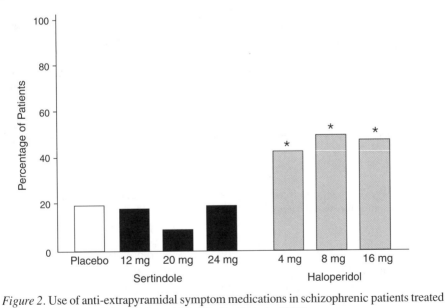

*Figure 2.* Use of anti-extrapyramidal symptom medications in schizophrenic patients treated with placebo, sertindole or haloperidol (Zimbroff et al., 1997).
An asterisk (*) indicates a significant differences between the haloperidol group and all three sertindole groups as well as placebo.

terms of the incidence of extrapyramidal side-effects (see Figure 2). In treating negative symptoms, sertindole and haloperidol seemed to be more or less equal in all dosages tested which produced an improvement of symptoms. Only 20 mg sertindole proved to be a superior to haloperidol in treating negative symptoms. This may imply that the advantages so far as negative symptoms are concerned, may not always be reproducible, especially in view of the fact that in another large study on sertindole, the best effects on negative symptoms were seen with 16 mg/d (Hale et al., 1996).

With respect to negative symptoms, the 7-arm-study on sertindole also resembles the situation faced when the results of various recent studies on new neuroleptics are reviewed. These are inconclusive to some extent, due to varying daily dosages or poor reproducibility in other aspects of the study (Peuskens, 1995; Marder & Meibach, 1994; Beasley et al., 1996a). However, not only better tolerability so far as extrapyramidal side-effects are concerned, but also a beneficial effect on negative symptoms has been demonstrated for several new neuroleptics, in methodologically demanding studies (see Figure 3).

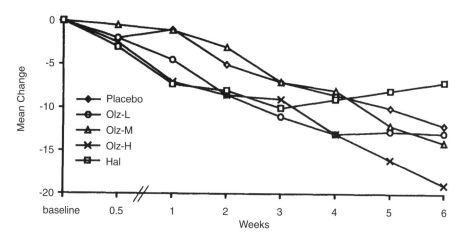

*Figure 3.* Weekly change in Scale for the Assessment of Negative Symptoms (SANS)-composite scores (observed cases); $p \leq 0.05$ (Beasley et al., 1996a).

In evaluating the effect on negative symptoms, there are the statistical and methodological problems that most studies were not undertaken with the aim of confirming efficacy for a defined dose of the substance. In most cases, the studies deal with this question only in an exploitative way. Therefore, the optimal dosage found in those studies has to be confirmed by further controlled studies.

Interpreting effects on negative symptoms becomes difficult when we consider neuroleptics which show different clinical profiles, so far as efficacy in treating productive symptoms, extrapyramidal tolerability, and improvement of depressed mood are concerned. All those variables influence negative symptoms and have to be kept in mind. This is especially true when an attempt is made to isolate a direct action on negative symptoms from other effects which indirectly influence the clinical appearance of these symptoms, such as changes in positive symptoms, extrapyramidal side-effects, and depressed mood. However, complex statistical analysis may be able to answer this question, as it has been done with risperidone by using the approach of path-analysis. The data of the American study on risperidone by using the approach of path-analysis. The data of the American study on risperidone, which showed advantages compared to haloperidol in negative symptoms, were reanalyzed using this statistical approach. This analysis was able to show that the benefits of risperidone are mostly due to a direct effect on negative symptoms (Möller et al., 1995; Möller & Müller, 1997). Later, this approach was also applied to other atypical neuroleptics, e.g., olanzapine and sertindole, with similar results (Tollefson & Sanger, 1997). Such an analysis, however, is still lacking for other drugs, e.g., the clinically approved clozapine. This statistical method though, is limited by the assumption of linearity of the relationships under consideration, which means that existing non-linear relationships escape firm analysis.

Another limitation is the fact that in most studies on new neuroleptics, effects on negative symptoms were only judged after the patient was hospitalized due to an acute episode of schizophrenia with predominant positive symptoms. To answer the question more accurately whether atypical neuroleptics are also effective in residual schizophrenia with chronic negative symptoms, controlled studies should be carried out in those particular patients. This is probably the most relevant clinical question, as chronic negative symptoms predict the course of the disease. Ideally, patients included in such a study would suffer from chronic negative symptoms without any chronic positive symptoms, in order to avoid difficulties in interpretation. Those patients could be best recruited from catamnestic studies, but are rarely found amongst current in- or out-patients. To fulfil the task of recruiting a set of patients with sufficient and predominating negative symptoms, it may be necessary to broaden the inclusion criteria and reduce the exclusion criteria, though possible factors which are capable of modulating negative symptoms should be excluded.

Recommendations for such a design have been developed by a peer-group of psychiatrists of university hospitals and specialized experts of the pharmaceutical industry (see Table 1) (Möller et al., 1994). These consensus-guidelines have been mostly adopted for the CPMP-guidelines for the evaluation of psychopharmacological effects on negative symptoms.

*Table 1.* Recommendations of the working group on negative symptoms in schizophrenia (Möller et al., 1994)

| |
|---|
| Aim: Evaluation of treatment effects on negative symptoms in schizophrenia |

1. Patient selection
    a) Positive symptoms not dominating the actual clinical picture, e.g., PANSS negative type
    b) Duration of negative symptoms > 6 months
    c) Stable condition of the schizophrenic illness > 6 months
    d) Flat affect and poverty of speech represent core negative symptoms
    e) No or low depression score

2. Design
    Double-blind comparison to placebo or active drug

3. Efficacy parameters
    BPRS or SANS or PANSS

4. Other scales
    Depression scales, EPS scales

5. Statistical analysis
    a) End-point comparison
    b) Interaction with productive symptoms, depression, EPS

However, studies which fully satisfy these standards have not yet been published. Apart from clozapine studies on patients with refractory positive symptoms, which in a narrow sense do not follow those designs, only one amisulpiride study comes close to these standards (Loo et al., 1997). This study shows a clear-cut advantage of 100 mg amisulpride compared to placebo, on negative symptoms, but it also gives rise to methodological questions. The dose of 100 mg is much lower than those used in other studies with patients with an acute exacerbation of schizophrenia which showed, beside good efficacy in treating productive symptoms, better effects on negative symptoms compared to haloperidol (Möller et al., 1997). Currently, there is one study with zotepine under way which fulfils all the criteria of the guidelines.

In the search for differential benefits of the various new neuroleptics, further controlled group studies are currently proceeding, comparing other atypical neuroleptics to risperidone, e.g., an olanzapine-risperidone and an amisulpride-risperidone study. However, when comparing two substances with similar atypical profiles, a large number of patients is needed to insure a statistical significance of differences ($\beta$-error-problem).

There have also been critical comments about the fact that the new neuroleptics were only tested against haloperidol, but not against other older neuroleptics. In this respect, risperidone is the exception, because it has been tested against zuclopenthixol, perphenazine, and clozapine, and was mostly able to prove its advantages (see Table 2).

*Table 2.* Summary of major published clinical trials of risperidone (Curtis & Kerwin, 1995)

| Study description | Daily dose (mg) | Duration (weeks) | No. of patients | Rating scale | Results Overall efficacy | Results Extrapyramidal effects | Reference |
|---|---|---|---|---|---|---|---|
| Open, dose-finding | 10–25 | 4 | 17 | BPRS, SARS, CGI | > placebo | <washout | Mesotten et al. 1989 |
| Open, dose-finding | 2–10 | 4 | 20 | BPRS, GTI, SARS | > placebo | <washout | Castelao et al. 1989 |
| Double-blind, HAL control | 2–20 | 8 | 60 | BPRS, CGI, NOSIE, ESRS | RIS = HAL | RIS ≤ HAL | Mesotten 1991 |
| Double-blind, placebo and HAL control | 1–10 | 6 | 160 | BPRS, SANS, CGI, ESRS, AIMS | RIS > placebo RIS ≥ HAL | RIS = placebo RIS < HAL | Borrison 1991 |
| Double-blind, LEVO and HAL control | 4–12 | 4 | 62 | PANSS, BPRS, PAS, CGI, ESRS | RIS > HAL RIS > LEVO | RIS = LEVO LEVO < HAL | Tatossian 1991 |
| Double-blind, placebo and HAL control | 2–16 | 8 | 523 | PANSS, CGI | RIS > HAL | RIS < HAL | Marder 1991 |
| Double-blind, PER control | 5–15 | 8 | 107 | PANSS, BPRS, CGI, ESRS, UKU | RIS > PER | RIS = PER | Remvig 1991 |
| Double-blind, RIS 1 mg and HAL control | 1–16 | 8 | 1362 | PANSS, BPRS, CGI, ESRS, UKU | RIS > HAL | RIS < or = HAL | Peuskens 1992 |
| Combined analysis of 3 long-term trials | 2–20 | 19 months | 264 | BPRS, GTI, ESRS, UKU | > placebo | < washout | Mertens 1990 |
| Double-blind, HAL control | 2–20 | 12 | 44 | SADS-C, PANSS, CGI, NOSIE, ESRS | RIS ≥ HAL | RIS ≡ HAL | Claus et al. 1992 |
| Double-blind, placebo and HAL control | 2–10 | 6 | 36 | BPRS, SANS, CGI, ESRS, AIMS | RIS ≥ HAL | RIS < HAL | Borison et al. 1992 |
| Double-blind, placebo and HAL control | 2–16 | 8 | 135 | PANSS, CGI, BPRS, ESRS, UKU | RIS ≡ or > HAL | RIS < or ≡ HAL | Chouinard et al. 1993 |

Table 2 (continued)

| | | | | | | | |
|---|---|---|---|---|---|---|---|
| Double-blind, parallel group, PER control | 5–15 | 8 | 107 | PANSS, CGI, BPRS, ESRS, UKU | RIS ≥ PER | RIS ≡ PER | Hoyberg et al. 1993 |
| Double-blind, CLOZ control | 4–8 | 4 | 59 | BPRS, CGI, SARS | RIS ≡ CLOZ | RIS ≡ CLOZ | Heinrich et al. 1994 |
| Double-blind, placebo and HAL control | 2–16 | 8 | 388 | PANSS, ESRS, CGI, BPRS | RIS ≡ or > HAL | RIS ≤ HAL | Marder a. Meibach 1994 |

Abbreviations and symbols: AIMS = Abnormal Involuntary Movement Scale; BPRS = Brief Psyciatric Rating Scale; CGI = Clinical Global Impressions scale; CLOZ = Clozapin; ESRS = Extrapyramidal Symptom Rating Scale; GTI = Global Therapeutic Impression; HAL = Haloperidol; LEVO = Levomepromazin (methotrimeprazine); NOSIE = Nurses' Observation Scale for Inpatient Evaluation; PANSS = Positive and Negative Syndrome Scale; PAS = Psychotic Anxiety Scale; PER = Perphenazin; RIS = Risperidon; SADS-C = Schedule for Affective Disorders and Schizophrenia – Change version; SANS = Scale for the Assessment of Negative Symptoms; SARS = Simpson and Angus Rating Scale; UKU = UKU Side Effect Rating Scale; ≡ indicates similar effect; ≤ indicates tendency towards greater effect; < indicates statistically significant lesser effect ($p<0.05$)> indicates statistically significant greater effect ($p<0.05$).

# Long-Term Controlled Studies and Open Trials (Phase-IV-Studies)

Beside the evaluation of efficacy in acute episodes, it is also important to test the efficacy and tolerability of a new neuroleptic in long-term treatment. Recently, the results of an open one-year trial of risperidone in about 400 patients have been published (Möller et al., 1997c). It appears that risperidone shows high efficacy and good tolerability in such long-term treatment. Most important is the observation that the drop-out rate due to side-effects was very low (6% of the study population), whilst that due to extrapyramidal side-effects was only 2%.

Controlled long-term studies (up to one year) have also been conducted for olanzapine and sertindole, each in comparison to haloperidol. The results mostly have been published yet, but it appears (Satterlee et al., 1996; Street et al., 1996; Krystal, 1996; Tollefson & Sanger, 1997) that patients on olanzapine or sertindole show clearly more favorable results than patients on haloperidol.

Special attention should be paid to another long-term study of ore than 400 patients with a first episode of schizophrenia, which started early in 1997. This was designed as a controlled group trial, comparing risperidone versus haloperidol for the first two years and then following a semi-naturalistic design, with the intention that, whenever possible, patients on risperidone should stay on risperidone. Its purpose is to compare the medium-term outcome of schizophrenic patients receiving either the atypical neuroleptic, risperidone or a typical neuroleptic drug from various (efficacy in treating positive and negative symptoms, extrapyramidal tolerability, cognitive impairment, life quality and socioeconomic) aspects. The hypothesis is that in patients with their first episode of schizophrenia, atypical neuroleptics such as risperidone, are able to modulate the long-term outcome of the disease in a positive manner. Recently, a large study of similar size was started with sertindole. Its aim is to monitor in a naturalistic design for several years the course of the disease in patients on sertindole compared to various other neuroleptics (Wehnert, 1998).

Though phase-III-studies on new antipsychotics were carried out with high methodological standards, the patients in them were highly selected, which clearly limits generalization of the results. There is a necessity to combine the results of phase-III-studies with experiences in the routine clinical use of a new psychopharmacological agent, after its introduction.

Due to the fact that risperidone has been available for several years, there is also a large amount of clinical experience, documented in open trials and case reports. Summarizing the most important results, the optimal effective and well tolerated dose of 4–8 mg of risperidone which has been evaluated in two large phase-III-studies also holds true for routine clinical use. For example, the average daily dose of risperidone was 4–8 mg in a so far unpublished open trial (Albus et al., oral communication on the 6th World Congress of Biological Psychiatry). There are also reports of a better extrapyramidal tolerability, compared to other high-potency standard neuroleptics in daily routine use. However, this advantage may disappear as soon as a high-dose treatment (10 mg or more) is needed in some patients. Another advantage of risperidone which emerged in these open trials is a shortening of the time in hospital, which in turn improves the life-quality of the patient and thus leads to a better acceptance of the drug. Furthermore, risperidone showed a positive effect on cognition, beside a better extrapyramidal tolerability which may also improve compliance (Franz & Gallhofer, 1997).

In this context, it is important that risperidone has also been tested in controlled phase-III-studies for these higher dosages, whereas olanzapine, for example, has never been evaluated in dosages higher than 20 mg in all large phase-III-studies. This might be a serious problem, as it contrasts with the already apparent clinical necessity of sometimes treating patients with higher doses than the maximum used in these studies.

## Clinical Perspectives of Atypical Neuroleptics

Atypical neuroleptics have a broad range of pharmacological profiles, reaching from the selective dopamine-antagonist amisulpride, the more or less selective $D_2$-$5HT_2$ receptor antagonists like risperidone, to pharmacological nonselective "rich drugs" (formally also called "dirty drugs") like clozapine or olanzapine, whose mechanisms of interaction with different CNS-neurotransmitter systems are very complex (see Table 3). Clearly, this results also in different clinical profiles.

For example, olanzapine, zotepine, and especially clozapine cause marked sedation, which is rarely observed with risperidone. Whereas sedation may be not only an unwanted side-effect but an advantage in the acute treatment of excited psychotic patients, the anticholinergic side-effects frequently seen with zotepine, olanzapine and, to a lesser extent, with clozapine are clearly unwanted. Beside cognitive impairment and subjective side-effects they may also limit the use of these drugs in patients who are particularly risk, e.g., gastrointestinal problems (constipation), increased intra-ocular pressure, and cardiac problems. This latter is especially important with respect to sertindole. Some cases of an increased QT-interval have been described, exceeding the critical limit of 500 ms. Therefore, patients with cardiac risk should be excluded and ECGs should be carried out regularly during sertindole treatment.

*Table 3.* Recently marketed atypical neuroleptics in Germany. The main criteria for ranking receptor affinity as high, medium or low, is relative to antipsychotic efficacy, a minor criteria its efficacy relative to other drugs. These data have to be considered as preliminary and need further confirmation by more controlled studies

| Neuroleptic Chemical group | Olanzapine Thienobenzodiazepine | Sertindol Phenylindol | Amisulpride Benzamide |
|---|---|---|---|
| Receptor affinity | | | |
| High | $D_2$ <br> $HT_{2A}$, $HT_{2B}$, $HT_{2C}$ <br> $\alpha_1$ <br> $H_1$ <br> $M_1$ | $D_2$ <br> $HT_{2A}$, $HT_{2C}$ <br> $\alpha_1$ | $D_2$, $D_3$ |
| Medium | $D_1$, $D_4$ <br> $HT_3$, $HT_6$ | $D_3$, $D_4$ | |
| Low | $HT_{1A}$, $HT_{1B}$ <br> $HT_{1D}$ | | |
| | | $H_1$ <br> $M_1$ | |
| Half lifetime (h) | 33–51 | 24–84 | ca. 12 |
| Drug dosage (mg/d) | 10–20 | 16–24 | 400–800 |
| Side effects | Headache <br> Weight gain <br> Agitation <br> Ataxie <br> Sommnolence <br> Sleeplessness <br> Rhinitis <br> Consitpation <br> Diarrhoea <br> Dry mouth <br> Nausea, Vomiting <br> Vertigo, Tremor <br> Pharyngitis <br> Increase of liver-transaminases <br> Increase of QT-interval <br> Paresthesia | Hypotonus <br> Sleeplessness <br> Feeling of stuffed nose <br> Constipation <br> Decreased volume of ejaculation <br> Dry mouth <br> Hypertonus <br> Headache <br> Somnolence <br> Vertigo <br> Orthostatic dysregulation <br> Unconsciousness <br> Tremor <br> Increase of QT-interval <br> Weight gain | Sleeplessness <br> Anxiety <br> Excitation <br> Somnolence <br> Vertigo <br> Constipation <br> Nausea <br> Vomiting <br> Dry mouth <br> Increase of plasma prolactine levels <br> Extrapyramidal side effects |

D: dopamine-receptors; HT: serotonin-receptors; $\alpha$: $\alpha$-adrenoreceptors; H: histamine-receptors; M: muscarinic-acetylchonline-receptor (modified and supplemented according to Bandelow & Rüther 1997).

Other drugs, as clozapine and sertindole, show a more pronounced $\alpha$-adrenalytic profile. This may lead to a decrease of blood-pressure and to orthostatic problems, which can be avoided by a slow titration of the drug. However, this will limit the feasibility of its use in the treatment of acutely psychotic patients. The occasional problem of a life-threatening agranulocytosis in clozapine, which led to restrictions of its use, seems not to be apparent with olanzapine. Compared to clozapine, zotepine and amisulpride, which have only medium antipsychotic potency, causing the necessity of relatively high daily doses, risperidone, sertindole, and olanzapine can be classified as high-potency neuroleptics. A possible advantage of zotepine may be its potent norepinephrine re-uptake inhibition, implying also antidepressant efficacy of the substance. This may be of special interest in mixed schizophrenic and affective symptoms, but the theoretical advantage has not been supported yet by control group studies (Wolfersdorf et al., 1994).

When using non-sedating atypical neuroleptics in the treatment of acutely excited psychotic patients, a combination with sedatives such as benzodiazepines should be recommended so as to avoid an unnecessary dose increase of the neuroleptic to ensure sufficient psychomotor calming. The combination of atypical neuroleptics in order to increase efficacy in refractory patients or sedation can be recommended only for short periods; otherwise, the advantage of a higher tolerability of atypical neuroleptics is at risk.

## Conclusion

Due to their better tolerability and partly better control of negative symptoms, atypical neuroleptics may increase the acceptance of neuroleptic treatment by patients, and consequently also ensure compliance for continued treatment. This may in turn also improve the prognosis of schizophrenia.

Very recently, the first controlled studies have been carried out to test the different neuroleptics, especially atypical compounds, for their effects on cognition in schizophrenic patients. As an example, these studies demonstrated that risperidone is superior to clozapine (Franz & Gallhofer, 1997; Meltzer, 1995; Meltzer et al., 1994; Lee et al., 1994; Gallhofer et al., 1996). This effect may be due to the lack of anticholinergic side-effects of risperidone, which are capable of causing cognitive impairment.

There should be no doubt that the available atypical neuroleptics differ from conventional ones, as far as their pharmacological profile (see Table 3), clinical efficacy, tolerability, and state of evaluation of these parameters are concerned. Likewise with conventional neuroleptics, there are a heterogeneous group in which one specific drug cannot be substituted for easily by another. The indications for each atypical neuroleptic have to be checked in every individual patient. However, comparing this new generation of atypical neuroleptics to the family of typical neuroleptics, their overall advantages should be highlighted.

# References

Bandelow, B. & Rüther, E. (1997) Antipsychotische Behandlung: Jüngste Weiterentwicklungen und pharmakologische Grundlagen. *Psychopharmakotherapie,* **4**, 1–18.

Beasle, C. M., Tollefson, G., Tran, P. V., et al. (1996a) Olanzapine versus placebo and haloperidol. Acute phase results of the North American double-blind olanzapine trial. *Neuropsychopharmacology,* **14**, 111–123.

Beasley, C. M., Jr., Sanger, T., Satterlee, W., et al. (1996b) Olanzapine versus placebo: Results of a double-blind, fixed-dose olanzapine trial. *Psychopharmacology Berl,* **124**, 159–167.

Curtis, V. A. & Kerwin, R. W. (1995) A risk-benefit assessment of risperidone in schizophrenia. *Drug Safety,* **12**, 139–145.

Franz, M. & Gallhofer, B. (in press) Risperidon – ein neuer Serotonin-/Dopamin-Antagonist zur Behandlung der Schizophrenie.

Gallhofer, B., Bauer, L., Lis, S., et al. (1996) Cognitive dysfunction in schizophrenia: Comparison of treatment with atypical antipsychotic agents and conventional neuroleptic drugs. *European Neuropsychopharmacology,* **6**, 13–20.

Hale, A., Burght, V. D., Wehnert., A., et al. (1996) *A European dose-range study comparing the efficacy, tolerability and safety of four doses of sertindole and one dose of haloperidol in schizophrenic patients.* Melbourne: CINP Congress.

Krystal, J. E. (1996) *Sertindole: A multi-center, one year, haloperidol controlled trial assessing the long term safety, efficacy and quality of life in stable schizophrenic patients.* Abstract, Puerto Rico: SCNP Congress.

Lee, M. A., Thompson, P. A. & Meltzer, H. Y. (1994) Effects of clozapine on cognitive function in schizophlenia. *Journal of Clinical Psychiatry,* **55** (suppl. B), 82–87.

Loo, H., Poirier-Littré, M. F. & Théron, M. E. (1997) Amisulpride versus placebo in the medium-term treatment of the negative symptoms of schizophrenia. *British Journal of Psychiatry,* **170**, 18–22.

Marder, S. R. & Meibach, R. C. (1994) Risperidone in the treatment of schizophrenia. American Journal of Psychiatry, **151**, 825–835.

Meltzer, H. Y. (1995) Role of serotonin in the action of atypical antipsychotic drugs. *Clinical Neuroscience,* **3**, 64–75.

Meltzer, H. Y., Lee, M. A. & Ranjan, R. (1994) Recent advances in the pharmacotherapy of schizophrenia. *Acta Psychiatrica Scandinavica,* suppl. **384**, 95–101.

Möller, H. J. (1995) Neuere Entwicklungen in der antipsychotischen Medikation. *Schweizer Archiv für Neurologie und Psychiatrie,* **146**, 230–239.

Möller, H. J. (1998) Atypische Neuroleptika: Definitionsprobleme. Wirkungsmechanismen und Wirksubstanzen. In *Schizophrenie – Moderne Konzepte zu Diagnostik, Pathogenese und Therapie* (Eds. Möller, H. J. & Müller, N.) Münchner Kraepelin Symposium. Wien, New York: Springer.

Möller, H. J., Boyer, P. & Fleurot, O. (1997) Improvement of acute exacerbations of schizophrenia with amisulpride a comparison to haloperidol, *Psychopharmacology,* **132**, 396–401.

Möller, H. J., Gagiano, A. C., Addington, D. E., et al. (in press) Long-term treatment of chronic schizophrenia with risperidone: an open-label, multicenter study of 386 patients. Submitted to *International Clinical Psychopharmacology*.

Möller, H. J. & Müller, H. (1997) Statistical differentiation between direct and indirect effects of neuroleptics on negative symptoms. *European Archives of Psychiatry and of Clinical Neuroscience*, **247**, 1–5.

Möller, H. J., Müller, H., Borison, R. L., et al. (1995) A path-analytical approach to differentiate between direct and indirect drug effects on negative symptoms in schizophrenia patients. A re-evaluation of the North American risperidone study. *European Archives of Psychiatry and of Clinical Neuroscience*, **245**, 45–49.

Möller, H. J., Van Praag, H. M, Aufdembrinke, B., et al. (1994) Negative symptoms in schizophrenia: Considerations for clinical trials. Working group on negative symptoms in schizophrenia. *Psychopharmacology*, **115**, 221–228.

Ögren, S. O., Florvall, L., Hall, H., et al. (1990) Neuropharmacological and behavioural properties of remoxipride in the rat. *Acta Psychiatrica Scandinavica*, **82** (suppl. 358), 21–26.

Petit, M., Raniwalla, J., Tweed, J., et al. (1996) A comparison of an atypical and typical antipsychotic, zotepine versus haloperidol in patients with acute exacerbations of schizophrenia: A parallel group double-blind trial. *Psychopharmacological Bulletin*, **32**, 81–87.

Peuskens, J. (1995) Risperidone in the treatment of patients with chronic schizophrenia: A multi-national, multi-centre, double-blind, parallel-group study versus haloperidol. Risperidone Study Group. *British Journal of Psychiatry*, **166**, 712–726.

Satterlee, W., Dellva, M. A., Beasley, C., et al. (1996) Effectiveness of olanzapine in long-term continuation treatment. *Psychopharmacological Bulletin*, **32**, 509.

Street, J. S., Tamura, R., Sanger, T., et al. (1996) Long-term treatment-emergent dyskinetic symptoms in patients treated with olanzapine and haloperidol. *Psychopharmacological Bulletin*, **32**, 529.

Tollefson, G. D. & Sanger, T. M. ( 1997) Negative symptoms: A path-analytical approach to a double-blind, placebo- and haloperidol-controlled clinical trial with olanzapine. *American Journal of Psychiatry*, **154**, 466–474.

Tran, P., Beasley, C. & Tollefson, G. (1996) *Acute and long-term results of the dose ranging double-blind olanzapine trial*. Melbourne: CINP Congress.

Wehnert, A., (1998) The European Post-marketing Observational Serdolect (EPOS) Project: Increasing our understanding of schizophrenia therapy.

Wolfersdorf, M., Konig, F. & Straub, R. (1994) Pharmacotherapy of delusional depression: experience with combinations of antidepressants with the neuroleptic zotepine and haloperidol. *Neuropsychobiology*, **29**, 189–193.

Zimbroff, D. L., Kane, J. M., Tamminga, C. A., et al. (1997) Controlled, dose-response study of sertindole and haloperidol in the treatment of schizophrenia. *American Journal of Psychiatry*, **154**, 782–791.

# The Pharmacologic Treatment of First Episode Schizophrenia

Brian Sheitman

A study of the psychobiology of first episode schizophrenia and schizoaffective disorder has been ongoing at Hillside Hospital, New York, since 1986, under the direction of Jeffrey Lieberman and John Kane. The first cohort described was of 70 Research Diagnostic Criteria (RDC) schizophrenic ($n$ = 54) and schizoaffective ($n$ = 16) first-episode patients. The criteria for inclusion into this study were: No prior psychotic episodes; a lifetime history of less than 12 weeks of antipsychotic medication use; age 16–40; no history of any neuromedical disorder that could influence either the diagnosis or the biological variables that were to be assessed; a diagnosis of definite or probable schizophrenia or schizoaffective disorder (mainly schizophrenia) by RDC. Patients that met the eligibility criteria and who were willing and able to give informed consent were enrolled into the protocol. The design of the study included first an acute treatment phase and then patients were followed up by research psychiatrists over the next five years (Lieberman et al., 1993 & 1996)

The subjects had been ill for extended periods of time before coming into treatment: The median duration of psychotic symptoms prior to entry was 52±82 weeks. Psychiatric symptoms were noted to have been present for even longer periods of time (151±176 weeks). This finding, though somewhat puzzling, is consistent with other first-episode patient samples.

The patient sample was 56% male, had a mean age at entry of 24.3 ± 6 years, was 44% Caucasian, 32% African-American, 17% Hispanic, and 7% Asian. Most patients were of the middle and lower social classes. Patients had a high level of psychopathology at entry. The Clinical Global Impression scores were 5.6 ± 1.2 (5 = markedly ill, 6 = severely ill), while the Clinical Global Assessment scores were 24.5 ± 9.3 (scores range from 0–100). Seventy seven percent of patients met criteria for a diagnosis of schizophrenia (19% paranoid, 54% undifferentiated, 3% disorganized, 1% catatonic) and 23% for schizoaffective disorder (7% manic, 16% depressed). Seventy percent of patients had received no antipsychotic treatment prior to entry into the study. All patients were free of antipsychotic medication for 14 days before baseline assessment.

A variety of structured psychometric instruments, including the Schedule for Affective Disorders and Schizophrenia-Change version, Scale for the Assessment of Negative symptoms, Clinical Global Impression Scale, Clinical Global Assessment Scale, Simpson-Angus Neurological Rating Scale, and Simpson Dyskinesia Scale were administered at baseline, twice weekly throughout the acute treatment using an open standardized algorithm and proceeded through this until remission criteria were met. The medication consisted of sequential trials of fluphenazine (20mg for 6 weeks, then 40mg for 4 weeks), haloperidol (20mg for 6 weeks, then 40mg for 4 weeks), molindone hydrochloride (up to 300mg/day), and finally clozapine (up to 900mg/day). Based on both positive and negative symptoms and Clinical Global Impression (CGI) scores, operational criteria were used to define full or partial remission.

Using a survival analysis to determine cumulative response rates, 83% of patients had met remission criteria by one year. The median and mean time required for remission was 11 and 36 weeks, respectively. Though the overall response rate was high, the time required to meet remission criteria was longer than had been expected. This may have been due to the stringent criteria used to define remission. Sixty two percent of the patients developed at least one form of an acute extra-pyramidal side effect, suggesting that first-episode patients are more vulnerable to the side-effects of antipsychotic medication. The length of time a patient had been ill (psychotic) prior to entry was found to be associated with a longer time to, and a lower level of remission. Brain pathomorphology and abnormal basal growth hormone secretion also significantly predicted time to remission.

Ten patients that did not meet remission criteria while treated with typical antipsychotic medication in the standardized protocol went on to receive a trial of clozapine. After clozapine treatment, only three of these 10 patients met response criteria that are typically used for improvement in refractory patients (20% reduction in Brief Psychiatric Rating scale scores and a Clinical Global Improvement score of 3 or less). The criteria for full remission were considerably more stringent. These results suggested that those patients who do not remit from their first episode are likely to be among the most severely ill schizophrenia patients.

Though the remission rates from the first episode cohort were much higher than are typically found in the treatment of chronic patient samples, relapse rates were also very high. Using a survival analysis, 86% of patients had at least one relapse over a five-year period. During this period, treatment was not as rigidly controlled, as in the initial study. Patients were advised to continue their medication for at least one year after meeting remission criteria. Preliminary data suggest that patients were five times more likely to relapse when medication-free. Psychosocial treatments were not standardized during this time.

Twenty two patients whose first episode remitted subsequently relapsed, and six patients had a second relapse. The median ±SE times to remission for the two-episode group were 8.4 ± 1.3 weeks for the first and 11.9 ± 2.3 weeks for the second episode. All 22 patients remitted after their first episode, while only 20 remitted after their first episode, while only 20 remitted from the second episode. The median ±SE remission times for the 6 patients who had three episodes were 4 ± 2.5 weeks, 7 ± 1.6 weeks, and 24.1 ± 2.5 weeks, respectively. Only four of the six patients have remitted from the third episode. However, preliminary evidence from the study of brain pathomorphology suggests that there may be changes in patients' cortical and ventricular volumes that are consistent with the clinical deterioration evidences in some of these patients.

Preliminary clinical data are also available describing the efficacy of the atypical antipsychotic drugs risperidone ($n$ = 16) and clozapine ($n$ = 30) in the treatment of a similarly defined cohort of patients. Of the risperidone-treated patients, 9 of 13 remitted, while 3 patients dropped-out of treatment; of the 23 clozapine-treated patients, 15 remitted, with 7 dropping-out of treatment. Side-effect rates were considerably higher than reported in chronic samples. Seven out of the first 11 risperidone-treated patients developed acute extra-pyramidal side-effects, while most of the clozapine-treated patients complained of sedation, increased salivation, and weight gain. This again suggests that the medication doses required for the treatment of a first episode of psychosis, typical or atypical, are lower than for a chronic multi-episode patient (Sheitman et al., 1997).

The remission rates from the first episode patients treated with atypical antipsychotic medication were higher than those found in chronic multi-episode patient samples, but not greater than the rates from the cohort of patients treated with typical antipsychotic medication. This was not surprising, since 83% of the typical antipsychotic-treated group had met response criteria by one year. Some trends did emerge which suggested that clozapine was more efficacious in the treatment of negative symptoms and depression than the treatment used in the other two groups. However, this must be interpreted with caution, since the doses of medication used for the risperidone – and typically – treated cohorts were likely to have been much higher than what now would be considered optimum, and resulted in considerable acute extra pyramidal side-effects.

Overall, the results of the treatment of first episode schizophrenia and schizoaffective patients demonstrated that these patients have a better response to antipsychotic medication than chronic multi-episode patient samples.

47

Nevertheless, most patients will go on to have future relapses, with some of these them showing deterioration across episodes. These data, in addition to those demonstrating that the duration of untreated psychosis predicted the time required to remit from the first episode, are suggestive of an active morbid process that occurs early in the illness. Since patients did not come into treatment until, on average, one year after the onset of psychotic symptoms, the early identification and treatment of psychosis should be of the utmost importance.

The long delay in seeking treatment, with its potential deleterious consequences, have led some to suggest that this should be considered a major public health problem.

# References

Lieberman, J. A., Koreen, A. R., Chakos, M., et al. (1996) Factors influencing treatment response and outcome of first-episode schizophrenia: Implications for understanding the pathophysiology of schizophrenia. *Journal of Clinical Psychiatry*, **57** (suppl. 9), 5–9.

Lieberman, J. A., Jody, D., Geisler, S., et al. (1993) Time course and biologic correlates of treatment response in first episode schizophrenia. *Archives of General Psychiatry*, **50**, 369–376.

Lieberman, J. A., Alvir, J. A. J., Koreen, A., et al. (1996) Psychobiologic correlates of treatment response in schizophrenia. *Neuropsychopharmacology*, **14** (3S), 13S–21S.

Sheitman, B. B., Lee, H., Strauss, R. & Lieberman, J. A. (1997) The evaluation and treatment of first-episode psychosis. *Schizophrenia Bulletin*, **23** (4), 653–661.

# Effect of Atypical Antipsychotic Drugs on Cognitive Function in Schizophrenia

Herbert Y. Meltzer and Susan R. McGurk

Patients with schizophrenia have widespread, multifaceted impairment in neurocognitive function: Cognitive impairment is an early feature of the illness (Saykin et al., 1994). Indeed, some aspects of the deficit may precede the development of psychotic symptoms. For most patients, once the deficit is established at the end of the first episode, the extent of impairment changes only marginally over time, although there are clearly significant numbers of patients in whom it is progressive and reaches the proportions characteristic of severe dementia (Goldberg, 1993). An enormous range of tests have been applied to patients with schizophrenia; the frequency and extent of abnormalities vary with the test. It has been estimated that about 40% of patients with schizophrenia have impaired neurocognition (Braff et al., 1991; Goldberg et al., 1988), but this may be a gross underestimate. The major deficits may be found in executive function (abstraction/flexibility), attention, learning, working memory, semantic memory, verbal and visual spatial memory, and psychomotor performance (Braff et al., 1991; Saykin et al., 1994). These abnormalities in cognition are believed to be the result of abnormalities in the frontal and temporal lobes and in the mechanisms of connectivity between these regions of the brain (Frith, 1987).

There is little question about the functional significance of these cognitive impairments. In a recent review of the functional consequences of neurocognitive deficits in schizophrenia, Green (1996) concluded that the most consistent finding was that verbal memory was associated with three types of outcome measures: 1) community survival and function; 2) social problem-solving; and 3) skill acquisition. Vigilance was related to social problem-solving and skill acquisition. Executive function/abstraction was related to community functioning but not to social problem-solving. Cognitive impairment is also highly correlated with quality of life measures (Sevy & Davidson, 1994).

The treatment of schizophrenia has, up until now, been mainly focused on positive symptoms. More recently, negative symptoms have also been targeted, but with much less success. There has been virtually no effort made to specifically ameliorate the cognitive deficits in schizophrenia or to understand their pharmacology – a strategy which may be likely to lead to therapeutic advances even more rapidly than the necessary efforts to identify the neuronal basis for these deficits. Recent studies which have established that function such as visual-spatial working memory are dependent on intact dopamine function in the prefrontal cortex and related do $D_1$ receptor function in particular, are of great importance in the process of determining whether deficits in specific neurotransmitters are the cause of the cognitive impairment in schizophrenia. It has recently been suggested that cognitive impairment should become the target of pharmacological intervention in schizophrenia (Davidson & Keefe, 1995). These authors proposed the use of pharmacological agents that are independent of any action on positive symptoms to correct cognitive deficits, and suggest that drugs which enhance cholinergic or dopaminergic activity might be beneficial.

There has been extensive investigation of the effect of typical neuroleptics on cognitive functioning. Typical neuroleptics are potent $D_2$ receptor antagonists and are reasonably effective in the treatment of positive symptoms. However, their efficacy in regard to the improvement of cognitive impairments, which will briefly be reviewed below, has generally been found to be minimal. The concept of an atypical antipsychotic drug was reintroduced to mainstream research in schizophrenia with the evitalization of interest in clozapine. Clozapine was first labeled as atypical because it produced an antipsychotic action without causing acute or chronic extrapyramidal side-effects such as parkinsonism, dystonia, and akathisia. Thioridazine also produced low extrapyramidal side-effects but not nearly so few as clozapine or some of the newer atypical antipsychotic drugs such as risperidone, olanzapine, sertindole, quetiapine, and ziprasidone. Of these drugs, only clozapine has been demonstrated to not cause tardive dyskinesia. Risperidone produces dose-dependent extrapyramidal side-effects, which has been attributed to the extent of $D_2$ receptor blockade at higher doses, so that it is not atypical at all doses. It is unclear whether the other newer agents produce significant EPS at higher doses.

As will be discussed below, there is increasing evidence that clozapine and risperidone may improve some aspects of cognitive function. For both of these agents, however, more studies are required before definitive conclusions can be reached. There are almost no data for the other atypical antipsychotic drugs, but it can be shown that these drugs have beneficial effects on cognition, it would provide a major reason for using them as the standard treatment of schizophrenia, given that improvement in cognition has important advantages for outcome in this disorder. In the case of clozapine, it might greatly alter the risk/benefit ratio for using it and greatly increase its cost-effectiveness.

# Effect of Typical Neuroleptics on Cognitive Function

Patients with schizophrenia demonstrate impairments in various neuropsychological domains such as attention, attainment and shifting of conceptual set, vigilance, verbal learning and memory, working memory, and motor functioning. Comparisons of performance on neuropsychological assessments of these domains in schizophrenia have been examined in both medicated and unmedicated patients. There appear to be some minimal advantages as well as liabilities in some areas of cognition, but overall it appears that conventional antipsychotics have little impact on the wide ranging and often severe neuropsychological deficits in schizophrenia.

Early studies of the effects of phenothiazines on two tests of attention, the Continuous Performance Test (CPT) and the Digit Symbol Substitution Test (DSST) demonstrated that single doses impaired performance on both tests (Kornestsky, 1957). However, chronic administration of chlorpromazine was found to improve performance on the CPT. This improvement in sustained attention with chronic administration of chlorpromazine has been replicated in several subsequent studies.

With regard to abstraction and set-shifting, reduced (rCBF) in the prefrontal cortex was found in medicated and unmedicated patients while attempting the Wisconsin Card Sort, and similar poor performance was found in both groups. It was concluded that neuroleptics had minimal effects on prefrontal functioning. Killian et al. (1984) failed to detect any effects of haloperidol, flupenthixol, or clozapine on the Stroop test, which is also a measure of prefrontal functioning. Additionally, there are no neuroleptic-induced alterations on the Trail Making Test – a measure of set-shifting and visuotracking. Evaluations of effects of typical neuroleptics on maze performance have demonstrated a beneficial effect (Gardner et al., 1955), a detrimental effect (Porteus, 1957), and no effects on performance (Small et al., 1972).

Numerous studies find no effects of acute or chronic administration of neuroleptics on verbal learning and memory. This was true despite the variety of assessments used to evaluate learning and memory, including the WMS-R Logical Memory and Paired Associate subtests, which measure both short- and long-term verbal memory. However, because of the well-established liability for memory that anticholinergic agents have both in animals and humans, the effects of neuroleptic treatment on this cognitive domain should be examined independent of concomitant anticholinergic treatment. With regard to the visuospatial and visuomotor domains, improved performance after chronic administration of chlorpromazine has been found in the WAIS-R Block Design and Picture Arrangement.

Acute administration of typical antipsychotic medication resulted in decrements in performance on tasks of motor dexterity as measured by the Finger Tapping Test and the Pursuit Rotar Tests. Chronic administration has no effect on performance on these tasks. Coull et al. (1995) demonstrated a non-specific slowing of reactions times following acute administration of 0.5 mg of haloperidol in a non-psychiatric population.

Thus, acute administration of neuroleptics impairs some tests of vigilance and motor performance, while chronic administration of neuroleptics may improve function for at least some complex cognitive tasks requiring sustained attention and problem-solving. It remains to be determined if this improved performance is due to the direct effects of medication on neuropsychological function or a result of improved clinical status.

# Effect of Atypical Neuroleptics on Cognitive Function: Clozapine

The first published study of the effect of clozapine on cognition reported that after an average of 15 months of treatment, there was no significant improvement in attention, memory, or higher level problem-solving in 13 patients with schizophrenia, despite significant improvement in symptoms. The test battery included the Wechsler Adult Intelligence Scale-Revised (WAIS-R), the Wechsler Memory Scale-Revised, the Digit Symbol, Trail Making Part B, the Category Test, the Wisconsin Card Sorting Test, Facial Recognition, Line Orientation, and Wide Range Achievement Test. The average symptom scores declined by 40%, and 10 out of the 15 were responders by conventional criteria. No measure of cognitive performance improved significantly over the course of the study; in fact, visual memory significantly worsened. The baseline was obtained on typical neuroleptic drug treatment. However, there were some factors in this study which might have influenced the outcome. The range of time on clozapine before the drug effect was tested was 3–24 months, but 14 of the 15 patients were tested after 6 months, which should have been sufficient to detect an effect if one had occurred. Six of the patients were receiving lithium in addition to clozapine. Others received fluoxetine, lorazepam, valproate, primdone, or levothyroxine. The authors related the inability of these patients to resume social functioning to their lack of improvement in cognition, despite the improvement in symptoms. The negative effect on visual memory was attributed to its anticholinergic effects. The baseline level of cognition in this group of patients was within the range expected for patients with schizophrenia.

A different pattern emerged in the study of Haggar et al. (1993) from his

52

laboratory. In that study, 36 treatment-refractory schizophrenic patients were studied before initiation of clozapine, and at 6 weeks and 6 months thereafter. Compared to 26 normal controls, the subjects as a group, were impaired at baseline on all the tests used: 1) the Wisconsin Card Sort to test Conceptual Sorting and Abstraction; 2) the Wechsler Intelligence Scale-Revised-Maze (WISC-R) test of executive function/planning and organization; 3) Controlled Word Association Test and Category Instance Generation test of semantic memory; 4) Digit Symbol Test of sustained attention; 5) The Consonant Trigram Test of working or primary memory; and 6) the Immediate and Delayed Recall test of long-term episodic memory using the Buschke and Fuld restrictive re-minding procedure. The majority of patients ($N=27$) were first studied off neuroleptics (mean 9.2 days), but because these patients were neuroleptic-re-sistant, they showed little or no worsening during this period of time. As noted below, patients studied pre-post clozapine with baselines on typical neurolep-tic drugs have also shown improvement on clozapine (Buchanan et al., 1994; Hoff et al., 1994; Galletly et al., in press). In a preliminary study, Haggar et al. found that no systematic improvement occurred in patients who performed the battery twice over a three-week period.

After six weeks of treatment with clozapine monotherapy, scores signifi-cantly increased on the Controlled Oral Word Association Test, decreased in the Consonant Trigram Test, and remained unchanged in all other tests. By six months, significantly improvement was noted in the Digit Symbol Test, The Category Instance Generation Test, the WISC-R Maze Test and the immediate condition of the Verbal List Learning Test. The Consonant Trigram Test had returned to normal. There was no change in the Wisconsin Card Sort Test at any time. Significant improvement in the Brief Psychiatric Rating Scale score and the Positive Symptom subscale was noted. Improvement in the cognitive test scores was predicted by improvement in BPRS Negative Symptom ratings more than in other domains of psychopathology.

The results suggested that clozapine can improve both frontal and temporal lobe function, with the exception of transient worsening of working memory, which is primarily a frontal lobe function. This may be related to the D1 an-tagonist properties of clozapine which are appreciable. The variability in the extent and time-course of response to clozapine may reflect the unique sys-tems which subserve each test and the possibility that the effects which medi-ate the response are not simply alterations in the release of or response to neurotransmitter and neuromodulators. It seems possible that long-term changes in synaptic plasticity may underlie these changes. The fact that clozapine could improve some aspects of memory, despite its marked anticholinergic proper-ties, may reflect the fact that it is a cholinomimetic agent as well. The ability of clozapine to increase dopamine release in the prefrontal cortex may be relevant to its ability to improve frontal lobe functions. It has been postulated that decreased dopaminergic activity in the prefrontal cortex may be related to negative symptoms. Although clozapine did not significantly improve negative symptoms in this group of patients, there was a clear relationship between the change in negative symptoms and the improvement in cognitive function. This suggests that there could be a common basis for the effect of clozapine on both negative symptoms and cognitive function.

Since the publication of this study, there have been several others which have reported improvement in cognitive function. No study has failed to find any improvement in cognitive function, as did Goldberg et al. (1988). These other studies will now be reviewed.

Lee et al. (1994) randomly assigned patients who were good responders to typical neuroleptic drugs to clozapine ($N$=35) or typical neuroleptics ($N$=29). They were administered the same battery as the patients in the Hagger et al. study at baseline and at 6 weeks, 6 months, and 12 months. Treatment with clozapine improved attention, verbal fluency, and executive function at 6 weeks; improvement in these measures was maintained throughout the 12-month period. The extent of improvement in these measures was usually greater in magnitude than that observed in treatment-resistant patients. Performance on the Controlled Oral Word Association test reached levels associated with normals. Evidence has been summarized elsewhere that the Controlled Oral Word Association test may reflect frontal lobe functioning. Worsening at 6 weeks followed by normalization was again found for the Consonant Trigrams test. This has not been observed with other atypical antipsychotic drugs (e.g., risperidone or melperone). Treatment with typical neuroleptics produced a significant time effect at 6 weeks, in immediate recall of word list at 6 months, and in the Wisconsin Card Sort Categories Formed at 12 months, but not at other times, despite the fact that these patients responded very well to haloperidol or other typical neuroleptics. This indicates that the improvement in psychopathology was not related to a learning effect or secondary to general well-being. There was no consistent relationship between improvement in psychopathology and neurocognitive testing in the clozapine-treated patients.

Buchanan et al. (1994) compared the effects of clozapine and haloperidol after 10 weeks of double-blind treatment in a total of 39 patients who were randomly assigned to either drug. These patients were partial responders to typical neuroleptic drugs. Patients on haloperidol showed deterioration at end-point on Category Fluency and WAIS-R Block Design. There were no differences in a variety of memory, visual spatial, and executive/attention measures. At the end of the 10 weeks, patients on clozapine were treated open-label and the haloperidol-treated patients were also treated with clozapine. Both groups were reassessed the end of 12 months. One year of clozapine treatment was associated with significant improvement in Verbal Fluency, Mooney Faces Closure, and WAIS-R Block Design. There were trend improvements in the Stroop Color-Word Interference Test, Category Fluency, and the Logical Memory WMS-ER subscale. Trails B performance significantly declined over the one-year period, but no change in Wisconsin Card Sorting was noted. There were significant relationships between change in neuropsychological test performance, especially verbal fluency and memory tests, and change in quality of life scale scores.

Hoff et al. (1996) studied 20 chronically hospitalized, refractory schizophrenic patients while on typical neuroleptics and again after 12 weeks of clozapine treatment. Improvement in the Controlled Oral Word Association Test (verbal fluency), Symbol Digit Modalities Test, and Finger Tapping (psychomotor) was noted. There was a trend for improvement in verbal list learning. In contrast, patients treated with clozapine made more errors on the Benton Visual Retention Test, a test of short-term visual memory, and the Wisconsin Card Sorting Test.

Grace et al. (1996) reported an open trial of clozapine in treatment-refractory hospital patients with schizophrenia. A repeated measures design was used. Thirty-one patients received both clozapine and psychosocial treatment. Data were collected at baseline 1, 2, and 3 years. Clozapine was associated with improvement in learning and recall, Trails A and B, verbal fluency, recall memory, attention, and psychomotor performance. However, the improvement in psychopathology was not well correlated with the improvement in cognition. Very little further improvement was noted between years 1 and 2 or 3.

Finally, Galletly et al. (in press) assessed cognitive function and quality of life in 19 patients treated with clozapine for an average of 6.5 months. These patients were described as having mild symptoms, but unlike the patients studied by Lee et al. (1994), their duration of illness was 10.3+/–5.3 years and the mean number of hospitalizations was 8.6+/–6.8. During the course of treatment with clozapine, there was a dramatic improvement in positive and negative symptoms, depression rating, and quality of life. The mean estimated premorbid IQ was 107.6. A MANOVA comparing the pre-clozapine neuropsychological test scores with the scores at endpoint was highly significant ($F = 16$, df = 1, $p = 0.001$). Significant changes were found in the Digit Symbol, the WAIS-R Block Design and Similarities, the delayed recall condition of Verbal List Learning, the Controlled Oral Word Association Test, and the Consonant Trigram. These results were very similar to those of Haggar et al. (1993), with the exception of the improvement in the test of working memory (Consonant Trigram). Also in agreement with the results of Haggar et al. (1993), there was a good relationship between improvement in quality of life and improvement in specific cognitive measures, e.g., the Digit Symbol Substitution Test and test of verbal memory and visual-spatial concept formation. Changes in positive symptoms correlated with improvement in verbal concept formation, visual attention and psychomotor speed, and immediate recall. This suggests a relationship between positive symptoms and attention. The reduction in negative symptoms was correlated with improved retrieval from verbal reference memory and delayed memory. The authors concluded that negative symptoms may be related to impaired ability to retrieve stored information.

In summary, the overwhelming body of evidence with regard to clozapine and cognitive function suggests that it can improve some but not all cognitive measures in a significant number of patients, regardless of whether they are very severely ill and chronic or more recent onset and mildly ill. Some domains of cognition such as verbal fluency and recall memory under the immediate condition appear particularly responsive to clozapine. On the other hand, the Wisconsin Card Sort test of executive function/abstraction and the consonant trigram are usually but not always unresponsive to clozapine. There is no evidence for impairment in long-term memory or attention. These results are very encouraging. The fact that at least four studies (Haggar et al., 1993; Buchanan et al., 1994; Lee et al., 1994; Galletly et al., 1997) show a relationship between quality of life and cognitive measures after clozapine treatment strongly suggests that this degree of cognitive improvement is functionally significant.

While most of the long-term studies are not controlled, with the exception of that by Lee et al. (1994), it is still possible to conclude that the effects of clozapine on cognition are enduring. The fact that not all tests improve on clozapine suggests that specific brain regions and functions are improved, rather than a non-specific mechanism which affects overall function.

# Risperidone

Risperidone, like clozapine, has high affinity for 5-HT2a receptors, relative to $D_2$ receptors (Leysen et al., 1988). It has been reported to be superior to haloperidol for the reduction of positive and negative symptoms, but to produce fewer extrapyramidal side-effects (EPS). Because risperidone reduces the need for treatment of EPS with anticholinergic agents, it is suggested that on this basis alone, it would improve cognition.

The effects of risperidone vs. haloperidol have been examined on two measures of cognitive functioning – spatial working memory and Trail Making. Spatial working memory tasks require subjects to view a target stimulus briefly and then indicate the location of the target after a delay. Accurate performance on this task requires the formation of an internal representation of spatial location to guide the delayed response. This function is supported by the dorsolateral prefrontal cortex (Goldman-Rakic, 1991) and is impaired in schizophrenia (Park and Holzman, 1992). Although animal studies indicate a role for both dopamine

(Williams and Goldman-Rakic, 1993) and acetylcholine (McGurk et al., 1990), the neurochemistry that supports spatial working memory in humans is not well understood. Data from a multi-site, double-blind, parallel comparison of halo-peridol and risperidone in treatment-resistant schizophrenia indicate a superior effect of risperidone on a task of spatial working memory.

The effects of risperidone vs. haloperidol on spatial working memory were examined in a double-blind study in treatment-resistant schizophrenia. It was found that following 4 weeks of treatment with 6 mg of risperidone or 15 mg of haloperidol, risperidone had a beneficial effect on spatial working memory, as compared to haloperidol (McGurk et al., 1996). This beneficial effect was explained, in part, by the differential coadministration of benztropine mesylate, an anticholinergic, to the haloperidol patients. However, after controlling for the effects of benztropine as well as symptom changes, the beneficial effect of risperidone on performance of this task remained. Therefore, these findings suggest that the favorable effects of risperidone on spatial working memory may be due to direct effects of risperidone.

Similar findings were demonstrated for Trail Making Part B. Risperidone was found to decrease significantly the amount of time to completion of Part B, as compared to haloperidol. Changes in positive and negative symptoms, differential coadministration of benztropine, and attention and psychomotor speed (as measured by Trail Making Part A) did not account for the improve-ment in Trail Making Part B for risperidone. Again, beneficial effects on pre-frontal functioning from the direct effects of risperidone are postulated.

# Conclusion

Cognitive impairment is apparent in every area of functioning in the patients included in this review, although not every patient shows every type of impair-ment and the degree of impairment ranges from mild to severe within indi-vidual subjects. These studies confirm that the impairment in cognition is more closely related to quality of life and overall function than to positive or nega-tive symptoms, but both are related to cognitive functioning as well, especially negative symptoms. There is some evidence for modest effects of typical neu-roleptic drugs on sustained attention, but also evidence for worsening in some studies, e.g., Buchanan et al. (1994). It may safely be concluded that typical neuroleptic drugs are without significant impact on cognitive function in schizo-phrenia. However, with regard to atypical antipsychotic drugs, much greater promise is evident. Clozapine in particular has now been found to improve selected aspects of cognition in five out of six studies. The only one which failed to find an effect was that of Goldberg et al. (1993); this was the smallest and included some polypharmacy, which may have compromised the effect of clozapine. The other five studies were in fairly good agreement as to which aspects of cognitive function were improved by clozapine, with a few exceptions. The main area of agreement was the effect on verbal fluency, as assessed by the Controlled Word Association Test. All five studies identified improvement in this test, usually between 6–12 weeks, but the study of Buchanan et al. (1994) did not observe the improvement until 12 months. The pattern of improvement suggests that clozapine improved both frontal and temporal lobe function, but not all aspects of either. Only one study found an effect on the Wisconsin Card Sorting Test, which is a predominantly frontal lobe test but also engages other cortical areas. The effect of clozapine on working memory requires further study. Both studies from our laboratory found worsening at 6 weeks in the Auditory Consonant Trigram Test.

Hoff et al. (1997) also reported worsening at 12 weeks on a measure of short-term visual memory. The Wisconsin Card Sorting Test, which is considered to have a working memory component, was resistant to improvement by clozapine. However, both Haggar et al. (1993) and Lee et al. (1994) noted normalization of this test at 6 and 12 months and Galletly et al. (1997) reported improvement with clozapine at 6 months in the Consonant Trigram Test. Additional tests of clozapine on working memory tasks are indicated. If working memory impairment continues to be demonstrated by treatment with clozapine, this may indicate the need for more prolonged trials with clozapine, before determining how beneficial it will be in the treatment of schizophrenia.

Risperidone improved both visuospatial and verbal working memory following 6 weeks of treatment, but it is unclear how it affects of areas of cognition. Patients with deficits in working memory may be specific candidates for risperidone.

Intensive study of other atypical antipsychotics, e.g., olanzapine, ziprasidone, quetiapine, iloperidone, etc. are needed to determine the ability of these drugs to improve specific cognitive functions. It could be that each drug will have one or more areas where it is most effective. This could be the basis for determining which drug to use in patients with prominent abnormalities in specific areas, e.g., verbal fluency, and relative sparing of other types of functions. If it should be found that clozapine is uniquely effective in improving cognitive function, this would clearly necessitate a reevaluation of the role of clozapine in treating schizophrenia. Clozapine has already been shown to be superior to other agents in treating neuroleptic-resistant patients, and not causing tardive dyskinesia. It may have advantages in treating psychopathology in the neuroleptic-responsive patients, decreasing suicidality, etc. but much more direct comparison with the newer agents is needed to test this in controlled trials.

58

# References

Braff, D. L., Heaton, R., Kuck, J., et al. (1991) The generalized pattern of neuropsychological deficits in outpatients with chronic schizophrenia with hetogeneous Wisconsin Card Sorting Test results. *Archives of General Psychiatry*, **48**, 891–898.

Buchanan, R. W., Holstein, C. & Breier, A. (1994) The comparative efficacy and long-term effect of clozapine treatment on neuropsychological test performance. *Biological Psychiatry*, **36**, 717–725.

Carpenter, W. T., Schooler, N. R., Wise, S. S., et al. (1988) Treatment, services and environmental factors. *Schizophrenia Bulletin*, **14** (3), 427–437.

Davidson, M. & Keefe, R. S. E. (1995) Cognitive impairment as a target for pharmacological treatment in schizophrenia. *Schizophrenia Research*, **72**, 161–166.

Galletly, C. A., Clark, C. R., McFarlane, A. C. & Weber, D. L. (1997) Relationships between changes in symptom ratings, neurophysiological test performance and quality of life in schizophrenic patients treated with clozapine. *Psychiatry Research*.

Goldberg, T. E., Calls, J. R., Weinberger, D. R., et al. (1988) Performance of schizophrenic patients on putative neuropsychological tests of frontal lobe function. *International Journal of Neurosciences*, **42**, 51–58.

Grace, J., Bellus, S. P., Raulin, M. L., et al. (1996) Long-term impact of clozapine and psychosocial treatment on psychiatric symptoms and cognitive functioning. *Psychiatric Services*, **4**, 41–45.

Hoff, A. L., Faustman, W. O., Wienecke, M., et al. (1996) The efffects of clozapine on symptom reduction, neurocognitive function, and clinical management in treatment-refactory state hospital schizophrenic inpatients. *Neuropsychopharmacology*, **15**, 361–369.

Killian, G. A., Holzman, P. S., Davis, J. M. & Gibbons, R. (1984) Effects of psychotropic medication on selected cognitive and perceptual measures. *Journal of Abnormal Psychology*, **93**, 58–70.

Lee, M. A., Thompson, P.A. & Meltzer, H. Y. (1994) Effects of clozapine on cognitive function in schizophrenia. *Journal of Clinical Psychiatry*, **55** (suppl. B), 82–87.

Leysen, J. E., Gommeren, W., Eens, A. & de Chaffoy de Courcelles, D. (1988) Biochemical profile of risperidone, a new antipsychotic, *J. Pharmacol. Exp. Ther.*, **247**, 661–670.

Nestor, P. G., Faux, S. F., McCarleyk, R.W., et al. (1991) Neuroleptics improve sustained attention in schizophrenia. A study using signal detection theory. *Neuropsychopharmacology*, **4**, 145–149.

Saykin, A. J., Gur, R. C., Gur, R. J., Mozley, D., et al. (1991) Neuropsychological function in schizophrenia: Selective impairment in learning and memory. *Archives of General Psychiatry*, **48**, 618–624.

Sevy, S. & Davidson, M. (1995) The cost of cognitive impairment in schizophrenia. *Schizophrenia Research*, **17**, 1–3.

Small, I. F., Small, J. G., Milstein, V. & Moore, J. E. (1972) Neuropsychological observations with psychosis and somatic treatment. Neuropsychological examinations of psychiatric patients. *Journal of Nervous and Mental Disease*, **155**, 6–13.

Williams, S. M. & Goldman-Rakic, P. S. (1993) Characterization of the dopaminergic innervation of the primale frontal cortex using a dopamine-specific antibody. *Cerebral cortex*, **3**, 199–222.

# Psychopharmacotherapy in Early Psychosis

Marco C. G. Merlo

This is the approach to psychopharmacological treatment of early psychosis aims at integrating modern findings of pharmacological research with clinical practice in order to achieve a stable therapeutic relationship and provide a basis for long-term compliance. Pharmacotherapy is part of a complex treatment program that focuses mainly on preserving and furthering the patients' psychological and social resources. At the same time, emphasis is put on reducing as much as possible the devastating effects of psychosis. It is also our contention that the beneficial effects of antipsychotic drugs are lost if clinicians administer them at unnecessarily high doses and without considering modern knowledge of receptor biology.

The treatment of first-episode psychosis necessitates an especially cautious approach, because the patient needs help but at the same time is often very much afraid of contacting a psychiatrist or psychiatric institution. His/her family members, partners, or friends (i.e., significant others) are also very insecure about which kind of help to seek and in whom to confide. Even today, many prejudices and misinterpretations exist concerning psychosis and psychiatric treatment. Strong feelings of shame make it difficult for people to talk frankly about psychotic experiences. Therefore, the first contact with a patient and his/her significant others is essential for the ensuing course of treatment. It determines whether or not a stable therapeutic relationship can be established and the patient will comply with medication. From the very beginning of treatment, clinicians should bear in mind that every psychosis is a sign of an *extreme crisis* and that it necessitates prolonged treatment. At best, 2–3 years of treatment should be offered.

It is important for the psychiatrist to consider the implicit models of illness that the patient and his/her significant others will have. Keeping this in mind, the psychiatrist can then try to conceive a treatment plan that will entail as few coercive measures as possible. The prescription of medication itself implies a medical model of psychosis that may not be shared by the patient or his/her

60

significant others. In contrast, if positive symptoms, i.e., hallucinations, delusions, and disorganized thinking, are present, findings of recent research have shown that a delayed initiation of antipsychotic pharmacotherapy may cause irreversible damage (Wyatt, 1991; Loebel et al., 1993). This knowledge may put the psychiatrist in a dilemma between the time spent in trying to convince the patient to take medication and the need for an early start of drug treatment. Nevertheless, even with the strong pressure of health economics there is no pharmacological argument for starting Dopamine-antagonistic(DA)/Serotonin-Dopamine-antagonistic (SDA) antipsychotic treatment during the first days of hospitalization. For the classification of antipsychotics, see Table 1.

*Table 1.* Classification of antipsychotic agents (modified from Kane & Marder, 1995; Lahti et al., 1996)

*Sedating antipsychotics*
Methotrimeprazine (Nozinan®), chlorprothixene (Truxal®), promazine (Prazine®), pipamperon (Dipiperon®), zuclopenthixol (Clopixol®)

*Dopamine antagonistic (DA) antispsychotics*
Haloperidol (Haldol®), fluphenazine (Dapotum, Lyogen®), flupenthixol (Fluanxol®)

*Serotonin-dopamine antagonistic (SDA) antipsychotics*
Risperidone (Risperdal®)

*Atypical or broad-spectrum antagonistic antipsychotics*
Clozapine (Leponex®), olanzapine (Zyprexa®), sertindole (Serdolect®)

During the early phase of joining the patient in order to convince him/her to take medication, information about its mechanisms of action may help to improve its acceptance. If the patient suffers from delusions of poisoning or of other self-threatening content, an agreement on the necessity for medication should be obtained from one significant other. Our experience on a specialized ward for first-episode psychotic patients (Merlo & Hofer, in press) has shown that substantial benefit is obtained by information exchanging about experiences with medication.

Although the initiation of antipsychotic treatment should be carefully discussed and well planned with the patient and his/her significant others, patients in an excited or highly suicidal state need immediate help. But even in these cases, there is little pharmacological evidence to support starting with DA or SDA antipsychotics immediately. Of much more importance is sedation. This initial sedation should be provided with low dosages of DA antipsychotics or SDA antipsychotics (van Kammen & Marder, 1995). Sedation is better achieved by applying benzodiazepines or low or middle potency

61

(also called sedating, see Table 1) antipsychotics (e.g., levomepromazine, zuclopenthixol).

Furthermore, the cautious approach to the treatment of first-episode psychosis has to take diagnostic insecurities into account before starting drug treatment. Paranoid-hallucinatory syndromes can occur in different diagnostic entities, e.g., mood disorders, mental disorders due to a general medical condition, or substance-related disorders (DSM-IV). Even the DSM-IV section on schizophrenia covers different forms of psychosis which may manifest a paranoid-hallucinatory syndrome. Acute first-episode psychosis with schizophrenic syndrome can be electrophysiologically divided at least into two sub-groups (Merlo et al., 1998). These sub-groups presented different time-courses of remission of the schizophrenic syndrome. While one group remitted after seven days (early responders), the other did so after four weeks (late responders). As the antidopaminergic action of DA and SDA antipsychotics takes effect after 2–3 weeks, research should be done to see if psychosis with early response could be treated only with sedating agents.

Since antipsychotic treatment with DA or SDA antipsychotics implies a duration of at least one year, the decision to put a drug-naive first-episode patient on to such medication is an important one. The possible benefits have to be weighed against the side-effects. In particular, extrapyramidal symptoms, secondary negative symptoms, and cognitive drug-induced dysfunction should be avoided. Finding the lowest effective dose of DA/SDA antipsychotic is the most important strategy to achieve these goals. Stet their seminal paper, Baldessarini et al. (1988) emphasized that moderate doses (i.e., 300–600 milligrams chlorpromazine-equivalent per day) are adequate for most patients with acute psychosis. Several studies have since been published which confirm this finding (e.g., McEvoy et al., 1991). Interestingly, the main support for low-dosage strategies comes from positron emission tomographic (PET) studies (Farde, 1997; Kapur et al., 1996, 1997) which investigate in vivo the receptor affinity of antipsychotic drugs. McEvoy et al. were amongst the first researchers who differentiated between dosages of first- and multi-episode psychotic patients. They found that 2.1 ± 1.1 mg haloperidol were enough in never-treated patients, compared to 4.3 ± 2.4 for patients previously exposed to neuroleptics. Several studies have confirmed the feasibility of low-dose antipsychotic treatment in early psychosis (see Table 2). Kopala et al. (1997) even found that lower doses of risperidone (2–4 mg) produced a better antipsychotic effect than higher dosages (5–8 mg).

The lowest effective dose also helps to avoid administration of anticholinergic drugs, which have been related to a growing incidence of tardive dyskinesia and to cognitive dysfunction (e.g., Spohn & Strauss, 1989). Akathisia and parkinsonism can be interpreted as indicating neuroleptic overdose (Merlo

*Table 2.* Studies on daily dose during psychopharmacological treatment of early psychosis

| Study | | Dosages | Comments |
|---|---|---|---|
| McEvoy et al., 1991 | haloperidol | 2.1±1.1 mg | never medicated patients; neuroleptic threshold |
| *Emsley et al., | haloperidol | 5.6 mg | double-blind, flexible |
| | risperidone | 6.1 mg | dose |
| Kapur et al., 1996 | haloperidol | 2 mg | open, fixed dose |
| *Zhang-Wong et al. | haloperidol | 2 mg | open, fixed, flexible dose |
| Kopola et al., 1996; 1997 | risperidone | 2–4 mg | open study |
| | | 5–8 mg | |

*see McGorry & Edwards, 1997

& Gerlach, 1995). Therefore, instead of masking this overdose with anticholinergic drugs, it is better to reduce the dosage of the antipsychotic medication. If strong extrapyramidal symptoms and secondary negative symptoms occur in very low doses, e.g., 0.5–1 mg risperidone, an early application of atypical antipsychotics should be considered. In a consensus paper (Merlo et al., 1997), Swiss psychiatrists assembled more than twenty years of experiences with clozapine and recommended applying this medication earlier in the course of illness. Further studies are necessary to find out if new atypical antipsychotics like sertindole and olanzapine will have the same effect on patients with treatment-resistant schizophrenia or with strong side-effects at minimal dosages.

Special aspects of the treatment of first-episode patients include the duration of psychotic symptoms prior to treatment, interactions with psychotropic substances, comorbidity and partial response or non-response (Merlo & Gerlach, 1995). The importance of reducing the duration of psychosis prior to treatment has been shown in a number of studies (e.g., Wyatt, 1991). Falloon et al. (1987) have developed family management strategies for the prevention of morbidity in schizophrenia, while McGorry & Edwards (1997) have published a manual for the early detection and treatment of psychosis which integrates psychosocial and psychopharmacological interventions.

In the last five years, we have implemented a neuropsychological laboratory in our specialized unit. Preliminary results of these data confirm the findings of Convit et al. (1991) that patients with neurological soft signs present stronger extrapyramidal side-effects. We also found that these patients suffer from stronger negative symptoms and that they have deficits in non-verbal communication abilities during social interaction (Altorfer et al., 1998). Interestingly, patients with higher dosages performed worse on the span of apprehension and in the Wisconsin Card Sorting Test and had more intermittent slow waves in EEG (Hofer et al., 1997, Merlo et al., 1997).

The treatment of early psychosis is also the place where pharmacological and psychosocial interventions take place. The University Psychiatric Services of Berne has had a specialized ward since 1989 (Merlo & Hofer, in press); its advantages are that it is small (12–14 beds) and that it provides a highly structured treatment plan during the daytime. The nursing staff is well trained and help to provide an anxiety-reducing ward atmosphere. A special treatment program for psychotic patients with individual, group, and family therapy is applied. In a retrospective, two-year follow-up, it was found that only 27% of the patients treated on this ward had to be readmitted, in contrast to about 50% of those patients with first-episode psychosis who had been treated in 1987 or 1988, before the initiation of the specialized unit. Also, the time to readmission was significantly longer for the patients of the specialized ward. In the last ten years, several first-episode units have been founded and promising experiences in early secondary prevention have been made in different countries (e.g., Australia, United Kingdom, The Netherlands).

The American Psychiatric Association (1997) has published guidelines for the treatment of patients with schizophrenia. The authors state that hospital treatment is often the preferred setting for first-episode patients because they can be carefully observed for side-effects. Our experience from the specialized ward confirms this statement, but we have found even more positive effects of such inpatient treatment, for instance a peer-group effect among the young patients, lower tension in high-expressed-emotion families, and the possibility of early rehabilitation. Unfortunately, the American guidelines do not recommend lower dosages for first-episode psychotic patients.

## Conclusion

The administration of the lowest effective dose of DA/SDA antipsychotics, which should not be used for sedation, as well as an early application of atypical antipsychotics, is advisable for the psychopharmacological treatment of first-episode psychosis. Benzodiazepines or sedating antipsychotics should be used for excitatory states, but should be avoided in stable phases, to minimize cognitive dysfunction. Specialized units are helpful in providing early diagnosis, intervention, and rehabilitation, which helps to reduce social and cognitive deterioration.

# References

Altorfer, A., Merlo, M. C. G., Kaesermann, et al. (1998). Deficit in nonverbal communicative abilities of early-psychotic patients during social interaction: Therapeutical efficacy of neuroleptic drug treatment. *Schizophrenia Research,* **29,** 65.

American Psychiatric Association (1994). *Diagnostic and Statistical Manual of Mental Disorders, Fourth Edition.* Washington DC: American Psychiatric Press.

American Psychiatric Association (1997). *Practice Guideline for the Treatment of Patients with Schizophrenia.* Washington, DC: American Psychiatric Press.

Baldessarini, R. J., Cohen, B. M. & Teicher, M. H. (1988). Significance of neuroleptic dose and plasma level in the pharmacological treatment of psychosis. *Archives of General Psychiatry,* **45,** 79–91.

Convit, A., Volavka, J., Czobor, P., et al. (1994). Effect of subtile neuroleptical dysfunction on response to haloperidol treatment in schizophrenia. *American Journal of Psychiatry,* **151,** 49–56.

Falloon, I. R. H., McGill, G. W., Boyd, J. L. & Pederson, J. (1987). Family management in the prevention of morbidity of schizophrenia: Social outcome of two year longitudinal study. *Psychological Medicine,* **17,** 59–66.

Farde, L., & Halldin, C. (1997). $D_2$-dopamine receptors in schizophrenia. In *Schizophrenia* (Eds. Fog, R., Gerlach, J. & Hemmingsen, R.), pp. 190–199. Alfred Benzon Symposium 38. Copenhagen: Munksgaard.

Hofer, H., Merlo, M. C. G. & Brenner, H. D. (1997). Wisconsin Card Sorting Test and EEG changes in early psychosis. *Schizophrenia Research,* **24,** 107.

Jackson, C., & Birchwood, M. (1996). Early intervention in psychosis: Opportunities for secondary prevention. *British Journal of Clinical Psychology,* **35,** 487–502.

Kapur, S., Remington, G., Zipursky, R., et al. (1995). The $D_2$ dopamine receptor occupancy of risperidone and its relationship to extrapyramidal symptoms: A PET study. *Life Science,* **57,** 103–107.

Kapur, S., Remington, G., Zipursky, R., et al. (1996). High levels of dopamine $D_2$ receptor occupancy with low-dose haloperidol treatment: A PET study. *American Journal of Psychiatry,* **153,** 948–950.

Kopala, L., Fredrikson, D., Good, K. P., & Honer, W. G. (1996). Symptoms in neuroleptic-naive, first-episode schizophrenia: Response to risperidone. *Biological Psychiatry,* **39,** 296–298.

Kopala, L. C., Good, K. P. & Honer W. G. (1997). Extrapyramidal signs and clinical symptoms in first-episode schizophrenia: response to low-dose risperidone. *Journal of Clinical Psychopharmacology,* **17,** 308–313.

Lahti, A. C., Lahti, R. A. & Tamminga, C. A. (1996*).* New Neuroleptics and Experimental Antipsychotics. In The new pharmacotherapy of schizophrenia (Ed. Breier, A.), pp. 57–87. Washington, DC: American Psychiatric Press.

Loebel, A. D., Lieberman, J. A., Alvir, J. M. J., et al. (1992). Duration of psychosis and outcome in first-episode schizophrenia. *American Journal of Psychiatry,* **149,** 1183–1188.

McEvoy, J. P., Hogarty, G. E. & Steingard, S. (1991). Optimal dose of neuroleptic in acute schizophrenia. A controlled study of the neuroleptic threshold and higher haloperidol dose. *Archives of General Psychiatry,* **48,** 739–745.

McGorry, P. D. & Edwards, J. (1997). *Early Psychosis Training Pack.* Macclesfield: Gardiner-Caldwell Communications.

Merlo, M. C. G., Brenner, H. D., et al. (1997) Empfehlungen für den therapeutischen Einsatz von Clozapin (Leponex). *Schweizer Archiv für Neurologie und Psychiatrie*, **148** (suppl. IV).

Merlo, M. C. G. & Gerlach, J. (1995). Treatment-resistant schizophrenia. *Reviews of Contemporary Pharmacotherapy*, **6**, 153–164.

Merlo, M. C. G., Hofer, H. & Brenner, H. D. (1997). EEG changes and performance in span of apprehension in patients with early psychosis. *Schizophrenia Research, 24*, 116.

Merlo, M. C. G. & Hofer, H. (in press) Systemic considerations for the inpatient treatment of first-episode, acute schizophrenic patients. In *Cognitive Therapy with Schizophrenic Patients: The Evolution of a New Treatment Approach*. (Eds. Merlo, M. C. G., Perris, C. & Brenner, H. D.)

Spohn, H. E. & Strauss, M. E. (1989). Relation of neuroleptic and anticholinergic medication to cognitive functions in schizophrenia. *Journal of Abnormal Psychology, 98*, 367–380.

van Kammen, D. P. & Marder, S. R. (1995). Dopamin Receptor Antagonists. In *Comprehensive Textbook of Psychiatry/VI*. (Eds. Kaplan, H. J. & Sadock, B. J.). Baltimore: Williams & Wilkins.

Wyatt, R. J. (1991). Neuroleptics and the natural course of schizophrenia. *Schizophrenia Bulletin, 17*, 325–351.

# Sertindole: An Atypical Neuroleptic

Rico Nil and A. Wehnert

A number of definitions of atypical antipsychotics have been proposed, but the only attribute common to all of this class is their improved extrapyramidal side effect (EPS) profile relative to conventional antipsychotics (Meltzer, 1995). Other proposed definitions have included efficacy against negative symptoms, reduced risk of tardive dyskinesia, either no or reduced stimulation of prolactin, and efficacy in treatment-resistant schizophrenia. All these proposed definitions highlight the major limitations of conventional antipsychotics.

## Pharmacological Aifferentiation of Conventional and Atypical Antipsychotics

Clozapine was the first antipsychotic recognized as having an atypical clinical profile, and it has become a model for the development of newer "atypical" agents. In contrast to conventional antipsychotics (e.g., haloperidol) which have a $D_2$-receptor occupancy of 70–85% *in vivo* (Farde et al., 1989), clozapine shows a relatively low $D_2$ occupancy but a much broader receptor affinity profile. This includes high affinity to $5\text{-HT}_{2A}$, $\alpha_1$, muscarinic, and histaminergic receptors (Arnt et al., 1997).

Newer atypical antipsychotics such as risperidone, olanzapine, ziprasidone, and sertindole share this relatively strong $5\text{-HT}_{2A}$ and $\alpha_1$ receptor antagonism, but also demonstrate more potent antidopaminergic activity (Arnt et al., 1997). In the case of sertindole, this activity is highly selective for the mesolimbic pathway. For example, after chronic administration in rats, sertindole selectively inhibited the ventral tegmental dopaminergic neurons of the mesolimbic/mesocortical dopamine pathway, but did not affect the substantia nigra pars compacta dopaminergic neurons which project to the striatum. This limbic selectivity, which is not seen with conventional antipsychotics, points towards a potent antipsychotic activity without causing extrapyramidal disturbances (Arnt et al., 1997).

# Clinical Experience

The safety and efficacy of sertindole have been studied in a series of large, placebo-controlled clinical trials which have included the conventional antipsychotic haloperidol as the active comparator (Hale et al., 1996; Zimbroff et al., 1997; van Kammen et al., 1996).

# Clinical Efficacy

*The Landmark study*

This paper focuses on the results of the most important of these studies, which was conducted in the USA and Canada (Zimbroff et al., 1997). The study was designed in conjunction with various regulatory authorities, and is representative of the other studies included in the sertindole clinical program. Since there is a lack of consensus regarding the optimal dose of haloperidol, the study employed a "double-dose-finding" design, including three dosage groups for haloperidol, three dosage groups for sertindole and a placebo group.

After completing a single-blind, 4–7-day placebo run-in phase, eligible patients were randomized to 8 weeks' therapy with either sertindole 12, 20, or 24 mg/day, haloperidol 4, 8, or 16 mg/day, or placebo. The initial dose was 4 mg and increased by 4 mg every third day until the full dose was reached (day 16 in the sertindole 24 mg/day group). Adult (18–65 years), hospitalized patients were eligible for inclusion if they had a DSM-III-R or DSM-IV diagnosis of schizophrenia, a minimal degree of positive symptoms (>8 points) in any of the Brief Psychiatric Rating Scale positive symptom items, and were either naïve to, or had previously responded to antipsychotic therapy. A total of 497 patients (77% male; mean age 38.7 years) were randomized. Of these, 66% were paranoid and 95% had at least one previous hospital admissions prior to study inclusion. The average duration of illness was 16 years.

The antipsychotic efficacy of either sertindole or haloperidol was confirmed by a statistically significant decrease in total PANSS (Positive and Negative Syndrome Scale) score in all active treatment groups compared with placebo (see Figure 1). Similarly, the PANSS positive symptom sub-scale score improved by a significantly greater extent in the sertindole 20 and 24 mg groups and the haloperidol 8 and 16 mg groups than with placebo.

Although the study population was not selected specifically for negative symptoms, analysis of the negative symptom sub-scale of the PANSS suggested that sertindole is also effective against negative symptoms (see Figure 2).

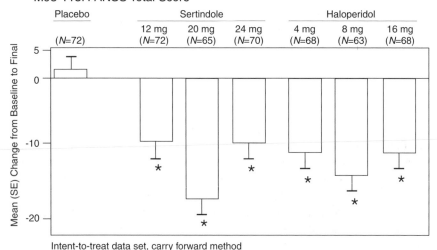

Intent-to-treat data set, carry forward method
* p≤0.05 vs. placebo

*Figure 1.* Change from baseline in Positive and Negative Symptom Scale (PANSS) total score after 8-weeks' treatment with sertindole, haloperidole or placebo (Zimbroff et al., 1997; *p≤0.05 vs placebo).

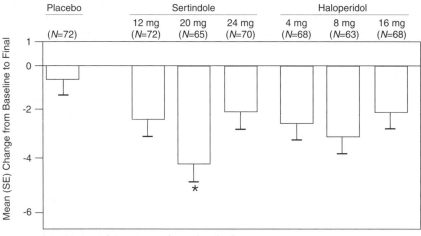

Intent-to-treat data set, carry forward method
* p≤0.05 vs. placebo

*Figure 2.* Change from baseline in Positive and Negative Symptom Scale (PANSS) negative sub-scale score after 8-weeks' treatment with sertindole, haloperidole or placebo (Zimbroff et al., 1997; *p≤0.05 vs placebo).

69

Compared with placebo, sertindole 20 mg/day was associated with a significant decrease in PANSS negative symptom sub-scale score, whereas none of the haloperidol groups demonstrated any significant advantage over placebo with respect to this parameter.

*Negative symptoms*

Data from subsequent studies supported the finding of the Landmark study results that sertindole is also effective against the negative symptoms of schizophrenia. For example, a similar US study (462 patients randomized to either sertindole 20 or 24 mg/day or to haloperidol 16 mg/day) also revealed a significant improvement in PANSS negative symptom sub-scale score with sertindole, although only in the 24 mg group. This benefit has since been confirmed in a European study in which 617 patients were randomized to sertindole 8, 16, 20 or 24 mg/day or haloperidol 10 mg/day. Compared with haloperidol recipients, patients receiving sertindole 16 mg experienced a significantly greater improvement on the negative symptom sub-scale (Hale et al., 1996).

It has been argued that the beneficial effects of atypical antipsychotics on negative symptoms may not be a direct effect, but may be attributable to improved extrapyramidal tolerability or an improvement in transient secondary negative symptoms (Möller, 1998). To separate such potential confounding effects statistically from any direct effects on negative symptoms, a Path analysis was applied to a pooled patient sample, including patients from the above-mentioned three studies (sertindole 12, 16, 20 and 24 mg and haloperidol 4, 8, 10 and 16 mg) (Wehnert et al., 1997a). The following potentially confounding variables were controlled for: (i) baseline PANSS negative symptom sub-scale score; (ii) depression component sub-scale score; (iii) extent of EPS [Simpson-Angus Scale (SAS), Barnes Akathisia Scale (BAS)]. This Path analysis confirmed that sertindole directly improves the negative symptoms of schizophrenia to a significantly greater extent than haloperidol (linear regression coefficient $= -1.9$; $p<0.05$).

*Long-term efficacy*

A long-term efficacy and safety comparison of sertindole and haloperidol revealed longer time intervals of remaining free of hospitalization for exacerbation, and of remaining medically compliant for the sertindole patient group (Daniel et al., 1998).

# EPS Profile

An improved extrapyramidal symptom (EPS) profile is characteristic of atypical antipsychotics and represents a clear advantage over conventional agents. In the Landmark study, there were no differences between sertindole and placebo in any of the EPS measures and no consistent dose-response relationship between sertindole and EPS. In contrast, all doses of haloperidol were associated with a substantially higher incidence of EPS than sertindole (see Figure 3).

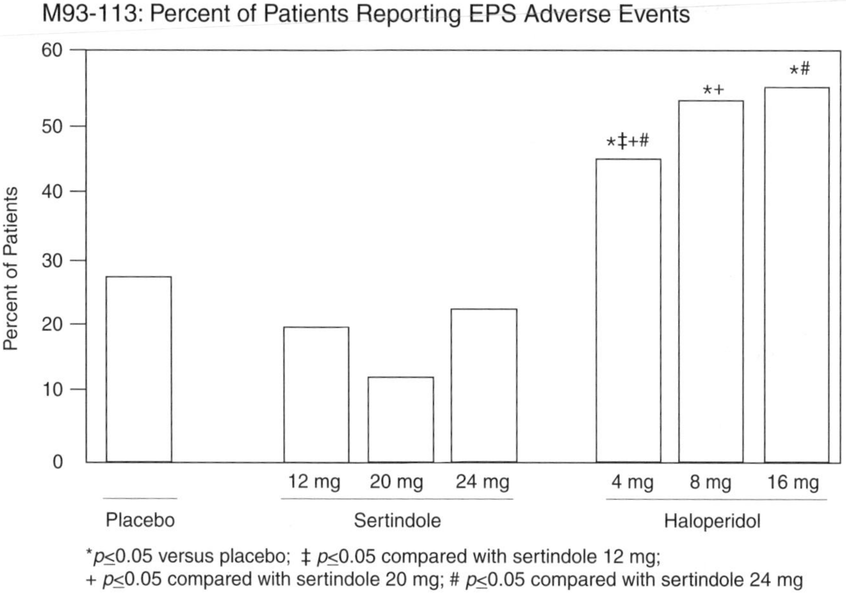

M93-113: Percent of Patients Reporting EPS Adverse Events

*$p \leq 0.05$ versus placebo;  ‡ $p \leq 0.05$ compared with sertindole 12 mg;
+ $p \leq 0.05$ compared with sertindole 20 mg; # $p \leq 0.05$ compared with sertindole 24 mg

*Figure 3.* Percentage of patients reporting extrapyramidal adverse events during 8-weeks' treatment with sertindole, haloperidole or placebo (Zimbroff et al., 1997; *$p \leq 0.05$ vs placebo; ‡$p \leq 0.05$ vs sertindole 12 mg; +$p \leq 0.05$ vs sertindole 20 mg; #$p \leq 0.05$ vs sertindole 24 mg).

Even the highest dose of sertindole (24 mg/day) produced significantly fewer EPS-related adverse events than the lowest dose of haloperidol (4 mg). This is despite a significantly higher use of anti-EPS medication by patients on haloperidol, which would to some extent mask any difference in EPS levels between the groups. Compared with placebo, haloperidol (all doses) was associated with a statistically significant deterioration from baseline in SAS score (see Figure 4a). In marked contrast, sertindole-treated patients had a statistically significant improvement in SAS and BAS scores compared with haloperidol recipients (see Figure 4b).

71

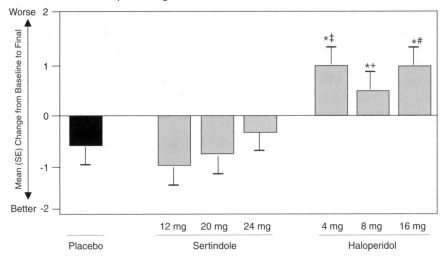

**A**  M93-113: Simpson-Angus Scale

*$p \leq 0.05$ versus placebo;  ‡ $p \leq 0.05$ compared with sertindole 12 mg;
+ $p \leq 0.05$ compared with sertindole 20 mg; # $p \leq 0.05$ compared with sertindole 24 mg

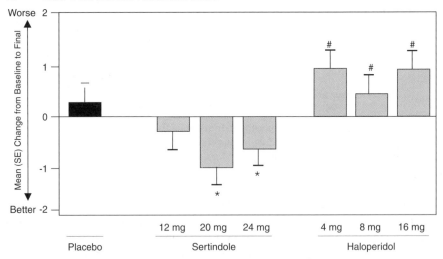

**B**  M93-113: Barnes Akathisia Scale

*$p \leq 0.05$ vs. placebo;  # $p \leq 0.05$ vs. one or more sertindole dose

*Figure.* Change from baseline in severity of extrapyramidal side effects as measured by **A** Simpson Angus Scale and **B** Barnes Akathisia Scale after 8-weeks' treatment with sertindole, haloperidol or placebo (Zimbroff et al., 1997; *$p \leq 0.05$ vs placebo; **$p = 0.01$ vs placebo; #$p \leq 0.05$ vs one or more sertindole doses).

72

The improvement in EPS profile in the sertindole groups might, to some extent, be explained by a wash-out effect from previous antipsychotic treatment. However, a survival analysis of time to first EPS has shown that the survival curves for placebo and sertindole follow similar patterns (Wehnert et al., 1997b). This provides further evidence that sertindole causes no more EPS than does placebo, and that the incidence of EPS-related adverse events in the sertindole and placebo groups can be attributed to similar factors, such as rebound akathisia, rebound parkinsonism, withdrawal dyskinesia or exacerbation of psychotic symptoms. In conclusion, data from clinical trials indicate that within the recommended dose-range, the level of EPS associated with sertindole is indistinguishable from that with placebo.

*Table 1.* Treatment-emergent adverse events reported statistically more frequently with sertindole or haloperidol than with placebo in short-term, placebo-controlled studies (data on file, H. Lundbeck A/S)

| Adverse event | No. (%) of patients | | | | | |
|---|---|---|---|---|---|---|
| | Placebo (n=231) | | Sertindole (n=520) | | Haloperidol (n=364) | |
| Any adverse event | 205 | (89) | 474 | (91) | 340 | (93) |
| Nasal congestion | 26 | (11) | 150 | (29)* | 59 | (16) |
| Dizziness | 18 | (8) | 71 | (14)* | 27 | (7) |
| Decreased ejaculatory volume+ | 5 | (2) | 58 | (11)+ | 7 | (2) |
| Dry mouth | 12 | (5) | 59 | (11)* | 27 | (7) |
| Hypertonia | 15 | (6) | 52 | (10) | 76 | (21)* |
| Akathisia | 17 | (7) | 27 | (5) | 96 | (26)* |
| Tremor | 21 | (9) | 28 | (5) | 71 | (20)* |
| Postural hypotension | 3 | (1) | 23 | (4)* | 10 | (3) |
| Arthralgia | 5 | (2) | 22 | (4) | 21 | (6)* |
| Peripheral edema | 1 | (<1) | 16 | (3)* | 1 | (<1) |
| Cogwheel rigidity | 6 | (3) | 14 | (3) | 30 | (8)* |
| Prolonged Q–T interval | 0 | (0) | 11 | (2)* | 0 | (0) |
| Paraesthesia | 0 | (0) | 10 | (2)* | 6 | (2) |
| Increased salivation | 4 | (2) | 10 | (2) | 25 | (7)* |

*$p \geq 0.05$ *vs* placebo; +males only: $n=187$ for placebo; $n=407$ for sertindole; $n=292$ for haloperidol.
NB: Detectable differences in haloperidol vs placebo comparisons are greater than those of sertindole vs placebo comparisons because of unequal sample sizes.

# Safety/Tolerability Profile

Adverse events occurring during short-term, placebo-controlled trials with sertindole are summarized in Table 1. Those occurring most frequently during sertindole therapy include nasal congestion, dizziness, dry mouth, and a decrease in ejaculatory volume. Nasal congestion and decreased ejaculatory volume may be attributable to sertindole's $\alpha_1$-blocking effect. The decrease in ejaculatory volume is reversible and is not accompanied by any other sexual dysfunction such as impairment of libido, erection, or orgasm. Mild weight gain was also observed during sertindole therapy, amounting to an average increase of 2.8 kg in the short-term studies.

The dose titration schedule in these studies meant that postural hypotension was rarely reported during the initiation of treatment. When it did occur, it was mild and transient and did not appear to be problematic. A slight prolongation of the QT interval was observed. Although no patients reported clinically related problems, sertindole is contraindicated in patients with cardiac diseases or hypokaliemia or patients under treatment with medication known to prolong the QT interval (Hale, 1998).

# Conclusion

An improved extrapyramidal side effect profile as a main criterion for an atypical neuroleptic was seen in all tested sertindole dose levels (Hale, 1998) as well as in long-term treatment (Daniel et al., 1998). The EPS levels were, in fact, indistinguishable from those of placebo. Although no direct comparative trials are yet available, the lack of any dose response relationship compares well with the atypical EPS profile of other neuroleptics such as olanzapine and clozapine (Bever and Perry, 1998, Gerlach et al., 1996). For risperidone an increase of the EPS risk above the placebo-level was observed in its upper dose range (Cohen, 1994). The importance of a favorable EPS profile in view of the development of tardive diskinesia has gained support from a study showing a significantly lower risk for tardive diskinesia for olanzapine than haloperidol (Tollefson et al., 1997a).

Antipsychotic efficacy of sertindole in the dose range of 12 to 24 mg was comparable to that of haloperidol (4 to 16 mg). It remains to be investigated with direct comparisons to what degree the antipsychotic efficacy of sertindole is also comparable with that of other atypical neuroleptics such as olanzapine, for which some superiority to haloperidol was reported (Tollefson et al., 1997b). The same holds true for efficacy against negative symptoms as a further indi-

74

cation of an atypical profile. It has generally been found that the atypical neuroleptics are more effective than conventional antipsychotics (Möller, 1998, Collaborative working group on trial evaluations, 1998) in this respect. As used for sertindole, path analyses appear to be appropriate to differentiate the effects on the primary and secondary negative symptoms. Further studies have been asked for to clarify whether specific components of primary negative symptoms respond to different atypical neuroleptics (Collaborative working group on trial evaluations, 1998).

In conclusion sertindole has established efficacy in both positive and negative symptoms of schizophrenia. Levels of EPS remained indistinguishable from those occurring with placebo. It possesses, therefore, all advantages of an atypical antipsychotic.

# References

Arnt, J., Skarsfeldt, T. & Hyttel, J. (1997) Differentiation of classical and novel antipsychotics using animal models. *International Clinical Psychopharmacology*, **12** (suppl. 1), 9–17.

Bever, K. A. & Perry, P. J. (1998) Olanzapine: A serotonin-dopamine-receptor antagonist for antipsychotic therapy. *American Journal of Health-System Pharmacology*, **55**, 1003–1016.

Cohen, L. J. (1994) Risperidone. *Pharmacotherapy*, **14**, 253-265.

Collaborative Working Group on Clinical Trial Evaluations (1998). Assessing the effects of atypical antipsychotics on negative symptoms. *Journal of Clinical Psychiatry*, **59**, 28–34.

Daniel, D. G., Wozniak, P., Mack, R. J. & McCarthy, B. G. (1998) Long-term efficacy and safety comparison of sertindole and haloperidol in the treatment of schizophrenia. The Sertindole Study Group. *Psychopharmacological Bulletin* **34**, 61–69.

Farde, L., Wiesel, F. A., Nordstöm, A. L., et al. (1989) $D_1$ and $D_2$ dopamine receptor occupancy during treatment with conventional and atypical neuroleptics. *Psychopharmacology*, **99**, 28–31.

Gerlach, J., Lublin, H. & Peacock, L. (1996) Extrapyramidal symptoms during long-term treatment with antipsychotics: Special focus on clozapine and $D_1$ and $D_2$ dopamine antagonists. *Neuropsychopharmacology*, **14** (suppl. 3), 35S–39S.

Hale, A., van der Burght, M., Friberg, H. H. & Wehnert, A. (1996) Dose ranging study comparing 4 doses of sertindole and 1 dose of haloperidol in schizophrenic patients. *European Neuropsychopharmacology*, **6** (suppl. 3), 61.

Hale, A. S. (1998) A review of the safety and tolerability of sertindole. *International Clinical Psychopharmacology*, **13** (suppl. 3), 65–70.

Meltzer, H. Y. (1995) Atypical antipsychotic drug therapy for treatment resistant schizophrenia. In *Schizophrenia* (Eds. Hirsch, S. R. & Weinberg, D. R.), pp. 485–502. Oxford: Blackwell Science Ltd.

Möller, H. J. (1998) Novel antipsychotics and negative symptoms. *International Clinical Psychopharmacology*, **13** (suppl. 3), 43–47.

Tollefson, G. D., Beasley, C. M. Jr., Tamura, R. N., et al. (1997a) Blind, controlled, long-term study of the comparative incidence of treatment-emergent tardive dyskinesia with olanzapine or haloperidol. *American Journal of Psychiatry*, **154**, 1248–1254.

Tollefson, G. D., Beasley, C. M. Jr., Tran, P. V., et al. (1997b) Olanzapine versus haloperidol in the treatment of schizophrenia and schizoaffective and schizophreniform disorders: results of an international collaborative trial. *American Journal of Psychiatry*, **154**, 457–465.

van Kammen, D. P., McEvoy, J. P., Targum, S. D., et al. (1996) A randomized, controlled, dose-ranging trial of sertindole in patients with schizophrenia. *Psychopharmacology*, **124** (1–2), 168–175.

Wehnert, A., Mack, R., Stilwell, C., et al. (1997a) Direct effects of sertindole on the primary negative symptoms of schizophrenia: A PATH analysis. *Biological Psychiatry*, **42**, 1–297.

Wehnert, A., Stilwell, C., Rasmussen, C., Mack, R. & Sloth-Nielsen, M. (1997b) Extrapyramidal symptoms and sertindole – analysis of three double-blind, haloperidol-referenced, phase III clinical trials. *European Neuropsychopharmacology*, **7** (S2), 218.

Zimbroff, D., Kane, J., Tamminga, C., et al. (1997) Controlled, dose-response study of sertindole and haloperidol in the treatment of schizophrenia. *American Journal of Psychiatry*, **154**, 782–791.

# Psychological and Psychosocial Therapies

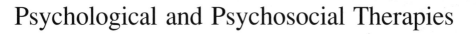

# Process-Targeted Cognitive Therapy for Schizophrenia: Effects and Mechanisms

William D. Spaulding, Dorie Reed, Mary Sullivan and Shelley Fleming

For more than ten years, evidence has been accumulating that the cognitive impairment which characterizes chronic schizophrenia in the residual phase can be reduced with various psychosocial treatment techniques (Spaulding et al., 1986; Reed et al., 1992; Corrigan & Storzbach, 1993; Storzbach & Corrigan, 1996). This evidence has been mostly in the form of anecdotal reports, case studies, and small-scale incompletely controlled clinical trials. However, our Nebraska research group has recently completed a large-scale controlled trial with a subject population of patients with particularly severe and treatment-resistant schizophrenia. A detailed description of the project and some initial findings have been given elsewhere (Spaulding et al., 1998). This report is a summary of the initial findings of the Nebraska outcome trial, including some new analyses of the possible mechanisms of the treatment effects.

## Method

The outcome study ran from 1990 to 1995. The treatment setting was the Community Transition Program (CPT), a fourty-bed unit for comprehensive psychiatric rehabilitation, housed in a public psychiatric hospital. The subjects were patients with severe and treatment-resistant psychiatric disorders in the schizophrenia spectrum.

Figure 1 shows the design of the outcome trial. The subjects were all patients in the CTP rehabilitation program. They were all receiving somewhat individualized treatment, but this always included psychopharmacological management, social and living skills training, occupational and recreational therapy, and intensive case management. Most required individualized contingency management programs to maintain engagement and participation in the various rehabilitation activities. The subjects entered the study after they were judged to be optimally medicated and clinically stable. They underwent an extensive assessment of their neuropsychological and behavioral functioning, including laboratory measures, milieu-based observational assessment with the NOSIE-30, and an elaborate assessment of social competence – the Assessment of Interpersonal Problem Solving (AIPS). After that, they were randomly assigned to the experimental or control condition. The experimental group received cognitive treatment, in the form of the cognitive subprograms of Integrated Psychological Therapy (IPT) as it existed in 1989 (except that it was translated from German into English before attempting its use with American patients). The control group received the same amount of supportive group therapy. After three months, all subjects began three highly structured therapy modalities, performed according to manuals and related materials distributed by the UCLA Center for Rehabilitation of Schizophrenia. The specific modalities were Medication Management, Interpersonal Problem-solving, and Leisure Skills Training. The skill training, the cognitive or supportive treatment, and the other rehabilitation activities continued for an additional three months. Then, six months after the first assessment, a second one was performed. Rehabilitation continued after that, and a follow-up assessment was performed after one year. Many of the subjects were discharged from hospital during that time, in which case the follow-up was performed in a community setting.

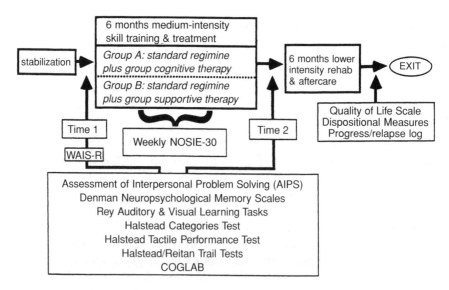

*Figure 1.* Experimental design of outcome study.

The experiment progressed with one cohort of 10 to 14 subjects, starting every six months for four years, yielding a final sample size of 91 subjects.

The clinical and research staff were all blind to the subject's assignment to experimental or control condition.

The primary outcome measure was the AIPS. This is because we expected that the primary effect of IPT would be to enhance the acquisition of social competence. The AIPS is a clinically meaningful measure, because there is strong evidence that improvements in social competence are associated with better long-term outcome. In addition, the AIPS gives us a detailed and fairly precise picture of a person's basic social functioning, within the time-frame in which we expect to see the effects of both cognitive treatment and social skills training.

In the AIPS assessment procedure, the subject view 10 videotaped vignettes portraying an interpersonal problem or conflict. After each vignette, subjects are interviewed to determine their apprehension of the problem, their ability to describe and understand it, and their ability to formulate a behavioral solution to the problem. Then they are asked to role-play a solution with the examiner. The entire assessment is videotaped, and later scored by trained observers. The scoring generates four subscales, which reflect performance in those various domains of apprehending and solving the problem.

# Results

Figure 2 shows the changes in the experimental and control groups, during the six months of cognitive or supportive therapy. All four of the AIPS subscales appear to show differential gains for the subjects receiving IPT, but the ANOVA interaction term reaches statistical significance for two, Articulation ($F=14.46$; $p<.0005$) and Content ($F=10.74$; $p<.002$). These subscales emphasize the subjects' ability to include relevant details in their formulation of the problem and its solution.

There was also a significant groups-by-repeated-measures interaction on the Disorganization factor of the BPRS ($F=5.00$; $p<.028$), but not on any other interview-based assessments of symptoms and interview behavior. On the PANS General Psychopathology subscale, there was a within-group change for the IPT group ($F=7.45$; $p<.01$) but not the Supportive group. This is probably a weak reflection of the same change as on BPRS Disorganization.

In the neuropsychological domain, there were significant groups-by-repeated-measures interactions on COGLAB Span of Apprehension measure ($F=9.98$; $p<.002$) and the COGLAB card sorting task ($F=4.63$; $p<.03$), which is

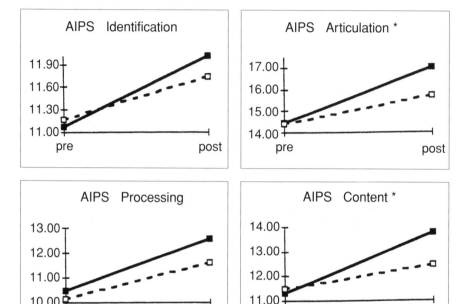

* ANOVA group by repeated measure interaction term $p<.01$

*Figure 2.* Effects of IPT and supportive therapy on performance on the Assessment of International Problem Solving (AIPS).

very similar to the well known Wisconsin Card Sorting Test. Also, the IPT subjects showed a within-group change on the Rey visual verbal learning task ($F=8.29$; $p<.003$) and Halstead Trails B ($F=7.18$; $p<.004$), while the Supportive subjects did not.

We have only just begun to analyze our longer-term data to determine the implications of these shorter-term treatment effects. We have completed one interesting evaluation – a study of rehabilitation staff perceptions of long-term outcome. We used an elaborate psychophysical sorting and scaling procedure, to construct a composite measure of the perceptions of key clinical staff about the relative success of all the subjects in the outcome study (Weilage, 1997). According to the perceptions of staff, the IPT subjects showed greater overall rehabilitation success. About 90% of the IPT subjects were sorted into the higher success categories, compared to about 74% of the Supportive Therapy subjects.

The initial results of the outcome study provide fairly strong evidence for the benefits of cognitive therapy, as done in the subprograms of IPT, on acquisition or reacquisition of social competence in chronic schizophrenia, as measured by the AIPS. There is also evidence for neuropsychological, behavioral and symptom domains. In contrast, there is no evidence for differential effects for the supportive therapy control condition. This is not to say that supportive therapy is without benefits: Supportive techniques are broadly distributed throughout rehabilitation modalities. The addition of a specific supportive therapy group may constitute a relatively minor proportional increment in the total "dose" of supportive treatment in a comprehensive rehabilitation program. The purpose of the supportive therapy condition in this study was to protect the blind and control for "staff attention" type placebo effects, not evaluate quantitatively the contribution of supportive techniques to psychiatric rehabilitation.

A number of non-specific treatment effects were observed across the domains of cognition, behavior, symptoms, and social competence. This experiment did not include a "no-treatment" condition, so one cannot be absolutely certain that such changes would not have occurred without comprehensive rehabilitation. However, previous studies have suggested that these changes do not occur spontaneously. In eagerness to develop better cognitive therapy techniques, the potential cognitive benefits of more conventional rehabilitation methods should not be overlooked.

Having demonstrated a unique contribution of cognitive therapy to psychiatric rehabilitation, we are currently performing multivariate analyses to clarify the nature and mechanisms of the treatment effect. This is an important step in the development of cognitive therapy techniques. While it may now be clear that cognitive therapy enhances the acquisition of social competence, it is not at all clear why that is the case. Our initial analyses of the short-term treatment effect indicate benefits across several domains of biobehavioral functioning. Does IPT work by strengthening basic cognitive processes which are a prerequisite to acquiring social skills, such as attention, memory or concept manipulation? Or is some other mechanism or pathway involved? Multiple regression and its elaborations in structural modeling and path analysis can shed some light on these issues.

The first analyses simply explored the patterns of statistical prediction of the treatment effects that occur in the data. To do this, the measures were transformed so that they reflect either a value at one point in time, or a value changing over time. The most simple of these transformations is the change score, the difference between "time two" and "time one" values. Statistical regression can also be used to remove the "time one" component of the *change score*. This yields a *residualized change score*, reflecting the degree of change which is independent of the initial value of the measure. The main effect of a one-way analysis of variance on the residualized change score is equivalent to the interaction term in a groups-by-repeated-measures analysis of variance.

Finally, we can also compute an *interaction term*, which can be used in statistical prediction to represent the interaction of one measure with another, as the two measures relate to the target variable. In this case, we are interested in the initial values of our various clinical and laboratory measures, as they interact with IPT. We can conceptualize our two experimental treatment conditions as a dose of IPT, of either 1 or 0 dosage units. We compute the interaction term as the product of the two measures involved in the interaction. The technique of using interaction terms is a way of improving conventional multiple regression analysis, which is limited by the assumption that the predictor variables in a regression equation do not interact with each other. However, in the behavioral sciences, they often do interact. In other words, a particular variable may behave differently in the presence of another variable. In these particular analyses, the interaction terms provide important clues about the mechanisms of the IPT treatment effect.

Attention is then focused on the two AIPS subscales that show a differential treatment effect for IPT – Articulation and Content. These subscales reflect the detail and completeness of the subjects' apprehension of the interpersonal problems or conflicts in the social competence assessment.

Figure 3 shows the best possible regression statistics for predicting change on the Articulation subscale, expressed as its residualized change score, predicted by pre-treatment values and change scores on the various clinical and laboratory measures. The numbers on the arrows are beta weights in the regression equation. The specific variables are selected for inclusion in the analysis because they show statistically significant bivariate correlations with the residualized Articulation change score.

The regression formula accounts for about 13% of the change in Articulation. This prediction is achieved by three variables. One is the dose of IPT, which is expected, because it is already known, that there is a differential treatment effect in the analysis of variance. The regression shows that the amount of change in Articulation can be predicted if it is known whether or not a subject received IPT. In addition, there is a relatively strong contribution of the *change score* for random errors on the COGLAB card sorting task. This means that patients who improved the most on this task also improved the most on AIPS Articulation, regardless of whether or not they received IPT. In contrast, the contribution of the *interaction term* – the degree to which IPT interacted with card sorting performance to produce AIPS Articulation change – is rela-

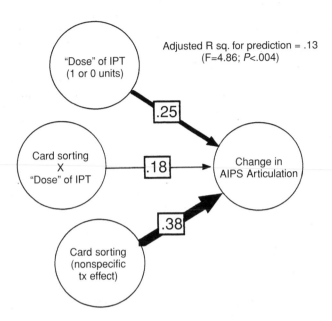

*Figure 3.* Path diagrams of contributions of treatment and cognitive changes to change in AIPS Articulation performance.

tively small. Although there is a significant bivariate correlation between the interaction term and the Articulation change, it is eclipsed by covariance with the other variables in the regression equation, and does not have a significant beta weight. This analysis is consistent with the interpretation that improvement in AIPS Articulation is brought about by IPT and is also associated with improvement in card sorting, but we have failed to identify any specific interactions between IPT and card sorting, or any other clinical or cognitive characteristics that could account for the IPT effect. It must be concluded that the mechanism of the IPT effect works in ways that are not captured by our assessment protocol.

Figure 4 shows the same analysis applied to AIPS Content. The regression formula is accounting for twice as much change in the outcome measure as the previous solution. Also, the formula includes not only the treatment dose, but two *interaction terms* which reflect the interaction of IPT with performance on the Rey VLT – a measure of verbal learning and memory – and a false alarms score from the COGLAB battery. This finding suggests that the benefits of IPT come about in large part through an interaction with the cognitive processes which these laboratory tasks measure. The false alarms score is presumed to be a measure of subjects' ability to adjust their signal detection characteristics, i.e., the biases toward making errors of omission vs. errors of commission, to the psychophysical characteristics of the task. In other words, IPT enhances the roles of intact memory and signal detection modulation in social skills training and related rehabilitation modalities. The direct prediction of AIPS Content change by the IPT dose is also statistically significant, although it is smaller than the interaction effects. This means that that part of the IPT effect on AIPS Content remains unexplained by our assessment protocol.

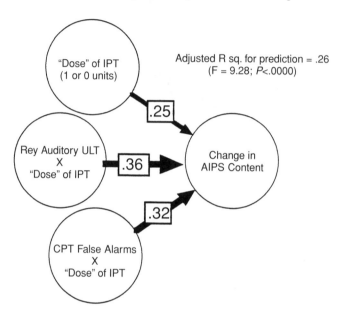

*Figure 4.* Contributions of IPT and cognitive changes to change in AIPS Context performance.

## Conclusion

As done in the cognitive subprograms of IPT – cognitive therapy appears to contribute uniquely and meaningfully to comprehensive rehabilitation. The effect of IPT is most observable with measures of the detail and completeness with which a patient can apprehend and understand an interpersonal situation. Within the cognitive system, this effect appears to be associated with improvements in memory and executive processing, although not all of these cognitive effects contribute directly to improvement in social competence. Conversely, cognitive therapy seems to improve social competence in ways that we have not yet accounted for with our neuropsychological, behavioral, and symptomatic measures. With further analyses, we hope to develop a more precise picture of how cognitive therapy effects operate, and of which patients may benefit the most.

# References

Corrigan, P. & Storzbach, D. (1993) The ecological validity of cognitive rehabilitation for schizophrenia. *Journal of Cognitive Rehabilitation*, **11**, 14–21.

Reed, D., Sullivan, M., Penn, D., et al. (1992) Assessment and treatment of cognitive impairments. In *Effective Psychiatric Rehabilitation* (Eds. Liberman, R. P. et al.) San Francisco: Jessey-Bass.

Spaulding, W., Reed, D., Storzbach, D., et al. (1998) The effects of a remediational approach to cognitive therapy for schizophrenia. In *Outcome and Innovation in Psychological Treatment of Schizophrenia* (Eds. Wykes, T. et al.) London: John Wiley.

Spaulding, W., Storms, L., Goodrich, V. & Sullivan, M. (1986) Applications of experimental psychopathology in psychiatric rehabilitation. *Schizophrenia Bulletin*, **12** (4), 560–577.

Storzbach, D. & Corrigan, P. (1996) Cognitive rehabilitation for schizophrenia. In *Cognitive Rehabilitation for Neuropsychiatric Disorders* (Eds. Corrigan, P. & Yudofsky, S.), Washington, D.C.: American Psychiatric Press.

# Estimating Rehabilitation Potential in Schizophrenic Subjects

K. H. Wiedl, J. Wienöbst and H. Schöttke

## Cognitive Remediation and Dynamic Testing

In cognitive remediation (Green, 1993), the goal is to improve cognitive deficits often found in schizophrenic persons with the help of cognitive or behavioral intervention. Main target areas are attention, memory, and concept-formation. Cognitive remediation is thus an important component of rehabilitation (see also Spaulding et al., 1994). In our studies, aspects of concept-formation are given special consideration.

At the beginning of cognitive remediation research, the predominant type of investigation, at least in the Anglo-American literature, was represented by "feasibility studies" (Green et al., 1997). They were undertaken as a first step within a comprehensive research strategy to determine whether and how performance can be improved in the respective variables.

Results from feasibility studies are quite promising for some of the target variables analyzed so far (see Green, 1993). However, besides the main effects found for the specific interventions, there are hints pointing to heterogeneous patterns of performance among schizophrenic persons and indicating that within the groups under study, the patients may systematically differ in their ability to profit from the interventions given. Discussing results from studies on concept formation, which are of particular interest for our work, some authors explicitly postulate different types of responders, calling them "learners" and "non-learners" (Green et al., 1990) or "good," "remediable," and "poor" (Stratta et al., 1994). Both groups of authors discuss their classifications with regard to possible implications for psychopathology, etiology and rehabilitational needs (see also Goldberg & Weinberger, 1994; van der Does & van den Bosch, 1992).

Indicators of heterogeneous patterns of performance in cognitive remediation are the starting-point of our approach: The goal is to investigate whether subgroups of patients in responsiveness to intervention, as applied in feasibility studies, can be established within groups of schizophrenic patients. Also, whether the learner status thus defined allows for the prediction of training proficiency in conceptually similar measures of clinical training and for generalizability to other cognitive target areas. An adjoining question is how intra-individual differences in responsivity to measures of cognitive remediation can be modeled theoretically.

The shift from a general perspective to a differential approach, as is implied in the latter statements, is congruent with the concept of Dynamic Testing: Inter-individual differences in learning, in profiting from instruction, training or compensatory interventions, or in resisting to the effects of strain on performance are the target concern of this approach to assessment (Wiedl, 1984; Guthke & Wiedl, 1996). These inter-individual differences are used as diagnostic information, which is related to concepts like Learning Ability, Learning Potential, Plasticity, Responsiveness to Instruction, Cognitive Modifiability, or Rehabilitation Potential (Wiedl et al., 1995; Guthke & Wiedl, 1996). Basically, assessment either follows a test-training-test paradigm or a paradigm of theory-guided within-test-interventions. Diagnostic information is based on change rates and/or the quality and amount of intervention needed. Dynamic Testing has a long, yet little known tradition both in European and American psychology and psychiatry (Lidz, 1987; Wiedl et al., 1995). Meanwhile, assessment devices have been developed (Learning Tests, Diagnostic Program) that follow principles of assessing intra-individual variability in a psychometrically controlled way for the fields of intelligence testing and educational psychology (Hamers et al., 1993; Guthke, 1993). Basic issues in the application of Dynamic Testing in clinical psychology have been discussed by Wiedl & Schöttke (1995).

In this chapter, we shall describe two studies that were undertaken in order to estimate whether feasibility studies on concept formation, using the Wisconsin Card Sorting Test (WCST, Berg, 1948) as a target variable, are promising for purposes of Dynamic Testing, e.g., for the assessment of rehabilitation potential in schizophrenic patients. In the first investigation, a pilot study, the goal was to verify attempts at classifying schizophrenic patients according to their learner status in the WCST, as reported in the literature, and relate this classification to a prognostic criterion that is relevant for rehabilitation. Since this study has been reported in detail elsewhere (Wiedl & Wienöbst, 1999; Wiedl et al., 1997), the present report will be confined to aspects relevant for the evaluation of this approach and the subsequent extension, that was made in our second study. There, generalizability of WCST-learner status to the function of verbal recall and the search for moderator variables will be reported in more detail than previously.

# WCST-Learner Status and Prognosis in Cognitive Rehabilitation Training

The Wisconsin Card Sorting Test is a test of cognitive abilities, which frequently shows performance deficits in schizophrenic patients. It is a neuropsychological test, thought to be related to frontal lobe functioning (Weinberger et al., 1991). The WCST is used for assessing the formation, maintenance, and change of concepts. The task is to sort a number of cards (standard version: 128) according to rules (color, form, number) which have to be inferred from "right" or "wrong" feedbacks given by the experimenter after each sort. No other feedbacks or helps are given. After 10 consecutive correct trials, the experimenter changes the rule without previous announcement. Main scores are the number of correct responses, of categories achieved, and of perseverative errors (for a description of procedures see Heaton, 1981).

A number of studies demonstrated the feasibility of performance change in this test with the help of different methods of intervention, among which elaborate trial-by-trial feedback, specifying the reasons for the correctness or incorrectness of each sort, seemed to be the most salient procedure (Goldberg et al., 1987; Bellack et al., 1990; Summerfelt et al., 1991; Green et al., 1992; Metz et al., 1994; Stratta et al., 1994; for a review and discussion see Goldberg & Weinberger, 1994). Whereas it was clearly shown that performance increased as long as training procedures were applied, it remained unclear, however, whether these improvements are maintained over time (see Goldberg & Weinberger, 1994). Our hypothesis was that these unclear findings can be clarified with the help of a differential approach, systematically distinguishing different types of learners, and further, that this distinction allows one to predict the patients' ability to profit from a (short) training in cognitive rehabilitation.

## Method

*Subjects*

23 patients form two psychiatric hospitals, diagnosed as schizophrenic according to ICD-9 or DSM-III-R, took part in the study after having given informed consent (subclassifications are 295.1:3, 295.2:1, 295.3:13, 295.6:6). The mean age was 29.2 (SD = 5.2), average length of education was 10.6 years (SD = 1.6). The patients had been ill for an average of 6 years (SD = 4.4), with a mean number of 4.6 hospitalizations (SD = 2.7). All patients were treated with

neuroleptics, with an average chlorpromazine equivalent of 593.7 mg per day. Twelve subjects were males, and eleven were females. Between the day of admission and the start of our test, there was an average time-interval of 18 weeks (SD = 34).

*Test administration*

The WCST was given in a pretest-test plus training-post-test arrangement within one session, with each block comprising 64 cards. Pre- and post-test were identical with the standard procedures described by Heaton (1981). The test plus training block was administered according to the trial-by-trial intervention procedures described by Green et al. (1992) and Goldberg et al. (1987):

> After finishing the first block, it was announced to the patients that they would now get help. Before starting the second block, the three sorting rules (color, form, number) were explained to them. After every card sort, the patients were additionally told why their choice was right or wrong (i.e., "this was wrong, we don't sort for color now, but for form or number"). Change of category was announced (i.e., "correct, you had to sort for color. Having performed ten consecutive correct sorts, the rule will change. You will now no longer sort for color but for form or number"). Between the three blocks, little breaks of approximately five minutes were provided. Altogether, WCST administration took between 30 and 45 minutes[1].

*Clinical rehabilitation training*

For a first check of external validity, units from the Integrated Psychological Therapy Program (IPT, Roder et al., 1988) were included. The IPT is a group program developed to ameliorate both cognitive dysfunctions and social behavioral deficits in schizophrenics. The Cognitive Differentiation unit was chosen for its conceptual similarity to the requirements of the WCST and for its clinical relevance. Two sessions were held where the patients worked in groups of about five with cards that had to be described and classified according to their various attributes, moving from single attribute to multiple attribute classifications in the course of the sessions. Each session took about 30 minutes. A multiple choice test comprising six classification items ("Classification Test") was developed according to psychometric criteria to evaluate the subjects' training proficiency, based on a pre-test-post-test comparison.

---

[1] A complete description of instructions can be obtained from the first author

# Results

For the analysis of changes in WCST performance following continuous verbal feedback, non-parametric statistics were used (Friedman Test, Wilcoxon Matched Pairs Signed Ranks Test), due to heterogeneity of variances (Bartlett-Box-Test). A significant effect of testing conditions for all WCST-measures selected was observed. Also, all mutual comparisons between T1, T2, and T3 proved to be significant ($\alpha$ adjusted to < .014 for multiple testing). The subjects as a group had thus improved their WCST performance under conditions of continuous feedback (T2) and had then fallen back to significantly lower level (T3) which, however, was still significantly higher than the baseline level (T1), thus proving the short-term effectiveness of the intervention applied.

For the classification of patients according to their learner status, the number of correct responses was selected due to distributional characteristics. For this measure, the group means were 35.91 (SD = 10.47) for the pre-test, 59.13 (SD = 2.36) for the test plus training, and 51.00 (SD = 8.18) for the post-test. According to an algorithm developed by Schöttke et al. (1993), based on indicators of reliability and the standard error of prediction and controlling for ceiling and ground effects, "Learners" were defined as those subjects, who had improved their performance from pre-test to post-test by 15 correct responses (1.5 SD). "High Scores" were those patients who had scored between an expected upper level of 58 and a lower level of 43 (upper level −1.5 SD) correct responses in the pre-test. "Non-Learners" did not meet either criterion. Following this algorithm, 12 subjects were classified as Learners, 6 as Non-Learners, and 5 as High Scores. There seemed to be a tendency of association between learner status and subclassification of schizophrenia, with a higher frequency of paranoid patients among High Scores and non-paranoid patients among Non-Learners. Statistical testing could not be performed, due to the low cell frequencies.

For the subsequent analysis of external validity of this learner typology, the 17 patients who had complete data sets were grouped according to training proficiency in the IPT, with the help of the Classification Test. Seven subjects had a considerable gain (improvement of 2 or more classification items), whereas eight did not improve or had only a small training gain (one item). For analyzing the relationship between WCST learner status and the patients' progress in cognitive differentiation training, the subjects were cross-classified. The result is illustrated in Table 1.

A clear prediction of training gain is possible for Non-Learners and High Scores, but not for Learners. A reduction of the 3 x 2 classification table to a 2 (Learners and High Scores vs. Non-Learners) x 2 (training gain) table yields a significant result: High Scores and Learners profit more from cognitive differentiation training than Non-Learners ($p$ = .02, Fisher's exact probability test).

Table 1. Cross-classification of training proficiency and WCST-classification

| | low | high |
|---|---|---|
| Learners | 5 | 0 |
| Non-Learners | 4 | 4 |
| High Scores | 0 | 4 |

By inclusion of a further variable – educational level – it seems that a clear prediction is possible also for the Learners: Those Learners with low educational level have low training proficiency, whereas those with high educational level do well in the IPT. No prediction was possible with variables of psychopathology. Incorporating results from additional studies, which showed that learner status seems to be related to length of overall stay in hospital and to the level of clinical rehabilitation programs to which the patients were admitted (Wiedl et al., 1997), these results were discussed with regard to a concept of "rehabilitation potential." The issue of generalizability was raised.

# Generalizability of WCST Learner Status

To check for the generalizability of WCST learner status, non-trivial results were expected for cognitive performance, which is not specific to frontal lobe functioning, but which can at least be attributed on the whole to temporal lobe functioning, a domain which also proves to be impaired in groups of schizophrenic patients (Levin et al., 1989). Empirical results indicate that measures of verbal recall may be particularly sensitive to these persons' impairment in this domain (Beatty et al., 1993; Brand et al., 1996). Further, the measures to be selected should allow observation of the progress of learning and of the implementation of interventions comparable to those applied in the dynamic version of the WCST. According to these criteria, the Auditiv-Verbale Lerntest (AVLT "Auditory Verbal Learning Test," Heubrock, 1992), which was originally designed by Rey (1964), was selected.

# Method

## Subjects

Subjects were 33 patients with a diagnosis of schizophrenia according to DSM-III-R or ICD-10, who were in a state of remission. The patients were recruited in a psychiatric hospital, a rehabilitation unit for the mentally ill, a day care unit, sheltered accommodation, and patients' clubs. Table 2a presents clinical and demographic data of this sample. Two-thirds of the patients belong to the paranoid (11) or residual (11) type, followed by the disorganized (5) and undifferentiated (4) type, and by schizoaffective disorder (2). All patients received neuroleptic medication.

*Table 2.* Demographic and clinical characteristics of two samples (a, b) of schizophrenic patients

|  | a | | | b | | |
|---|---|---|---|---|---|---|
|  | M | SD | N | M | SD | N |
| Age | 34.94 | 10.49 |  | 32.91 | 7.17 |  |
| Gender:   m |  |  | 23 |  |  | 23 |
|          f |  |  | 10 |  |  | 10 |
| Years of school attendance | 11.24 | 1.56 |  | 10.66 | 1.64 |  |
| Premorbid Intelligence (WST) | 99.30 | 13.70 |  | 96.70 | 15.33 |  |
| Age at first admission to hospital | 23.23 | 4.27 |  | 24.60 | 6.70 |  |
| Total time of being ill (years) | 11.27 | 10.61 |  | 8.8 | 5.52 |  |
| Number of admissions to hospital | 4.48 | 3.43 |  | 6.39 | 5.74 |  |
| Total stay in hospital (weeks) | 62.00 | 93.31 |  | 62.00 | 62.8 |  |

*Test administration*

The WCST was administered following the procedures described above.

In the standard procedure of administering the AVLT, a list of 15 nouns is read to the subjects with the instruction to reproduce these after the termination of their presentation. No feedback is given by the tester. This procedure is repeated five times, followed by a second list, used to assess the effects of interference, and again by a last check for the recall of the first list.

To make this test more comparable to our dynamic version of the WCST, this standard procedure was modified as follows. After the second and third reproductions, the subjects were given a short feedback concerning the number of correctly recalled nouns, these nouns were quoted, and a reinforcing

94

statement was added. Then, an extended instruction was given for the next (third or fourth) trial with the purpose of motivating the patients and ensuring adequate attention (..."you are able to recall one or two more words ..., ... listen exactly ..., ... focus your concentration on the words ..., don't let yourself be distracted by noise or other things"). This instruction is about four times as long as the standard instruction and was also given in a standardized way [1].

Test performance was to be measured by the number of correct reproductions. For the assessment of moderator variables, the Pair Frequency Index can be used to estimate the tendency towards subjective organization of the learning material. Further, the effects of interference can be estimated in terms of proactive and retroactive inhibition.

# Results

*Effects of intervention on WCST performance and the discrimination of learner types*

Application of non-parametric tests (Friedman Test, Wilcoxon Matched Pair Signed Rank Test) due to heterogeneity of variances (Bartlett-Box-Test) yielded a significant main effect for testing conditions on number of correct responses ($\chi^2 = 49.29$, $p \le .001$). Also, all mutual comparisons proved to be significant ($p \le .0001$). As in the pilot study described above, there is a significant increase of performance under intervention (test plus training) and a significant drop of post-test-scores. However, the latter performance was significantly higher than the pre-test-level found at first testing (level of significance adjusted for attenuation; similar results for the other WCST-scores).

Next, learner types were determined with the help of single case analysis, using the algorithm described above. Results showed 16 High Scores, 10 Learners, and 7 Non-Learners. Although these proportions seem to be different from the ones found in the first study, the distributions of the learner types did not differ significantly ($\chi^2 = 4.38$, df = 2). No associations between learner status and subclassification of schizophrenic disorder could be detected. Figure 1 shows the WCST scores for the whole sample and the three learner types. According to this result, the test performance of this sample was equivalent to the performance of the sample described above.

---

[1] A complete description of instructions can be obtained from the first author

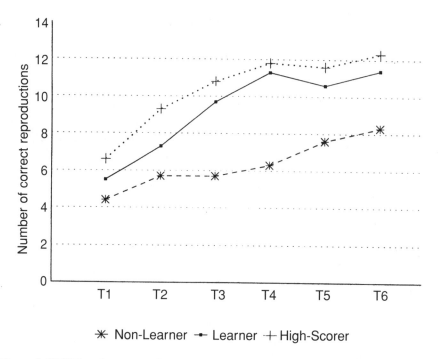

✳ Non-Learner ‑•‑ Learner ╶+╴ High-Scorer

*Figure 1.* WCST-performance of schizophrenic patients under different conditions of test administration.

*WCST learner status and AVLT performance*

Generalization of WCST learner status was assumed on the basis that the three groups proved to be different in level of AVLT performance with a rank order of High Scorers, Learners, and Non-Learners. Also, it was assumed that performance change would be significantly different in Learners and Non-Learners.

Figure 2 illustrates the results, revealing impressive differences between the groups. Analysis of variance demonstrates a significant difference of WCST-learning-groups in the level of recall performance (F = 9.58, df = 2, $p \leq .01$), a significant effect of repeated testing (F = 4.97, df = 5, $p \leq .0001$) and a significant interaction (F = 2.18, df = 10, $p \leq .022$). Post-hoc comparisons show that the WCST learning groups only differed in their increase in recall performance from trial 2 to trial 3 ($p \leq .012$) and trial 3 to trial 4 ($p \leq .008$). The reason is that the Learners had a clear rise in performance after trial 2 (introduction of specific interventions), whereas the Non-Learners tended to stagnate at this point. Generalization, as defined above, is thus proved by our results.

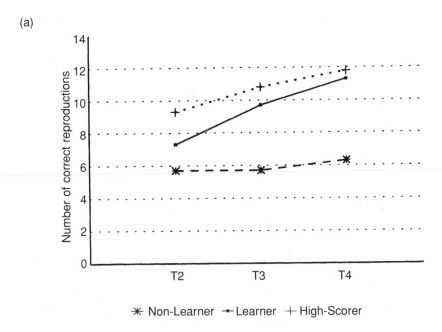

(a)

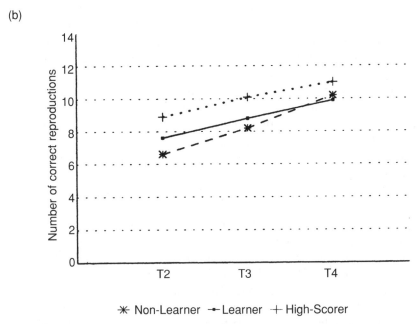

(b)

*Figure 2.* Performance of WCST-learner-types in a dynamic version of the Auditory Verbal Learning Test (AVLT).

Hints on variables that may moderate the difference in recall performance levels of the WCST learner types may be gained from the indicators that are provided by additional analysis of AVLT performance. Computation of the Pair Frequency Index (relative frequency of recalling nouns pair-wise, which had also been listed pair-wise in the first presentation) shows the highest score for the High Scorers (.69), followed by Learners (.26), and Non-Learners (-.26; Kruskal Wallis, $\chi^2 = 7.46$, p .024). The subjective organization of memory content may thus be a variable that accounts for differences in verbal recall performance in the different WCST learner groups.

The comparison of the groups with indicators of interference did not yield significant effects. In retroactive inference, the groups almost scored equal (.09, .08, .10; F = .023, p = .98). There was a tendency, however, for Non-Learners to be more effected by proactive interference (–.12) than Learners (.01) and High Scorers (.27; $\chi^2 = 4.07$, p = .13, Kruskal Wallis computed due to heterogeneity of variances). From inspection of the data, it seems that significance was not achieved because of the large variances within the groups. The fact that Non-Learners learned about one-quarter less after introduction of the interference list (B) indicates, however, that proactive inhibition may yet be a factor that mediates differences in recall performance between Learners and Non-Learners.

Concerning the different learning rates over AVLT-trials following verbal intervention, the hypothesis is plausible that Learners and Non-Learners may be different in their capacity to work with and profit from verbal context-information. If this hypothesis is valid, these two groups should not differ when the AVLT is presented without additional context information, i.e., in standard administration. In this case, Learners and Non-Learners should show equal progress over trials, yet at a different level: For WCST-Learners, the pronounced increase of performance after the introduction of specific verbal intervention should disappear, whereas for Non-Learners, stagnation should not be found any more.

With the help of a sample of schizophrenic patients from a different part of our project, we were able to test this hypothesis experimentally. Thirty-three subjects, comparable with the sample described above in clinical and demographic characteristics (see Table 2b, subtypes: 15 paranoid, 10 residual, 4 schizoaff., 2 schiz.simpl.), were given the dynamic version of the WCST and the standard version of the AVLT. WCST-performance was again classified as described above (12 High Scorers, 16 Learners, 5 Non-Learners). A three-factor analysis of variance conducted on the salient AVLT trials T2, T3, T4 (second factor) yielded significance for the main effects of the WCST learner status (F =5.50, $p = .016$) and AVLT-trials (F = 59.83, $p = .0001$), but not for groups (special intervention / no intervention in AVLT). However, and of high relevance for our hypothesis, a significant interaction of the three factors was found (F =3.70, $p$ = .007). The nature of this intervention is illustrated in Figure 3: As expected, differential effects of repeated AVLT administration in Learners and Non-Learners were found, depending on the presence or absence of specific verbal interventions. This result remains stable in an analysis of covariance, using first-trial recall performance as a covariate.

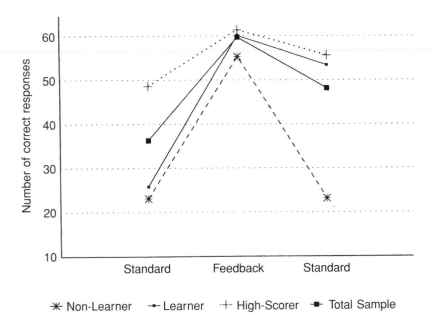

*Figure 3.* Recall-Peformance of WCST-learner-types under dynamic (a) and standard (b) conditions of applying the Auditory Verbal Learning Test (AVLT).

## Discussion

We have presented the first results from a project where the goal is to relate research on cognitive remediation with the concept of dynamic assessment, aiming at finding a method for the estimation of rehabilitation potential. The studies reported here have to be replicated, extended, and differentiated. This is particularly important for the association between learner status and psychopathology and its implication for prediction and generalization. At the present state of knowledge, three aspects of our results seem to be worthy of special consideration.

First, we were able to show that for the measure of cognitive remediation under study – the WCST assessing the formation, maintenance, and change of concepts – about two-thirds of our patients either proved to have a high level of performance throughout or were capable of catching up to such a level after a short within-test-intervention. Only a small proportion of the patients showed the "stubborn deficit" (Green et al., 1992, p. 62) which is commonly attributed to this group of subjects and seems to be related to a dysfunction of the frontal lobes. Our results thus cast doubt on the assumption of general performance deficits in schizophrenic patients using the WCST; also, they seem to imply a need for differentiating and further developing the frontal-lobe hypothesis of schizophrenic disorders.

Second, it became evident that WCST learner status, which represents patients' responsivity to verbal intervention in this test of concept formation, not only permits prediction of performance in a short, clinical training of cognitive rehabilitation, but also generalizes to the function of verbal recall. According to our results, factors that might mediate prognostic validity and generalizability should be related to premorbid educational level, the subjective organization of recall memory, and the utilization of verbal context information related to the specific intervention. The latter processes constitute components of working memory (see Brand et al., 1996) and are thus also related to frontal lobe functioning. For the variable of interference or resistance to effects of interference, which also counts among the functions of the frontal lobes and is also relevant to an effective working memory, significant results were not found, but might be verifiable for the aspect of proactive interference and with the help of a larger sample. Taking the different results together, it seems that inter-individual differences in the functioning of working memory might be a promising point of access for the estimation of rehabilitation potential in schizophrenic patients. Whether differences in the effectiveness of working memory in the different WCST-learner-types are caused by structural abnormalities of the frontal lobes (for a review and meta-analysis see Schöttke, 1996), which interact with characteristics of the specific intervention applied, cannot be answered with the help of our data.

In respect of the intervention used, there are both quantitative and qualitative aspects to be considered. The quantitative argument would imply that the amount of verbal information transferred could not be adequately processed or stored to guide further performance, and that it even interfered with learning. Under a more qualitative perspective, the question is whether or not the differences in verbal recall between Learners and Non-Learners may be related to the impact of specific patterns of interpersonal relations, which are activated in the context of the intervention applied and which may differentially trigger or impede the functions of working memory in these groups of patients.

Our third point deals with the heterogeneity of the disorder which is by tradition named schizophrenia. Our results indicate that apart from subclassifications based on psychopathology or etiology, groups of patients can be meaningfully distinguished according to their responsivity to intervention. How this classification relates to other, more traditional attempts at classifying schizophrenia is open to research. Regardless of this open question and based on principles of scientific logic, the intrapersonal conditions guiding the pathogenesis and psychopathological appearance of a disorder and those conditions that mediate its modification through intervention need not necessarily be identical. Our approach may thus be a promising supplement to existing systems of classification, including aspects of the phenomenon – cognitive modifiability or rehabilitation potential – which otherwise may not be taken into account sufficiently. Our data indicate that these aspects may be helpful to estimate the quantitative and qualitative differences in rehabilitational needs of different groups of persons suffering form schizophrenia.

# References

Beatty, W. W., Jocic, Z., Monson, N. & Staton, R. D. (1993) Memory and frontal lobe dysfunction in schizophrenia and schizoaffective disorder. *Journal of Nervous and Mental Disease*, **181**, 448–453.

Bellack, A. S., Mueser, K. T., Morrison, R. L., et al. (1990) Remediation of cognitive deficits in schizophrenia. *American Journal of Psychiatry*, **147**, 12, 1650–1655.

Berg, E. A. (1948) A simple objective technique for measuring flexibility in thinking. *Journal of General Psychology*, **39**, 15–22.

Brand, A., Hildebrandt, H. & Scheerer, E. (1996) Gedächtnisstörungen bei schizophrenen Erkrankungen. *Fortschritte der Neurologie und Psychiatrie*, **2** (64), 49–65.

Goldberg, T. E. & Weinberger, D. R. (1994) Schizophrenia, training paradigms, and the Wisconsin Card Sorting Test redux. *Schizophrenia Research*, **11**, 291–296.

Goldberg, T. E., Weinberger, D. R., Berman, K. F., et al. (1987) Further evidence for dementia of the prefrontal type in schizophrenia? A controlled study of teaching the Wisconsin Card Sorting Test. *Archives of General Psychiatry*, **44**, 1008–1014.

Green, M. F. (1993) Cognitive remediation in schizophrenia: Is it time yet? *American Journal of Psychiatry*, **149**, 62–67.

Green, M. F. (1996) What are the functional consequences of neurocognitive deficits in schizophrenia? *American Journal of Psychiatry*, **153** (3), 321–330.

Green, M. F., Ganzell, S., Satz, P. & Vaclav, J. F. (1990) Teaching the Wisconsin Card Sorting Test to Schizophrenic Patients. Letter to the editor. *Archives of General Psychiatry*, **47**, 91–92.

Green, M. F., Satz, P., Ganzell, S. & Vaclav, J. F. (1992) Wisconsin Card Sorting Test performance in schizophrenia: Remediation of a stubborn deficit. *American Journal of Psychiatry*, **149**, 62–67.

Green, M. F., Hellman, S. & Kern, R. S. (1997) Feasibility Studies of Cognitive Remediation in Schizophrenia: Grasping the Little Picture. In *Towards a Comprehensive Therapy for Schizophrenia* (Eds. Brenner, H. D., Böker, W. & Genner, R.), pp. 79–93. Seattle: Hogrefe & Huber Publishers.

Guthke, J. (1993) Developments in Learning Potential Assessment. In *Learning Potential Assessment: Theoretical, Methodological and Practical Issues* (Eds. Hamers, J. H. M., Sijtsma, K. & Ruijssenaars, A. J. J. M.). Amsterdam: Swets & Zeitlinger.

Guthke, J. & Wiedl, K. H. (1996) Dynamisches Testen. *Zur Psychodiagnostik der intraindividuellen Variabilität.* Göttingen: Hogrefe.

Hamers, J. H., Sijtsma, K. & Ruijssenaars, A. J. (1993) Learning Potential Assessment. *Theoretical, Methodological and Practical Issues.* Amsterdam: Swets & Zeltinger.

Heaton, R. K. (1981) Wisconsin Card Sorting Test Manual. *Psychological Assessment Resources.* Odessa: Florida.

Heubrock, D. (1992) Der Auditiv-Verbale-Lerntest (AVLT) in der klinischen und experimentellen Neuropsychologie. Durchführung, Auswertung und Forschungsergebnisse. *Zeitschrift für Differentielle und Diagnostische Psychologie,* **3,** 161–174.

Levin, S., Yurgelon-Todd, D. & Craft, S. (1989) Contributions of clinical neuropsychology to the study of schizophrenia. *Journal of Abnormal Psychology,* **98,** 341–56.

Lidz, C. S. (1987) Dynamic Assessment. *An Interactional Approach to Evaluating Learning Potential.* New York: Guilford Press.

Metz, J. T., Johnson, M. D., Pliskin, N. H. & Luchins, D. J. (1994) Maintenance of training effects on the Wisconsin Card Sorting Test by patients with schizophrenia or affective disorders. *American Journal of Psychiatry,* **151,** 120–122.

Rey, A. (1964) *L'examen clinique en psychologie.* Presses Universitaire de France.

Roder, V., Brenner, H. D., Kienzle, N. & Hodel, B. (1988) *Integriertes Psychologisches Therapieprogramm für schizophrene Patienten (IPT).* München: Psychologie Verlags-Union.

Schöttke, H. (1996) *Neuropsychologie der Minus- und Plussymptomatik. Eine Mehrebenenanalyse.* Münster: LIT-Verlag.

Spaulding, W. D., Sullivan, M., Weiler, M., et al. (1994) Changing cognitive functioning in rehabilitation of schizophrenia. *Acta Psychiatrica Scandinavica,* 1994, **384,** 116–124.

Stratta, P., Mancini, F., Mattei, P., et al. (1994) Information processing strategy to remediate Wisconsin Card Sorting Test performance in schizophrenia: A pilot study. *American Journal of Psychiatry,* **151,** 915–918.

Summerfelt, A. T., Alphs, L. D., Funderburk, F. R., et al. (1991) Impaired Wisconsin Card Sort performance in schizophrenia may reflect motivational deficits (letter). *Archives of General Psychiatry,* **48,** 282–283.

Van der Does, A. J. & Van den Bosch, R. J. (1992) What determines Wisconsin Card Sorting performance in schizophrenia? *Clinical Psychology Review,* **12,** 567–583.

Weinberger, D. R., Berman, K. F. & Daniel, D. G. (1991) Prefrontal Cortex Dysfunction in Schizophrenia. *In Frontal Lobe Function and Dysfunction* (Eds. Levin, H., Eisenberg, H. & Benton, H.), pp. 275–287. New York: Oxford University Press.

Wiedl, K. H. (1984) Lerntests: nur Forschungsmittel und Forschungsgegenstand? *Zeitschrift für Entwicklungspsychologie und Pädagogische Psychologie,* **16,** 245–281.

Wiedl, K. H. & Schöttke, H. (1995) Dynamic assessment of selective attention in schizophrenic subjects: The analysis of intraindividual variability of performance. In *European Contributions to Dynamic Assessment* (Ed. Carlson, J. S.), pp. 185–208. London: JAI Press Ltd.

Wiedl, K. H. & Wienöbst, J. (1999) Interindividual differences in cognitive remediation research with schizophrenic patients – indicators of rehabilitation potential? *International Journal of Rehabilitation Research*, **50** (11), 1411–1419.

Wiedl, K. H., Guthke, J. & Wingenfeld, S. (1995) Dynamic Assessment in Europe: Historical Perspectives. In *European Contributions to Dynamic Assessment* (Ed. Carlson, J. S.), pp. 33–82. London: JAI Press Ltd.

Wiedl, K.H., Wienöbst, J., Schöttke, H. & Kauffeldt, S. (1997) Differentielle Aspekte kognitiver Remediation auf der Grundlage des Wisconsin Card Sorting Tests. Osnabrück: *Psychologische Forschungsberichte aus dem Fachbereich 8 der Universität Osnabrück.*

103

# Generalization of Skills Training to the Natural Environment

Robert Paul Liberman, Karen E. Blair, Shirley M. Glynn, Stephen R. Marder, William Wirshing and Donna Ames Wirshing

More than two decades of empirical and evaluative research on social skills training have amply documented its efficacy as a psychosocial treatment for persons who have schizophrenia or other disabling mental disorders (Dilk & Bond, 1996; Benton & Schroeder, 1990; Smith, Bellack & Liberman, 1996). Efficacy has been measured in controlled studies that have determined the positive impact of social skills training on:

1. Acquisition of skills that have been taught during the training procedure(s);

2. Maintenance of the skills for at least one year, when the duration and intensity of the training procedures were adequate;

3. Generalization of the skills learned in a hospital or clinic setting into the natural, life space of the individual;

4. Generalization of the training to broader domains of social, vocational, and family functioning;

5. Reduced symptoms, hospitalization time, readmissions, and relapses.

Of the various dimensions studied and listed above, the question of *generalization* of skills learned in the training setting into the patient's "real world" has produced the most controversy. While a debate has raged between those who question the extent of generalization and those who assert that transfer of training does occur, there is general agreement that greater generalization would be desirable, as would methods for measuring its extent. Up to the present time, naturalistic confederate tests have been used to demonstrate generalization (Wallace & Liberman, 1985) as well as interviews that investigate social and independent functioning in everyday life (Marder et al., 1996; Blair et al., 1998). In this paper we shall review the strategies that can be used to promote generalization, and then describe a new strategy, *In Vivo Amplified Skills Training,* or IVAST, that is currently undergoing a test of its impact on schizophrenic persons' extending the use of skills learned in the from clinic to community life.

## Strategies for Promoting Generalization

Just as behavioral learning principles have been used in the training of social and independent living skills (Liberman, DeRisi & Mueser, 1989), the same principles are integrated into methods for promoting the *transfer of skills from clinic to community*. What are the requirements for generalization to take place? Answering this question can lead to the pathways for successful generalization. The requirements for generalization of skills can be measures that strengthen *intrapersonal attributes responsible for generalization, techniques to strengthen the individual's capacity to use skills in a panoply of environments,* and *environmental supports*. These are summarized in Table 1.

*Table 1.* Techniques for promoting generalization of social skills into the natural environment

---

*Intrapersonal Attibutes*
    Neurocognitive functioning
    Cognitive remediation (e.g., Integrated Psychological Therapy)
    Procedural learning (e.g., modelling, behavioral rehearsal)
    Overlearning
    Self-monitoring and self-reinforcement

*Coping Capacities*
    Modules for social and independent living skills
    Problem-solving "response set"
    Homework assignments

*Social Support*
    *In vivo* amplified skills training
    Behavioral family therapy
    Multiple family therapy
    Psychosocial self-help clubs

---

*Intrapersonal variables* that may promote or impede generalization are the neurocognitive functioning of the individual (e.g., problems with working memory, secondary memory, vigilance, and accuracy in social perception can all conspire to block the transfer of skills learned in a clinic to the community).

105

The use of active-directive techniques such as behavioral rehearsal, coaching, and role playing builds on the parts of the brain that are responsible for *procedural learning,* i.e., the learning that takes place without awareness and reliance on verbal facility. While there is evidence that verbal learning and awareness of the contingencies of reinforcement may be impaired in schizophrenia, procedural learning is relatively well preserved in this disorder (Kern et al., 1996); hence, active-directive training of skills may be expected to have more durability from one setting to another, bridged by the relatively greater "automatic" and habitual processes regulating memory, concentration, and discrimination of cues. Additional methods that can make skills more "habitual" are *overlearning* and the use of *booster training sessions.*

From the vantage point of the variables within the individual that govern generalization, *cognitive remediation* procedures may aid in the subsequent acquisition and use of social skills. The foremost example of this type of "preparatory" cognitive training is *Integrated Psychological Therapy,* or IPT, developed and validated in a series of studies by Brenner and his associates in Berne (Brenner et al., 1995). In IPT, social perception and cognitive differentiation skills are trained in a hierarchy, prior to training in interpersonal problem-solving and social skills.

Other methods of cognitive remediation, while validated through lavoratory and analogue studies, may hold promise for building stronger bridges from the "rate limiting" brain mechanisms for skills training to generalized use of the skills in the natural environment. For examples, an errorless learning paradigm was used to normalize the performance of persons with treatment-refractory schizophrenia on a putative test of prefrontal cortex functioning, the Wisconsin Card Sorting Task (Kern et al., 1996). Similarly, monetary incentives and instructions were used to normalize performance on a test of early visual processing of information, The Span of Apprehension Task (Kern, Green & Goldstein, 1995).

*Self-monitoring* and *self-reinforcement* are other interpersonal routes to increasing generalization. This can be done by the use of wrist counters, notepads, pagers, and cellular telephones. The patient is taught how to keep track of his behavior in certain situations and to use checklists and rating forms. For example, the "Warning signs checklist" is used by patients to record daily the presence and severity of any prodromal symptoms that may herald relapse of psychosis (mania or schizophrenia). Each night, the patient checks a box on the checklist corresponding to that day's experiences – "Not Present," "Mild," "Moderate," or "Severe." Increases in the severity of warning signs result in a call or visit to the psychiatrist on the mental health team for responsible review and consideration of intervention (e.g., temporary increase in medication or removal of stressors). The patient delivers self-reinforcement for monitoring his or her warning signs, and also receives positive feedback from the responsible clinician(s).

## Strengthening Coping Capacity to Use Skills

While self-monitoring is used in the modules for training social and independent living skills, the key element in promoting the generalized use of the knowledge and skills taught in the modules is the acquisition of a "problem-solving" approach to the challenges of everyday life. Modules in the *UCLA Social & Independent Living Skills Program* (Liberman et al., 1993), rely heavily on self-monitoring and self-evaluation, e.g., in the learning of medication self-management, and relapse prevention (Liberman et al., 1993). It is also a key element in the modules for teaching social and independent living skills *(Workplace Fundamentals, Substance Abuse Management, Recreation for Leisure, Basic Conversation Skills, Community Re-Entry, Medication Management and Symptom Management)*. When faced by unanticipated obstacles to using skills in the natural environment, it is important for a mentally disabled person to be able to "shift gears" and "semi-automatically" fall back on *problem-solving methods*. The structured techniques of problem-solving include learning to use a variety of resources to put skills into use (e.g., money, people, transportation, communication devices like telephones, to generate various options that might solve problems. The person should also be able to consider pros and cons of each, before selecting and implementing an action plan. The use of structured problem-solving has been described in detail in several publications (e.g., Liberman & Corrigan, 1993; Wallace et al., 1985). This techniques may be viewed as a "social prosthesis" for individuals who are stymied in their efforts to meet daily hassles, major stressors, and challenges to their use of coping skills.

Additional techniques that are imbedded in the modules and implemented by therapists to promote generalization include giving *homework assignments* and conducting *in vivo practice*. Homework motivates patients to initiate and complete activities, just as it does students, especially if the trainer or therapist inquires about the homework every day. If the homework is given to carry out assignments in the "real world," and its completion is prompted and reinforced, this method will make an impact. Over the years, our group has found that over 75% of our patients give positive reports on their having completed their homework assignments. These reports are honest and candid when no negative consequences are attached to failure and a "problem-solving response set" is established. When *in vivo* practice is used, the therapist goes part of the way into the natural environment with the individual who is doing an assignment from the skills training class or group, offering encouragement, prompts, and reinforcement for approximations to completing the task.

A certain degree of generalization has been found to occur following participation in the modules. For example, in a two-year study of 80 schizophrenic patients who were randomly assigned to receive low-dose fluphenazine decanoate plus modules vs. the same maintenance medication plus supportive group psychotherapy, only the patients who participated in 200 hours of skills training showed significant improvement in their self-rated social adjustment (Marder et al., 1996).

In the same study, patients were rated on their demonstrated knowledge and skills in self-management of medication and symptoms by their psychiatrists who were "blind" to their patients' psychosocial treatment condition. This evaluation (see Table 2) indicated that patients who received clinic-based training in the Medication and Symptom Management Modules were found to have significantly greater knowledge and skills in these areas by their psychiatrists.

Training programs for social skills can also promote generalization through the use of *multiple exemplars,* and *fading techniques.* Multiple exemplars involve the participation of many different group members to simulate the targeted others in the patient's life who may come in contact with the patient

Table 2. Psychiatrist ratings of patients' knowledge and skill in medication and symptom self-management at the end of study. Means and (Standard Deviations) are shown for patients randomly assigned to skills training or supportive group therapy

|  | Skills Training (N=42) | Supportive Training (N=34) |
|---|---|---|
| Understanding reasons for taking medication | 1.79 [2] (0.87) | 1.38 (0.78) |
| Regularly assesses benefits and side effects of medication | 0.62 [4] (0.55) | 0.04 (0.11) |
| Reacts constructively to bothersome side effects | 1.74 [2] (0.99) | 1.24 (0.95) |
| Understands prodromal symptoms (warningssigns) | 1.21 [3] (0.64) | 0.75 (0.57) |
| Monitors warning signs of relapse | 0.79 [4] (0.54) | 0.30 (0.39) |
| Takes action and seeks intervetnion for warning signs | 1.25 [1] (0.71) | 0.71 (0.71) |

Differences between means (df=74) Skills Training Group MANOVA
[1] $p = 0.05$; [2] $p = 0.03$; [3] $p = 0.001$; [4] $p = 0.0001$

when the latter uses his/her skills. For example, if the patient is learning how to converse with teachers or potential employers, it is helpful to have as many different people role-playing those persons, so that the patient will be prepared to interact successfully with many different personal "styles." Fading of the frequency, duration, and degree of structure in the social skills training also promotes generalization by reducing the dependence of the individual trainee on the specific parameters of the training setting, including the trainer. At the same time that the patient is moving toward less frequent contact with the trainer and training procedures, he/she is getting *intermittent reinforcement* which is well-known to yield more durable behavior that is resistant to extinction than frequent or continuous reinforcement.

## Social Support

Environmental support as a means of promoting generalization can be organized in a variety of ways: (1) peer-mediated case management; (2) psychosocial self-help clubs; (3) assertive case managers with outreach into the community; (4) educating the family or other community caregivers about the nature of schizophrenia and how to assist in promoting greater social adaptation and independence for the patient (Liberman, 1992). An important feature of environmental support is to engineer *opportunities, encouragement,* and *reinforcement* for the individual who is trying to apply skills in the community. One way to create these beneficial exigencies in the community economically is through a new approach termed, *In Vivo Amplified Skills Training.*

## What is *In Vivo* Amplified Skills Training?

In Vivo Amplified Skills Training, or IVAST, builds upon the assertive, outreach case management techniques that were pioneered by Stein and Test in their innovative work with the Program for Assertive Community Treatment (PACT) in Madison, Wisconsin (Stein & Test, 1980; Test, 1992). The primary goals of assertive community treatment were to: (1) reduce use of hospitalization through the provision of on-site support and rapid response to emergencies, and (2) improve the client's quality of life by linking him/her to extant social services. IVAST supplies the missing ingredient that has proven to be an obstacle in the efforts of assertive community case managers to inculcate durable social and independent living skills to clients – i.e., the use of an expert or specialist (Test, 1991) who utilizes highly prescriptive and structured behavioral techniques to teach clients to function more autonomously.

In contrast to the indefinite and comprehensive assertive case management, IVAST is a more focused, time limited, skills training intervention. The IVAST trainer uses behavioral techniques to assist clients to make use of the skills they have learned in clinic-based module groups. The IVAST trainer liases with the clinic-based module trainer to keep abreast of the skills that are being taught. Contact is also maintained with other members of the client's treatment team (e.g., psychiatrist, nurse, case manager); hence, the IVAST model is compatible with a broad array of models of case management. The community-based and specialized IVAST trainer also enriches the case management team by consulting the client's natural support system (e.g., family members, rehabilitation, housing, social security, mental health agencies) to promote opportunities, and reinforcement for the generalization of social skills learned in the clinic, day hospital, or mental health center. To allow time for community-based services by the IVAST trainer, typical case management tasks (e.g., arranging non-emergency medical appointments and completion of disability applications) are deferred to other members of the case management team. The IVAST trainer has a small case load of approximately 10–20 clients, yielding sufficient time to work co-operatively and individually with each client to set and achieve personal goals. As shown in Table 3, the IVAST trainer utilizes behavioral techniques to promote the client's use of self-management rating sheets in using medication management skills, symptom management skills, and social problem-solving skills.

Each IVAST session is based on five tasks for the therapist or case manger: (1) to use behavioral techniques such as shaping, prompting, rehearsal, fading, coaching, and positive reinforcement to promote the client's daily use and maintenance of skills that have been learned in clinic-based module training; (2) to encourage the client to assume the primary responsibility for achieving his or her goals, with the IVAST trainer serving as a consultant to help the client achieve success and autonomy; (3) to facilitate the client's identifying opportunities for developing natural supports in the community; (4) to approach every challenging situation in the community with a formal problem-solving orientation; (5) to assign IVAST homework in addition to the module homework assignments to further reinforce use of skills in community settings.

The IVAST trainer's manual (Blair, 1994) was designed to operationalize the five overarching IVAST tasks, by using a structured and systematic format which directly parallels the seven learning activities in each skill area of the modules in the UCLA Program for Social and Independent Living Skills. The IVAST trainer's manual provides a "how to" approach for using behavioral techniques, identifying opportunities to use module skills, reinforcing the use

110

*Table 3.* IVAST Skill Attainment Record

| Module Skill/Activity | Trial Date | Number of Trials (Maximum of 3) |
|---|---|---|
| Client demonstrates 6 steps to take medication in home environment | _____ <br> _____ <br> _____ | _____ <br> _____ <br> _____ |
| | Skill Mastery ___Yes ___No | |
| Client knows the 3 rules for taking medication safely | _____ <br> _____ <br> _____ | _____ <br> _____ <br> _____ |
| | Skill Mastery ___Yes ___No | |
| Client demonstrates understanding of information on medication label | _____ <br> _____ <br> _____ | _____ <br> _____ <br> _____ |
| | Skill Mastery ___Yes ___No | |
| Client uses Self-Assessment Rating Sheet | _____ <br> _____ <br> _____ | _____ <br> _____ <br> _____ |
| | Skill Mastery ___Yes ___No | |
| Client demonstrates a place to keep medications that meets criteria | _____ <br> _____ <br> _____ | _____ <br> _____ <br> _____ |
| | Skill Mastery ___Yes ___No | |

of skills, and expanding the client's support network in the community. For example, one IVAST activity focuses on using the skills required to make an appointment with a doctor to report a side-effect. Thus, the manual provides prescriptive, *in vivo* activities for each of the seven learning activities in each skill area, for each module that is being taught to the client in the clinic. These community-based interventions aim to bridge the gap between clinic-based training and the use of learned skills in the natural environment. The IVAST trainer also completes an IVAST Skill Attainment Record for each client, as module skills are demonstrated in the community.

In one example of the use of IVAST, outpatients with stabilized forms of schizophrenia attend four different clinic-based Social and Independent Living Skills groups which include the Medication Management and Symptom Management modules twice a week for 90-minute sessions, each for six months, followed by a Social Problem Solving module twice a week for 90 minutes, for four months. The skills training concludes with weekly, one-hour groups for six months of Personal Effectiveness for Successful Living (Liberman et al., 1989), in which participants work toward achieving individualized and personally-relevant goals.

The IVAST trainer engages each of these outpatients for an average of two hours per week, but the actual amount of time varies across the 15-month period. For example, contacts for initial orientation and alliance building during the engagement phase of IVAST may exceed two hours per week. After completing the Medication Management and Symptom Management modules, longer sessions may be scheduled when clients are learning to use Social Problem Solving and completing their homework assignments to achieve personal goals as part of the Personal Effectiveness for Successful Living group. During the final fading phase in the last two months of the 15-month period, the IVAST trainer decreases weekly meetings to every other week.

Every IVAST activity is recorded using a Contact Rating Sheet format, as shown in Table 4. An IVAST Contact Rating Sheet is completed to detail the actual content of each session. The IVAST trainer receives weekly consultation from an expert community skills trainer, as well as clinical supervision from a psychologist. Feedback about the appropriateness of IVAST interventions is given to the trainer during the weekly supervision with the psychologist, using completed IVAST Contact Rating Sheets as guides. The psychologist also assists the IVAST trainer in crisis intervention, and carries out quality assurance monthly by accompanying the IVAST trainer into the community.

## Case Study of IVAST

Jim was a 35-year-old, single Caucasian male, who had a 20-year history of psychiatric admissions at the Veterans Administration hospital for recurrent exacerbations of paranoid schizophrenia. Medication non-compliance was notorious and contributed to his relapses. His psychosocial functioning was poor with social isolation, dependence on his parents, and no work or organized recreation activities. Several months before beginning skills training, Jim moved out of his parents' home and into a board-and-care home. He did little socializing with other residents there, and spent most of his time watching television.

*Table 4.* IVAST contact rating sheet

Patient Name _____ Evaluation Date _ _/ _/ _
                                                                                  m m d d y y
Session # _____ Session Time _ _ _
_____(in minutes)
Money Spent $ _ _._ _                          Total Miles _ _ _


*Appointment Location:*

1. Veteran's Administration            7. Recreation area
2. Patient's house or apartment        8. Shopping area
   with caretaker includes session
3. Patient's house or apartment        9. Vocational
   without caretaker includes session
4. Doctor's office                     10. Pharmacy
5. Coffee shop or restaurant           11. Residential care
6. Social Service Agency               12. Other _____: _____


*Session Activites:* (Circle all that occured in session)

1. Obtain tangible resource            7. IVAST Medication Management Module

# _____
2. Review IVAST homework assigned      8. IVAST Symptom Management Module
   in last session

# _____
3. Identify and/or meet people who can 9. IVAST Social Problem Solving, Step
   be a resource to patient

# _____
4. Crisis intervention                 10. IVAST Successful Living Assignment
5. Review notebook                     11. Assigned IVAST Homework _____
6. Family session                      12. Other: _____


*Self Monitoring* (Circle all that apply.) Based upon review of the patient's notebook and environment, indicate if the patient has completed rating sheets for:

1. Medication Self-Management Rating Sheet
2. Warning Sign Rating Sheet
3. Persistent Symptoms Rating Sheet
4. Coping Techniques for Persistent Symptoms

113

*Table 4 (continued)*

---

*Evaluation of Homework Assignment From Prior Sessions:* (Circle all that apply)

1. Completed IVAST homework successfully.
2. Did not attempt IVAST homework assignment because _____
3. Attempted IVAST homework but did not complet because _____
4. No IVAST homework assigned.

*Obstacles reported by patient or observed during session that interfered with obtaining rehabilitation goals:* (Circle all that apply)

1. Lack of needed resources
2. Warning signs flaring up
3. Side effects causing discomfort
4. Family/caregiver stressor
5. Use of street drugs or alcohol since last visit

6. Enviromental stressor
7. Persistent Symptoms
8. Other: describe _____
For next week _____

---

He refused to leave the home or take the bus anywhere. His only source of income was his Social Security Disability Benefits, which barely covered his monthly expenses, but he was able to budget his limited income and live frugally.

Jim's highest educational achievement was a bachelor's degree in music, when he held the first-chair violinist position in his university's orchestra. On graduating, he taught the violin lessons while seeking employment, but during that year, suffered his first psychotic episode. For a period of time, he was able to teach the violin part-time to a few private students, but this was interrupted by frequent relapses because of his deficits in symptom and medication management skills, and non-compliance with treatment. Eventually, with exacerbations of symptoms becoming more severe, his disability increased and he retreated to his room in almost complete social isolation. His parents' tolerance for his residing at home ended when Jim's visual hallucinations and persecutory delusions provoked him to jump through a window.

*Assessment and goal setting*

At the beginning of the IVAST intervention, Jim had benefited from a brief hospital admission, symptom stabilization, and return to his board-and-care home, where his medication was dispensed to him daily. He had no insight into his illness. He described his personal motivation to achieve independent living goals, but felt hopeless in achieving them. He lacked structure in his daily living routines and felt badly that his relationship with his parents had become

114

so stressful and alienated. He knew that his parents relied upon his income to help sustain their living needs, and were having financial problems as a result of his absence from the household.

Jim set goals to re-evaluate his living situation, do a better job of controlling his symptoms, and learn more about his need for maintenance antipsychotic medication. He also decided to increase his leisure time recreational pursuits to at least one activity each week, and to improve his relationship with his parents.

*Medication and symptom management modules*
During his first six months of IVAST sessions, Jim was helped to integrate the medication management and symptom management skills he had learned in the clinic-based groups into his daily routine. The IVAST trainer used coaching, modeling, role-playing, homework assignments, and monitoring techniques to encourage Jim's ability to report symptoms and side-effects to his doctor and to develop a method to take his medication reliably. The IVAST trainer helped Jim identify a place that was visible to keep his medication and a Self-Assessment Rating Sheet. He kept his rating sheet in a notebook on a shelf beside his medication. Jim also linked taking his daily doses of medication to breakfast-time and dinner-time each day. The IVAST trainer prompted and reinforced Jim to take his medication daily, then gradually reduced prompts and reinforcement to intermittent visits to the board-and-care home.

*Social problem-solving group*
In the Social Problem-Solving group, Jim learned skills to: (1) identify social problems, (2) generate alternative solutions, (3) prioritize possible solutions, and (4) implement a solution using communication skills effectively. As he learned these skills in clinic-based groups, Jim practiced the skills in the community, with encouragement from his IVAST trainer.

To help him achieve his goal of a fuller social life, the IVAST trainer provided Jim with *in vivo* support to help him identify the places, people and specific situations where he could practice using conversational skills in the community. After practicing the skills, with the trainer's prompting, modeling, and role-playing, Jim was given homework assignments to implement his independent use of conversational skills. A typical assignment was to start a brief conversation with someone he knew at his board-and-care home and write down the results. A later assignment was to introduce himself to people he did not know, and have a brief conversation with these people three times a week.

The IVAST trainer helped Jim to identify a coffee shop within walking distance of his board-and-care home, which they visited twice a week for two weeks. The IVAST trainer encouraged Jim to start conversation with some of the "regulars" at the coffee shop, and then gave him homework assignments to walk there at least twice a week independently. He completed his homework assignments without fail and as a result, began to experience pleasant, low-key social interactions with others at the coffee shop. He even developed a relationship with a woman who also frequented the same place. Before long, Jim got into a new routine. Each day, after eating breakfast and taking his medication, he walked to the coffee shop to enjoy a "second cup of coffee" with his new friend. He also began to initiate activities with fellow residents at the board-and-care home, such as getting a small group together to watch weekend football games on the television.

*Personal effectiveness for successful living group*
The final skills training group he attended for five months was *Personal Effectiveness for Successful Living*. In this group, he set a goal to improve his relationship with his father. He also set a recreational and leisure goal to begin playing the violin five days a week, for a minimum of 15 minutes a day. Jim formulated the component steps or short-term goals to achieve his long-term goals, and received IVAST support and coaching in the community to achieve each step in his plan. For example, the first step that he achieved with support from the IVAST trainer was identifying ways he could spend "quality" time with his father and yet get an additional benefit from the activity as a recreational or leisure activity.

Jim was able to execute a plan for every step in his pathway to achieve this two-pronged successful living goal. He decided that he would like to make a record or "Memory Book," with photographs, of his father's achievements during the latter's career as a landscape architect. The IVAST trainer modeled how to ask his father's permission to make a record of his work. Through role-playing this conversation, Jim demonstrated the effective use of conversational skills, and was given a homework assignment to discuss the idea with his father. Jim completed his assignment successfully and in the next week, his father helped him identify locations of the commercial and residential landscape gardens he had designed during his career, which were still intact.

To accomplish his goal of travelling to remaining sites and taking photographs for the "Memory Book," Jim had to learn how to obtain bus schedules, change buses, and travel for several hours each way on a bus to get to the more distant locations. The IVAST trainer accompanied him to obtain a bus schedule, modeled how to read it and then with Jim, role-played how to read the time-table. Jim learned how to identify the correct bus route for a desired destination. After the IVAST trainer accompanied him on several trial runs to a community site, Jim set a goal to travel to two sites a week independently, which he was able to accomplish successfully. During the third week, the IVAST trainer accompanied him to assess his skills in using the bus schedules and to provide booster sessions on using the bus system, as needed. Learning to use the bus schedules and travelling alone on the bus was a significant accomplishment for Jim. On entry into the study, he was barely able to tolerate the stress of taking the bus to his parents' house. Now, he was able to travel on the bus for two hours in each direction, which began to expand his "life space" significantly.

Jim successfully achieved his goal to increase his recreational and leisure activities, and took steps to improve his relationship with his father. After he visited several gardening sites, he would sit down with his father and ask him questions about the horticulture designs. He would take notes and then type up a description and paste it under the photograph. His father spent many hours telling him stories about each site, and their relationship became warm and close.

*Two-year follow-up*
Nine months after completing 15 months of skills training in the clinic, Jim continued to report to his case manager there on a regular basis for follow up. He attended all his clinic appointments, reporting changes in his personal warning signs of relapse, as well as the stressors that he was unable to resolve through using his own problem-solving skills. He maintained his medication compliance and did not suffer any relapses during this two-year period of follow-up.

Jim completed enough of the Memory Book to have a representative sample of his father's work. When his father's physical condition worsened, Jim decided to move back to his parent's home because there wasn't anyone else to care for his physically debilitated parents. He had confidence in his problem-solving skills as protection against the stressors he would encounter. His parents were grateful for Jim's improved mental health and poignantly described how they had "got their son back again." As the daily demand increased to attend to his father's care and keep the household operating, Jim was able to use his newly acquired problem-solving skills to identify the community agencies that could come to their home to provide weekly house-cleaning and daily cooking services. When Jim moved back to his parents' house, he hoped that he might have some extra money to use for recreational activities, but unfortunately, all the family's money was needed to pay for the extra help to assist with cleaning and cooking. Jim barely had enough pocket money to meet his girlfriend at the coffee shop on the days when extra help came to help with household chores. He managed to budget one hour of time, three days a week and enough money for coffee.

For the next year, Jim never missed a clinic appointment and demonstrated his ability to use his medication and symptom management skills, even while managing the demands placed upon him each day by his aged and ill parents. His daily activities were demanding, with cooking, cleaning, bathing his father, feeding his mother, taking his medication, administering his parents' medication, and stretching the family budget. He was able to carve out a respite of 15 minutes a day to call his own, which was usually in the evening after taking his medication and preparing his parents for bedtime. During this precious period each day, he brought beauty into his parents' waning lives by playing a medley of Strauss waltzes and a Brahms lullaby on his violin.

## Summary

There is increasing evidence from studies with both psychiatric inpatients and outpatients that social skills training does *generalize* from clinic-based or hospital-based training situations to the everyday life of patients in the community. The data to support this conclusion come from the self-report of patients themselves, from relatives and significant others, and from psychiatric personnel responsible for the patients' supervision. There is also convergent validation of generalization from cross-national studies conducted in Europe, the USA, South America, and Asia (Liberman, 1998),

The lessons learned from IVAST suggest the need for further innovations in promoting generalization of clinic-based skills training into the everyday life of clients with schizophrenia. For example, self-monitoring may allow the individual to judge the effectiveness of the skills being used in the natural environment, and determine future selection of skills or needs for learning alternative skills. Therefore, teaching self-monitoring and other self-management strategies may add to the use of skills "where the rubber hits the road" (Chadsey-Rusch, 1986). Long-term follow-up services that go far beyond the usually limited lives of research projects may be needed to maintain skills that have tenuous survival value in natural settings that are not always supportive (Cuvo & Davis, 1983). For instance, the use of low-cost, self-help, psychosocial clubs may be of value in this respect (Beard et al., 1982; Bond et al., 1984; Jacobs et al., 1988; Jacobs, 1984). Procedures can also be organized to sharpen gradually eroding skills or to meet the needs of new environments that the client moves into (Ford et al., 1984). Fading and overtraining procedures during clinic-based learning, and structured reinforcement program implemented by peers after clinic-based training may also be effective in maintaining skills acquired in the clinic (Huang & Cuvo, 1997).

Generalization can be facilitated by interventions that focus on the individual patient, as in overcoming neurocognitive deficits and teaching problem-solving skills, as well as by those that focus on increasing the opportunities, encouragement and reinforcement that patients receive from their natural environments for using the skills that they have learned in clinic or hospital-based training programs. With the advent of new, atypical antipsychotic drugs that hold out the promise of improving the neurocognitive functioning of persons with schizophrenia (Green et al., 1997), as well as cognitive remediation strategies (Brenner et al., 1995), there is every reason to be optimistic that generalization of social and independent living skills will enlarge the scope of community functioning of persons with schizophrenia, improve the quality of their lives, and promote their recovery.

# References

Beard, J. H., Probst, R. N. & Malmud, T. J. (1982) The Fountain House model of rehabilitation. *Psychosocial Rehabilitation Journal*, **5**, 47–53.

Benton, M. K. & Schroeder, H. E. (1990) Social skills training with schizophrenics: A meta-analytic evaluation. *Journal of consulting and Clinical Psychology*, **58**, 741–747.

Blair, K. E., Glynn, S., Liberman, R. P. L., et al. (1998) *In vivo* amplification of skills training promoting generalisation of independent living skills for clients with schizophrenia. *In press*.

Blair, K. E. (1994) *In Vivo* Amplified Skills Training: Trainer's Manual. *Unpublished Manual*.

Bond, G. R., Dincin, J., Setze, P. J. & Witheridge, T. F. (1984) The effectiveness of psychiatric rehabilitation: A summary of research at Threshold. *Psychosocial Rehabilitation Journal*, **7**, 7–21.

Brenner, H. D., Roder, V., Hodel, B., et al. (1995) *Integrated Psychological Therapy for Schizophrenic Patients*. Toronto: Hogrefe & Huber.

Chadsey-Rusch, J. (1986) Identifying and teaching valued social behaviors. In *Competitive Employment: Issues and Strategies* (Ed. Rusch, F. R.), pp. 273–287. Baltimore: Brooks.

Cuvo, A. J. & Davis, P. K. (1983) Behavior therapy and community living skills. In *Progress in Behavior Modification* (Eds. Hersen, M., Eisler, R. M. & Miller, P. M.), pp. 126–172. New York: Academic Press.

Dilk, M. N. & Bond, G. R. (1996) Meta-analytic evaluation of skills training research for individuals with severe mental illness. *Journal of Counseling and Clinical Psychology*, **64** (6), 1337–1346.

Ford, L., Dineen, J. & Hall, J. (1984) Is there life after placement? *Education and Training of the Mentally Retarded*, **19**, 291–296.

Green, M. F., Marshall, B. D., Wirshing, W. C., et al. (1997) *Risperidone's effects on verbal working memory*. Paper presented at the International Congress on Schizophrenia Research, Colorado Springs, CO.

Huang, W. & Cuvo, A. J. (1997) Social skills training for adults with mental retardation in job related settings. *Behavior Modification*, **21**, 3–44.

Jacobs, H. E. (1988) Vocational Rehabilitation. In *Psychiatric Rehabilitation of Chronic Mental Patients* (Ed. Liberman, R. P.), pp. 245–284. Washington, D.C.: American Psychiatric Press.

Jacobs, H. E., Kardashian, S., Kreinbring, R. K., et al. (1984) A skills-oriented model for facilitating employment among psychiatrically disabled persons. *Rehabilitation Counseling Bulletin*, **28**, 87–96.

Kern, R. S., Green, M. F. & Goldstein, M. J. (1995) Modification of performance on the span of apprehension, a putative marker of vulnerability to schizophrenia. *Journal of Abnormal Psychology*, **104**, 385–389.

Kern, R. S., Green, M. F. & Wallace, C. J. (1997) Declarative and procedural learning in schizophrenia: A test of the integrity of divergent memory systems. *Cognitive Neuropsychiatry*, **2**, 39–50.

Liberman, R. P. L. & Corrigan, P. (1993) Designing new psychosocial treatments for schizophrenia. *Psychiatry*, **56**, 238–249.

Liberman, R. P. L., De Risi, W. J. & Mueser, K. (1989) *Social Skills Training for Psychiatric Patients*. New York: Pergamon Press.

Liberman, R. P. L. & Wallace, C. J. (1992) Innovations in skills training for the seriously mentally ill: *The UCLA Social and Independent Living Skills Modules*, **2**, 43–60.

Marder, S. R., Wirshing, W. C., Mintz, J., et al. (1996) Behavioral skills training versus group psychotherapy for outpatients with schizophrenia: Two-year outcome. *American Journal of Psychiatry*, **153**, 1585–1592.

Smith, E. E., Bellack, A. S. & Liberman, R. P. (1996) Social skills training for schizophrenia: Review and further directions. *Clinical Psychology Review*, **16**, 599–617.

Stein, L. I. & Test, M. A. (1980) Alternative to mental hospital treatment, I. Conceptual model, treatment program and clinical evaluation. *Archives of General Psychiatry*, **37**, 392–397.

Test, M. A., Knoedler, W. H. & Allness, D. J. (1991) Long-term community care through an assertive continuous treatment team. In *Advances in Neuropsychiatry and Psychopharmacology, Vol. I. Schizophrenia Research.* (Eds. Tamminga, C. & Schulz, S. C.), pp. 239–246. New York: Raven Press Ltd.

Test, M. A. (1992) The training in community living model: Delivering treatment services through a continuous treatment team. In *Handbook of Psychiatric Rehabilitation* (Ed. Liberman, R. P.), pp. 153–170. New York: MacMillan.

Wallace, C. J. & Liberman, R. P. L. (1985) Social skills training patients with schizophrenia: A controlled clinical trial. *Psychiatry Research*, **15**, 239–247.

# Further Advancement of the Integrated Psychological Therapy Program for Schizophrenic Patients: Intervention Methods and Results

K. Andres, H.D. Brenner, B. Hodel, M. Pfammatter and V. Roder

Despite a long-standing lack of sufficient evidence to support the efficacy of psychosocial approaches in the treatment of schizophrenia, research on psychological therapy has made significant progress over the past fifteen years. Neuroleptic medication, deinstitutionalization, and the stress-vulnerability model have been particularly salient in prompting the development of psychological treatments. There are four avenues that are now particularly promising, when provided in conjunction with neuroleptic medication: (I) social skills training; (II) cognitive-behavioral methods of remediating neuropsychological deficits and of modifying or coping with positive symptoms; (III) psychoeducational programs for patients and their relatives; (IV) coping-oriented therapy (Bellack & Mueser, 1993; Penn & Mueser, 1996).

For many years, a considerable part of the research at our hospital has focused on impaired social functioning, which has always figured in clinical practice as one of the central problems in the treatment of schizophrenia. Various levels of functioning have to be assessed in a differentiated manner in connection with such theoretical constructs as social skills and social competence. Patients with schizophrenia suffer from a wide range of cognitive disorders in the areas of attention, information-processing, social perception, problem-solving ability, and social interaction. These disorders, which are both instrumental and interpersonal, increase the likelihood of tense, stressful interaction and social isolation. On the other hand, improved cognitive functions and interpersonal skills facilitate the development of social resources. They are important factors in determining the particularly fragile balance between stress and vulnerability that marks the illness and its course (Liberman et al., 1994; Smith et al., 1996).

# The Integrated Psychological Therapy Program

The Integrated Psychological Therapy (IPT) Program was originally based on the conceptual model illustrated in Figure 1: In this model, there is a dynamic interaction between basic cognitive processes and higher order ones: Dysfunctions at lower levels of cognitive functioning necessarily result in dysfunctions at higher levels, which in turn interact with lower order processes. Moreover, these cognitive dysfunctions prevent the development and implementation of social and instrumental skills, and thus hinder competence. Poor and instru-

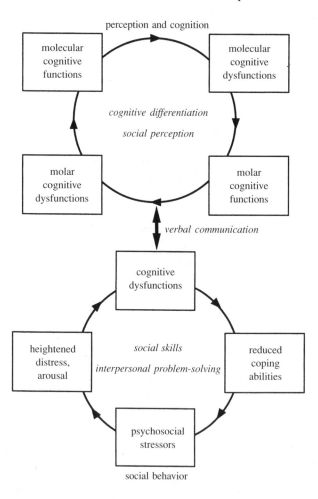

*Figure 1.* Theoretical and clinical rationale of the Integrated Psychological Therapy Program (IPT).

mental social competence increases the likelihood of the individual being over-whelmed by social stressors, while at the same time decreasing the capacity to cope with adverse situations. The psychophysiological arousal caused by psy-chosocial stress leads to the information processing that had been limited due to cognitive deficits becoming even more impaired. Interventions that attempt to interrupt these vicious circles thus have to focus on both cognitive and so-cial impairment (Brenner et al., 1992a).

As a result, the IPT Program consists of five hierarchical subprograms (see Figure 2) that are administered in a set sequence. The focus of training gradu-ally progresses from cognitive tasks in information processing (cognitive dif-ferentiation, social perception) to more complex tasks in social behavior (ver-bal communication, social skills, interpersonal problem-solving) (Roder et al., 1992; Brenner et al., 1994).

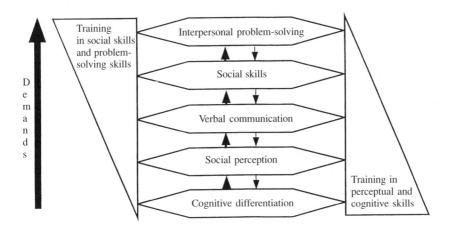

*Figure 2.* The five subprograms of the Integrated Psychological Therapy Program (IPT).

A series of controlled studies have been undertaken by several research groups in different treatment settings (in-patient, day care, outpatient). The results of this research on the effects and mechanisms of the treatment are summarized elsewhere. (cf. Brenner et al., 1994; Theilemann & Peter, 1994). Taking together, they did not support the assumption that improved cognitive functions have a pervasive effect on more complex levels of behavioral organi-zation. An improvement in cognitive functioning seems to be a necessary but not a sufficient prerequisite for socially competent behavior in schizophrenic patients. Furthermore, both the results of some studies and clinical observations suggest that the positive effects which improvements in cognitive levels of functioning have on social ones and vice versa are most likely translated into action in a protective therapeutic environment. On the other hand, skills that might have been acquired in therapy can be partially lost through emotional stress in real-life situations. It also appeared that unsatisfactory generalization and maintenance of social skills and problem-solving skills that had been learnt in therapy might be related to the extent to which the IPT subprograms are tailored to the specific demands of independent community life (Roder et al., 1997).

## Further Development of the Program

Consideration of the available research led to the advancement of the IPT Program in three main directions. Hodel et al. (1996a,b) devised a treatment approach for Coping with Maladaptive Emotions (Emotional Management Training, EMT) in an effort to improve emotional information processing in schizophrenia (see Figure 3). Its main objective is to reduce affective vulnerability, i.e., to loosen the close relationship between emotional stress and an increase in both cognitive dysfunction and maladjusted behavior, and particularly to teach preventive strategies that can be generalized to other situations. Strategies spontaneously employed to cope with emotions are analyzed, and then more appropriate coping strategies are elaborated and rehearsed. Training proceeds in several well defined steps, the ability to identify overarousal and upsetting situations is practiced, and a self-verbalization technique is taught to reduce arousal and correct misinterpretations of normal bodily sensations that may have negative consequences (Hodel & Brenner, 1997).

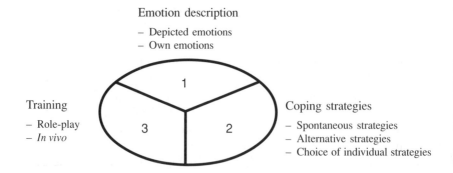

*Figure 3.* Emotional Management Training.

The problem of the poor generalization and transfer of the skills that were acquired prompted Roder et al. to shift the prime focus of training to the specific social and problem-solving skills that equip patients to lead independent lives in the community. The aim of the resulting Residential, Vocational, and Recreational Skills Training Program (RVR) is to build behavioral skills that enable patients to cope with the major problems of rehabilitation over a sustained period of time (Roder et al., 1997). A direct approach to remedying cognitive deficiencies is incorporated into therapy by providing cognitive skills training that is related to concrete situations in social life. Figure 4 depicts the structure of this program. Proceeding from simple tasks to more complicated ones, patients are first sensitized to their individual needs and possibilities, so that they become capable of solving residential, occupational, and recreational problems in their lives with the help of their therapists. The fact that cognitive and instrumental skills training focuses on difficulties that actually arise in the course of rehabilitation makes the problem-solving process highly relevant to everyday life. That is why the first part of therapy focuses on imparting behavior-oriented cognitive skills, whereas the prime focus in the second part shifts to the practical implementation of skills. Problems that emerge in the course of attaining individualized goals and then sustaining them in the long run are dealt with in the third part of the program.

Schaub et al. developed a coping-oriented treatment approach that is a further development of the original IPT Program in a third direction (Schaub et al., 1997; Andres et al., 2000). On the one hand, this approach is based on

- Introduction and motivation
- Cognitive restructuring
- Brainstorming of ideas
- Decision training (needs, interests, obstacles, etc.)
- Social skills training
- Coping with emotional problems

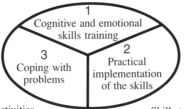

- Problem analysis for activities
- Problem-solving
- Establishing coping behavior

- Skills training *in vivo*
- Self verbalization and self-reinforcement
- Knowing different activities practically
- Anticipation of problems

*Figure 4.* Treatment Program "Residential, Vocational, Recreational Functioning" (RVR).

125

available psychoeducative programs, and on results of research on coping behavior in patients with schizophrenia (Andres et al., 1998). It also incorporated elements of the coping-oriented therapy approaches developed by Süllwold & Herrlich (1990) and by Wiedl (1994).

The resulting program is divided into four parts (see Figure 5). The primary objective of the first part is to impart information about the illness in general, diagnostic terms, the vulnerability-stress model, early warning signs, and the course of the disorder. Crisis strategies and possible treatments are also discussed. In the second part, a definition of stress is elaborated, before a stressful situation selected by the group is considered. This situation is analyzed from cognitive, emotional, physiological, and behavioral standpoints, and stressors commonly experienced in various spheres of life are identified. Following this, forms of appropriate coping behavior are practiced by using role play techniques. Concepts of health and health behavior in general are central to the third part of the program. Potentially pleasant situations are identified and ways to structure the day, leisure-time activity, and physical fitness discussed; whenever feasible, these are practiced in real-life situations. In addition, various relaxation techniques are learned. The fourth part comprises psychoeducative sessions with family members. The purpose of these meetings is to alleviate emotional stress and impart information about the disorder and its treatment. A list of early warning signs is drawn up and a crisis strategy developed as a preventive measure against relapse.

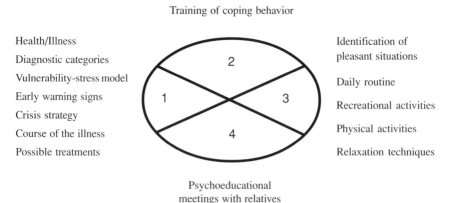

*Figure 5.* Coping-oriented Treatment Program.

Manuals describing the therapeutic procedures used and topics discussed in all three versions of the IPT Program have been elaborated. A series of ongoing controlled studies funded by the Swiss National Foundation are currently being undertaken to evaluate their effectiveness and efficiency (Hodel & Brenner, 1996; Roder et al., 1996; Schaub et al., 1997). The design and methods used are comparable and be illustrated here by reporting on one of these studies in more detail.

## Study on the Effectiveness of the Coping-Oriented Treatment Program

*Design, Subjects, and Methods*

For the purpose of this study, the coping-oriented therapy approach was compared to a supportive group therapy control condition in which the patients were given free choice in the topics they wished to discuss. In both the experimental and control conditions, the patients' relatives were offered the opportunity of taking part in informative discussion sessions. Patients were successively assigned to the alternating coping-oriented or supportive therapy groups. A total of 24 ninety-minute sessions, spread over a period of three months, were provided. The assessments were performed immediately prior to and after therapy, as well as at intervals of 6, 12, and 18 months after completion of therapy. Thirty-three patients (22 male and 11 female), all diagnosed with schizophrenia spectrum disorders according to ICD-10, were included in the study. Of these, 17 took part in coping-oriented therapy and 16 in supportive therapy. Twenty-two subjects were diagnosed as having schizophrenia, and 11 schizoaffective disorders. The average age at index hospitalization was 31.5 years (SD = 7.9), the mean duration of illness 7.7 years (SD = 5.6 years), the average number of hospital admissions 4.8 (SD = 3.5), the total duration of hospitalization for all subjects 77.4 months (SD = 70.7 months), the length of school attendance 10.1 years (SD = 1.6), and the chlorpromazine-equivalent medication dose 180.6 (SD = 141.2). At the beginning of therapy, the patients were either in inpatient or day care, but towards the end, most were outpatients. Although clinical requirements precluded the possibility of randomization, no significant differences in these variables were ascertained between the control and experimental conditions.

The following assessments were undertaken. Using specially adapted scales, patients were requested to rate the degree of importance they attached to receiving general information on the disorder and particular instruction on early warning signs. They subsequently indicated their satisfaction with the information provided. The significance of discussing the disorder with others and the importance of and satisfaction with pharmacotherapy were also appraised. The Tower of Hanoi Test (Goldberg et al., 1990) was used to assess procedural learning and problem-solving skills. To evaluate the scope of knowledge about the disorder and the pharmacotherapy provided, patients completed a modified version of the Knowledge Questionnaire developed by Hahlweg et al. (1995). Measures of psychopathology were assessed using the Brief Psychiatric Rating Scale (BPRS) (Overall & Gorham, 1962) and the Scale for the Assessment of Negative Symptoms (SANS) (Andreasen, 1984). The Scale for Concept of Illness (KK) (Linden et al., 1988) served to ascertain the degree of confidence in the attending doctor and trust in medication. Coping behavior was operationalized by means of the Stress Coping Questionnaire (SVF) by Janke et al. (1985), the Freiburg Questionnaire on Coping with Illness (FKV) (Muthny, 1989), the Competence and Self-control Questionnaire (CCQ) (Krampen, 1991), and the Questionnaire on Coping with Stress in the Course of Illness (UBV) (Reicherts & Perrez, 1993). Psychosocial functioning was assessed by means of the Frankfurt Self-Concept Scale (FSKN) (Deusinger, 1986) and the Social Interview Schedule (SIS) (Hecht et al., 1987).

In addition to more traditional methods of analyzing the resulting data, effect sizes were calculated by using an indicator from Rosenthal (1991, p. 15, Formula 2.12), which reflects intragroup changes in the patients' condition immediately prior to and after therapy. The mean difference between pre- and post-assessment was divided by the dispersion of the differential values.


# Results

Prior to treatment, the patients participating in the coping-oriented therapy condition had been in full inpatient treatment for an average of 173.9 days during a one-year period; following therapy, the average was 82.1 days for the same time span. For patients in the supportive therapy control condition, these mean values were 131.3 and 81.8 days, respectively. The reduction in the number of days spent in inpatient care is significant for the experimental group ($p = .012$), but not for the control group ($p = .314$). In this connection, the varying initial levels of hospitalization may have played a part, but the study of the duration of inpatient care over extended periods by Rosenheck et al. (1993) suggests that the more favorable results found in the experimental group cannot solely be attributed to varying initial levels.

The sum-scores of the BPRS, which reflect the degree of severity in overall symptomatology, were significantly reduced in both conditions. In the same way, negative symptoms were significantly diminished in both therapy conditions, but no differential effects could be determined between the two conditions.

Cognizance of the disorder and its treatment improved to a marked extent in both the experimental and control conditions ($p = .000$, respectively $p = .003$). Analysis of variance indicated that this improvement was more pronounced in the experimental group ($p = .038$).

Moreover, both groups showed considerable improvement with regard to individual variables of psychosocial functioning, e.g., in the quality of housing and leisure time activities. As opposed to the control condition, the coping-oriented therapy approach achieved an improvement in the quality of social interaction and a heightened ability to deal with people. On the other hand, the control group proved to have benefited more in the organization of leisure time.

Significant improvements in coping-behavior were not achieved in either condition. The only exception to this was in the supportive therapy group, which demonstrated a significant improvement in the self-assessment of depressive coping style. The effect sizes, with values between .80 and 1.46 for both conditions, were highest in the areas of knowledge and psychopathology. In addition, the patients participating in coping-oriented therapy rated the importance of and satisfaction with pharmacotherapy considerably higher than those in the control group. In conjunction with the comparatively greater augmentation of knowledge, this can be viewed as a consequence of devoting more time to the discussion of pharmacotherapy in the experimental condition.

The effect sizes regarding improvements in social parameters lay within the medium range with an average of .40 and .22 for the experimental and control groups respectively. In view of the subjects' high level of chronicity, these values do not seem inconsiderable. By contrast, the mean effect sizes for improvement in coping behavior, at .13 and .17 respectively, appear modest. If the effect sizes over all 33 examined variables for the coping-oriented and supportive therapies are averaged, respective values of .38 and .25 result. As these do not differ significantly, there is little reason to infer a globally differentiated effectiveness. A possible explanation for this may be provided by a comparison of the contents of both therapy forms (see Table 1).

All the topics of discussion proposed by the coping-oriented therapy group were also suggested by the participants in the supportive therapy group. The only differences were in the emphasis given to individual themes. Topics which were not specified for discussion in the coping-oriented group occupied only 14% of the total time allotted to the supportive therapy group. To evaluate

*Table 1.* Percentage of time spent on different topics in both treatment groups

| Topic | Coping-oriented therapy | Supportive therapy |
|---|---|---|
| Coping strategies | 23 | 23 |
| Early warning signs, coping with crises, prevention | 18 | 2 |
| Strain (definition, analysis of demands) | 18 | 14 |
| Illness, symptoms, cours | 15 | 27 |
| Medication | 8 | 3 |
| Vulnerability-model | 6 | 1 |
| Leisure time | 5 | 11 |
| Recognition of resources | 5 | 14 |
| Therapies | 2 | 1 |
| Other subjects (drugs, meaning of life, religion, esoteric themes, psychoanalysis, interpretation of dreams, ecology) | 0 | 14 |
| **Total** | **100** | **100** |

better what direction further developments of the coping-oriented therapy approach should take, endeavors were made to determine which therapeutic dimensions were linked to the course of the disorder. Various variables assessed immediately after the conclusion of therapy served as predictors of this course. The following variables were analyzed and defined as outcome criteria: Number of days of hospitalization within 12 months after completion of therapy and the sum-scores of both the BPRS and the SANS, one year after therapy. The computation of these outcome criteria was based on one random sample taken from both the coping-oriented and supportive therapy groups.

The variables of learning ability, confidence in medication and the attending doctor, individual aspects of psychosocial functioning, coping-behavior, and problem-solving skills were tested for their predictive value on the three outcome criteria, after the conclusion of therapy. For this purpose, potential predictors were correlated with the outcome criteria, and subsequently the three predictors with the highest bivariate correlation values per criterion were further evaluated by regression analysis. In Table 2, factors are shown that predict the number of days in hospital, the psychopathological condition as measured by the BPRS, and negative symptoms as measured by the SANS.

The ability to learn as operationalized in the Tower of Hanoi test, although in itself not a relevant variable in coping-oriented therapy, is nonetheless of particular interest, because it had the highest predictive power for forecasting the number of days in hospital. However, the markedness of active coping behavior proved to be of nearly equivalent predictive strength. Objective hous-

Table 2. Prediction of outcome one year after therapy by variables assessed immediately after the conclusion of therapy

| Criterion | Predictors | Bivariate correlation between predictors and criterion | Standardized $\beta$ weight | Adjusted $r^2$ $F$ $p$ | Regression equation |
|---|---|---|---|---|---|
| Hospitalization days within one year | SIS[1]: objective housing condition Tower of Hanoi: progress in learning of three picture elements FKV-F[2]: active coping | −.58 .55 −.55 | −.26 .46 −.40 | .47 5.155 .018 | |
| BPRS[3] sum-score one year after therapy | FKV-F: active coping KK Scale[4]: trust in medication FKV-F: depressive coping style | −.68 −.45 .43 | −.55 −.39 .33 | .60 6.921 .010 | |
| SANS[5] sum-score one year after therapy | FKV-F: active coping SIS: objective work situation FKV-F: depressive coping style | −.60 −.53 .53 | −.59 −.43 .34 | −.63 8.417 .004 | |

[1]Social Interview Schedule; [2]Freiburg Questionnaire on Coping with Illness, rated by others; [3]Brief Psychiatric Rating Scale; [4]Scale for Concept of Illness; [5]Scale for the Assessment of Negative Symptoms

ing conditions at the end of therapy was another highly relevant factor. The following variables proved to be particularly relevant for the prediction of the severity of overall symptomatology one year after completion of therapy: Active coping behavior, confidence in medication, and depressive coping style. Active coping behavior, together with the work situation and a depressive coping style were also valid predictors for the degree of severity of negative symptoms, as measured at the one-year follow-up (see Table 2).

Regression analyses showed that approximately half the variance in the criteria could be explained by means of three predictors each. It is remarkable that the patients' knowledge of the disorder and its treatment – aspects which were most distinctly influenced by therapeutic intervention – turned out to be poor predictors of the duration of hospitalization and symptomatology, as measured one year after therapy.

# Discussion

The limited sample size and the explorative approach of our study permit only preliminary conclusions to be drawn from the findings. Because of the limited sample size, only very distinct treatment variations became significant. Furthermore, as the therapeutic contents of both treatment settings strongly overlap, numerous differential effects were hardly to be expected. This similarity is exemplified by the unexpected congruence in the topics of discussion, as proposed by both the patients in the supportive therapy group and those in the coping-oriented group. For 86% of the total duration of therapy, topics of interest were discussed in the supportive therapy group which were also central to the coping-oriented therapy approach. This overlapping can be viewed as favorable, inasmuch as it substantiates patients' interest in the content of coping-oriented therapy. One instance of dissimilarity between the two groups, however, was the emphasis placed on questions of pharmacotherapy: considerably more time was devoted to this topic in the coping-oriented therapy group.

This disparity was manifested by the greater increase in performance on the questionnaire on knowledge (which also covers questions pertinent to pharmacotherapy) shown by the patients who had participated in coping-oriented therapy, as opposed to those in the control group. Three additional findings further support the assumption that coping-oriented therapy offers more advantages, most particularly in the area of clarifying questions on medication. The importance of pharmacotherapy was rated significantly higher in the coping-oriented group after therapy than before, which was not the case in the control group. Satisfaction with and confidence in pharmacotherapy increased more distinctly in the coping-oriented therapy group without, however, reaching a statistically significant difference. These differences are primarily reflected in considerably higher effect sizes. Non-specific treatment effects were demonstrated in the degree of overall symptomatology, in the prominence of negative symptomatology, and in individual aspects of the level of psychosocial functioning.

A significant reduction in the duration of hospitalization during the period of 12 months prior to and 12 months after treatment was only established in the experimental group. The non-significant reduction for the supportive therapy group may be linked to the lower initial levels for these patients; the initial levels alone, do not suffice as an explanation for the differences found.

Neither of the treatment conditions brought about decisive changes in coping behavior. Indeed, the mean effect sizes in this respect were the most modest. Possible explanations for this may be that both forms of therapy were ineffectual in this respect, or that the measures used were insufficiently sensitive to change. In this connection, the various unresolved problems in areas of conceptualizing and operationalizing coping should be borne in mind.

Inasmuch as the coping-oriented therapy approach negligibly effected patients' coping behavior, it may be judged to have missed one of its central goals, the clinical relevance of which is underlined by regression-analytical evaluation. The fact that active coping behavior was shown to be a relevant predictor for the three outcome criteria in this study, i.e., duration of hospitalization, degree of severity of overall psychopathology, and negative symptomatology one year after conclusion of therapy, indicates the appropriateness of focusing on coping-behavior aspects by emphasizing active coping strategies in the therapeutic setting.

Coping-oriented therapy obviously had limits with respect to improving cognitive performance, which proved to be an important predictor for the criterion of duration of hospitalization. This is hardly surprising in view of the fact that improving cognitive performance was not an explicit therapeutic objective within the framework of this study.

Only marginally significant correlations were observed between the therapy goal of improved cognizance of the disorder and its treatment – which was best attributed to the coping-oriented therapy approach – psychopathology, and length of hospitalization as measured at the one-year follow-up after therapy. It is conceivable that the process of imparting knowledge to the subjects also fosters confidence in pharmacotherapy, but that the latter need not proportionally correlate with a higher level of cognizance. This supposition may serve to elucidate the finding that confidence in pharmacotherapy, and not knowledge of the disorder and its treatment, is predictive with regard to the severity of overall symptomatology.

Since the relapse rate is heavily dependent on compliance, interventions aimed at enhancing compliance deserve particular attention in the clarification of specific effect factors in psychoeducative and coping-oriented treatment programs. To date, investigations have seldom addressed the issue of whether these approaches may be contingent upon improved compliance, and thus only fulfil an adjuvant role in pharmacotherapy, or if they display specific, broader effects. Resolving this question is pivotal to eliminating ambiguity in these therapy approaches. Should it prove the case that the effects achieved are mainly ascribable to heightened compliance, then one should refer, in a more specific way, to "compliance therapy" (Kemp & David, 1996). However, the objective of our coping-oriented therapy approach, as practiced in Berne, is clearly not to be found only in improved compliance, but most particularly in engendering responsible behavior on the part of our patients in dealing with psychosocial stress, early warning signs, and the symptoms of illness.

# Conclusions

This paper described attempts at further advancement of the Integrated Psychological Therapy Program that have been engaged in over the past few years, and first results of research on their effectiveness. On the one hand, the results confirm data collected by other research groups supporting the efficacy and efficiency of such cognitive-behavioral interventions when used as an integral part of a coordinated and comprehensive treatment plan. On the other hand, they also underscore the need for more active participation on the part of both patients and relatives to improve the generalization and transfer of skills acquired in therapy to real-life situations. Efforts to improve the effectiveness of treatment programs like these would, however, also have to involve giving more systematic attention to other questions. These include differential indications, specific components, and processes of effect, as well as the optimal combination with various strategies of drug treatment or far-reaching psychosocial rehabilitative measures. One of the limitations of our present knowledge is that it is based on research that evaluated separately the efficacy of cognitive behavioral programs and the efficacy of different mental health service systems. Future therapy research has to stop separating these aspects. There is therefore a need for a new generation of therapy research that would combine evaluation of therapeutic interventions and of service delivery. However, there are a number of reasons why this ambitious goal will be difficult to reach. Due to the rather small differences between effect sizes, criteria that are required for controlled, randomized studies can only be fulfilled in large-scale multi-center studies. Since there is no support for psychotherapy research on this scale, research endeavors are usually limited to individual projects with small samples. A great deal would be achieved if some research groups from different centers were to join forces and work together on collaborative projects of this kind.

# References

Andreasen, N. C. (1984) *Scale for the Assessment of Negative Symptoms (SANS)*. The University of Iowa, Iowa City.

Andres, K., Pfammatter, M., Garst, F., et al. (2000) Effects of coping-oriented group therapy for schizophrenia and schizoaffective patients: A pilot study. *Acta Psychiatrica Scandinavia,* **101** (4), 318–322.

Bellack, A. S. & Mueser, K. T. (1993) Psychosocial treatment for schizophrenia. *Schizophrenia Bulletin,* **19**, 317–336.

Brenner, H. D., Hodel, B., Kube, G. & Roder, V. (1987) Kognitive Therapie bei Schizophrenen: Problemanalyse und empirische Ergebnisse. *Nervenarzt,* **58**, 72–83.

Brenner, H. D., Hodel, B., Genner, R., et al. (1992a) Biological and cognitive vulnerability factors in schizophrenia. Implications for treatment. *British Journal of Psychiatry,* Suppl. 18, 154–163.

Brenner, H. D., Hodel, B., Roder, V. & Corrigan, P. (1992b) Treatment of cognitive dysfunctions and behavioral deficits in schizophrenia. *Schizophrenia Bulletin,* **18,** 21–25.

Brenner, H. D., Roder, V., Hodel, B. & Kienzle, N. (1994) *Integrated Psychological Therapy for Schizophrenic Patients (IPT).* Seattle: Hogrefe & Huber.

Deusinger, I. M. (1986) Die Frankfurter Selbstkonzeptskalen (FSKN). Göttingen: Hogrefe.

Goldberg, T. E., Saint-Cyr, J. A. & Weinberger, D. R. (1990) Assessment of procedural learning and problem solving in schizophrenic patients by Tower of Hanoi type tasks. *Journal of Neuropsychiatry,* **2,** 165–173.

Hahlweg, K., Dürr, H. & Müller, U. (1995) *Familienbetreuung schizophrener Patienten: ein verhaltenstherapeutischer Ansatz zur Rückfallprophylaxe; Konzepte, Behandlungsanleitung und Materialien.* Weinheim: Beltz Psychologie Verlags-Union.

Hecht, H., Faltermaier, A. & Wittchen, H. U. (1987) *Social Interview Schedule (SIS).* Regensburg: Roderer Verlag.

Hodel, B. & Brenner, H. D. (1996) Weiterentwicklungen des "Integrierten Psychologischen Therapieprogrammes" für schizophrene Patienten (IPT): Erste Ergebnisse zum Training "Bewältigungen von maladaptiven Emotionen." In *Integrative Therapie der Schizophrenie.* (Eds. Böker, W. & Brenner, H. D.), pp. 170–188. Bern: Huber.

Hodel, B. & Brenner, H. D. (1997) Kognitive Therapieverfahren bei schizophren Erkrankten. In *Behandlung schizophrener Psychosen.* (Eds. Böker, W. & Brenner, H. D.), pp. 90–110. Stuttgart: Enke.

Janke, W., Erdmann, G. & Boucsein, W. (1985) *Stressverarbeitungsfragebogen (SVF).* Göttingen: Hogrefe.

Kemp, R. & David, A. (1996) Psychological predictors of insight and compliance in psychotic patients. *British Journal of Psychiatry,* **169,** 444–450.

Krampen, G. (1991) *Fragebogen zu Kompetenz und Kontrollüberzeugungen (FKK).* Göttingen: Hogrefe.

Liberman, R. P. & Green, M. F. (1992) Whither cognitive behavioral therapy for schizophrenia? *Schizophrenia Bulletin,* **18,** 27–35.

Liberman, R. P., Kopelowicz, A. & Young, A. S. (1994) Biobehavioral treatment and rehabilitation of schizophrenia. *Behavioural Therapy,* **25,** 89–107.

Linden, M., Nather, J. & Wilms, H. U. (1988) Zur Definition, Bedeutung und Messung der Krankheitskonzepte von Patienten. Die Krankheitskonzeptskala (KK-Skala) für schizophrene Patienten. *Fortschritte in Neurologie und Psychiatrie,* **56,** 35–43.

Muthny, F. (1989) *Freiburger Fragebogen zur Krankheitsverarbeitung, FKV.* Weinheim: Beltz Test.

Overall, J. E. & Gorham, D. R. (1962) The Brief Psychiatric Rating Scale. *Psychol. Rep.,* **10,** 799–812.

Penn, D. L. & Mueser, K. T. (1996) Research update on the psychosocial treatment of schizophrenia. *American Journal of Psychiatry,* **153,** 607–617.

Reicherts, M. & Perrez, M. (1993) *Fragebogen zum Umgang mit Belastungen im Verlauf, UBV.* Bern: Huber.

Roder, V., Brenner, H. D., Hodel, B. & Kienzle, N. (1992) *Integriertes psychologisches Therapieprogramm für schizophrene Patienten.* Weinheim: Bells.

Roder, V., Jenull, B., Brenner, H. D. & Zorn, P. (1996) (Re-)Integration schizophren Erkrankter in die Gesellschaft durch verhaltenstherapeutische Interventionen. In *Integrative Therapie der Schizophrenie.* (Eds. Böker, W. & Brenner, H. D.), pp. 225–246. Bern: Huber.

Roder, V., Zorn, P. & Brenner, H. D. (1997) Verhaltenstherapeutische Ansätze zu sozialen Fertigkeiten und Problemlösefertigkeiten schizophrener Patienten. Ein Überblick. In *Behandlung schizophrener Psychosen.* (Eds. Böker, W. & Brenner, H. D.), pp. 111–135. Stuttgart: Enke.

Rosenheck, R., Massari, L. & Frisman, L. (1993) Who Should Receive High-Cost Mental Health Treatment and for How Long? *Schizophrenia Bulletin,* **19**, 843–852.

Rosenthal, R. (1991) *Metaanalytic Precedures for Social Research.* Rev. Ed. Sage Publications, Newbury Park.

Schaub, A., Andres, K., Brenner, H. D. & Donzel, G. (1997) Developing a group format coping-orientated treatment programme for schizophrenic patients. In *Towards a Comprehensive Therapy for Schizophrenia.* (Eds. Brenner, H. D., Böker, W. & Genner, R.), pp. 228–251. Göttingen, Seattle, Toronto, Bern: Hogrefe & Huber Publishers.

Smith, T. E., Bellack, A. S. & Liberman, R. P. (1996) Social skills training for schizophrenia: Review and future directions. *Clinical Psychological Review,* **16**, 599–617.

Süllwold, L. & Herrlich, J. (1990) *Psychologische Behandlung schizophren Erkrankter.* Stuttgart: Kohlhammer.

Theilemann, S. & Peter, K. (1994) Zur Evaluation kognitiver Therapie bei schizophren Erkrankten. *Zeitschrift für Klinische Psychologie,* **23**, 20–33.

Wiedl, K. H. (1994) Bewältigungsorientierte Therapie bei Schizophrenen. *Zeitschrift für Klinische Psychologie und Psychopathologie,* **42**, 89–117.

# Treatment of Substance Abuse in Persons with Severe Mental Illness

Gregory J. McHugo, Kim T. Mueser and Robert E. Drake

Clinical knowledge and research findings have increased steadily in recent years regarding the problem of co-occurring substance use disorder (SUD) and severe mental illness (SMI) – often referred to as "dual disorders" or "dual diagnosis" (Drake & Mueser, 1996; Lehman & Dixon, 1995). Clinical and epidemiological data indicate that the rate of comorbid SUD in persons with SMI is substantially greater than in the general population (Cuffel, 1996). The Epidemiologic Catchment Area study (Regier et al., 1990) found that in the United States, persons with schizophrenia or bipolar disorder were 4.6 and 6.6 times as likely, respectively, to have had a SUD in their lifetimes as the general population.

SUD among persons with SMI has been associated with an array of negative outcomes: increased vulnerability to relapse (Linszen et al. 1994; Swofford et al. 1996), rehospitalization (Haywood et al., 1995); depression and suicidal behavior (Bartels et al.1992); violence (Cuffel et al. 1994); incarceration (Abram & Teplin, 1991); inability to manage finances (Shaner et al., 1995); non-compliance with medication and other treatments (Owen et al. 1996); increased vulnerability to HIV infection (Cournos et al., 1991); lower satisfaction with familial relationships (Dixon et al. 1995); and higher service use and costs (Dickey & Azeni, 1996). Persons with dual disorders are also strongly predisposed to homelessness, largely because their substance abuse leads to disruptive behavior, loss of social support, financial problems, and inability to maintain stable housing (Belcher, 1989; Benda & Datallo, 1988; Drake & Wallach, 1989; Lamb & Lamb, 1990). Once homeless, they have greater general difficulties, require more services, and are more likely to remain homeless than other subgroups of homeless persons (Fischer, 1990).

Traditionally, patients with dual disorders were treated in separate mental health, housing, and substance abuse treatment systems, either in a sequential or parallel fashion (Ridgely et al. 1987). Yet, research showed that patients with dual disorders fared poorly within the traditional treatment system, with

137

high rates of rehospitalization, homelessness, and other adverse outcome and persistence of their substance use disorders (Drake et al. 1996).

Over the past 10 years, several models for integrating mental health and substance abuse treatments have been described (Daley et al. 1993; Drake & Mueser, 1996; Lehman & Dixon, 1995; Miller, 1994; Minkoff & Drake, 1991; Solomon et al. 1993). Most of the existing approaches to integrated treatment for patients with dual disorders have been based on assertive community treatment (ACT; Test, 1992) These models generally include multidisciplinary case management teams, dual-disorder group interventions, assertive outreach, and a stage-wise approach to substance abuse treatment (Carey, 1996; Drake et al. 1993; Mueser et al. 1992).

Several recent open clinical trials (Detrick & Stiepock, 1992; Drake et al. 1993; Durell et al. 1993; Godley et al. 1994; Meisler et al., 1997) support the effectiveness of integrated treatment for dual disorders. However, integrated services have not been as successful when they have relied solely on residential care (Bartels & Drake, 1996; Blankertz & Cnaan, 1994; Rahav et al., 1995), have not included assertive outreach to link the patients with the intervention (Hellerstein et al. 1995), or have attempted brief, time-limited intervention (Burnam et al., 1995).

The purpose of the present paper is to summarize briefly the substance use and housing outcomes from two large-scale, longitudinal evaluations of integrated treatment for dual disorders, and to draw conclusions from these studies for improving clinical practice. In both studies, the more intensive and integrated services were expected to produce more progress towards recovery from substance abuse and higher levels of community tenure.

One key feature of the integrated service model in both studies was the stage-wise approach to substance abuse treatment and recovery, based on the four-stage model described by Osher and Kofoed (1989). This model prescribes that patients were first engaged in a working alliance (engagement stage) and then helped to develop motivation to acknowledge that substance abuse is a problem and to accept reduction or abstinence as a goal (persuasion stage); they next participate in actively reducing their substance use to non-harmful levels or to abstinence for longer periods of time (active treatment stage), and finally they continue to maintain their recovery process by remaining aware of their vulnerability to relapse and by addressing other goals in their lives (relapse prevention stage). In both studies, individual and group intervention differed as a function of a person's stage of treatment.

Self-report regarding substance abuse in persons with severe mental illness is problematic because of denial, minimization, failure to perceive that substance abuse is related to poor adjustment, distortions due to cognitive, psychotic, and affective factors, and the inappropriateness of traditional instruments for this population (Drake et al. 1993). In both studies reported here, a team of independent raters, blind to study condition, considered all available data on substance abuse and treatment involvement to establish separate consensus ratings on the Substance Abuse Treatment Scale (SATS), the Alcohol Use Scale (AUS), and the Drug Use Scale (DUS), following procedures validated previously (Drake et al. 1995). The SATS is an 8-point scale for rating clients' progress through the stages of substance abuse treatment (McHugo et al. 1995), and the AUS and DUS are 5-point scales for the diagnosis of substance use disorder according to DSM-IIIR criteria (Drake et al., 1990).

# New Hampshire Dual Disorders Study

ACT and standard case management (SCM) programs for persons with dual disorders were compared in seven community mental health centers (CMHCs) in New Hampshire. Referrals were screened, assessed at intake, and assigned randomly to ACT or SCM programs, after which they were followed for three years. Extensive information was obtained from participants, clinical staff, families, and community-based and mental health service providers. The programs, methods, and results of this study have been described elsewhere in greater detail (e.g., Clark et al., 1998; Drake et al., 1998; Drake et al. 1990; Teague et al. 1995).

*Participants*

Of the 240 eligible referrals, 223 completed intake assessment and entered the clinical trial. The study group was largely male, Caucasian, and young. The majority had never been married or were not currently married, had completed high school or higher education, and were unemployed. Three-quarters were diagnosed with schizophrenia or schizoaffective disorder, and alcohol use disorder was more common than disorders involving other drugs. During the three years of the study, 20 of the original 223 participants (9%) were lost to attrition; the remaining 203 participated in the research assessments for three years.

*Programs*

Implementation criteria for the ACT teams included nine essential features (services provided in the community, assertive engagement, high intensity of services, small caseloads, continuous 24-hour responsibility, team approach, multidisciplinary team, work closely with support system, and continuity of staffing) and four additional criteria that focused on dual disorders (direct substance abuse treatment by members of the team, use of a stage-wise dual disorders model, dual-disorders treatment groups, and an exclusive team focus on patients with dual disorders). The SCM programs incorporated many of these same principles, but clinicians had caseloads of twice the size (25:1 vs. 12:1), provided fewer services directly, and implemented fewer of the features of the ACT model.

*Measures*

Research psychiatrists established co-occurring diagnoses of SMI and SUD, using the Structured Clinical Interview for DSM-III-R (SCID; Spitzer et al. 1988). The baseline client interview contained the following measures from the substance use and housing domains: The Time-Line Follow-Back (TLFB) (Sobell et al., 1980) to assess days of alcohol and drug use over the previous six months; the substance use section from the Addiction Severity Index (ASI) (McLellan et al. 1980); and detailed chronological assessment of housing history and institutional stays using a self-report calendar supplemented by outpatient and hospital records (Clark et al. 1996). In addition, case managers rated clients every six months on the AUS, DUS, and SATS, and urine samples were collected at each interview to detect drugs of abuse. The research interview also included items relating to demographic information, medical and legal status, objective and subjective quality of life, current psychiatric symptoms, and service use. Follow-up interviews were conducted every six months.

*Group equivalence and attrition*

The SCM ($n = 114$) and ACT ($n = 109$) groups were equivalent at baseline. Attrition was higher in the SCM group than in the ACT group (14.0% vs. 3.7%), and after attrition, the SCM ($n = 98$) and ACT groups ($n = 105$) differed on 3 of the 45 baseline variables (age, number of residential moves, and disorganization symptoms). Analyses comparing the 203 completers to the 20 dropouts revealed only two significant differences at intake (GAS score and number of residential moves).

*Process analysis*

We assessed the ACT and SCM teams according to the 13 ACT criteria listed above (Teague et al. 1995). The implementation ratings showed that ACT differed significantly from SCM on five criteria: Smaller caseloads, greater intensity of services, dual disorders as a specialization, more of a team approach, and more individualized substance abuse treatment. ACT and SCM did not differ in several other key dimensions, such as providing services in the community, assertive outreach to engage patients, using a dual disorders model, having multidisciplinary teams, and using dual disorders groups. These data also revealed that considerable treatment diffusion occurred due to extensive statewide training, proximity of teams, and in many cases sharing of staff such as psychiatrists across teams. In addition, there was considerable variation in implementation among the ACT teams.

*Substance abuse and housing outcomes*

We examined five measures of substance use: Researchers' SATS, AUS, and DUS ratings, and participants' reports of days of alcohol and drug use on the six-month TLFB calendar. Mixed-effects regression analyses showed consistent main effects for time, indicating substantial improvements for both groups on all measures over three years. In addition, group-by-time effects were significant for the SATS and AUS scales, both favoring ACT. The primary housing measure was community days, which refers to the number of days living in stable community residences, thereby excluding hospital and jail stays, as well as days homeless and in other institutional settings. Figure 1 presents mean SATS ratings (Panel 1) and mean community days (Panel 2) for the ACT and SCM groups, showing the substantial gains over time by both groups. Including age, gender, and psychiatric diagnosis as covariates in statistical models did not change the results. Figure 2 shows progress through the stages of substance abuse treatment (SATS ratings) by persons with schizophrenia (Panel 1) and bipolar disorder (Panel 2), with the latter showing more rapid progress.

# Washington, DC Dual Disorders Study

Homeless, dually diagnosed persons were recruited for an 18-month quasi-experimental evaluation of integrated treatment. The research demonstration was located in southeast Washington, DC, a predominantly African-American area

## Panel 1

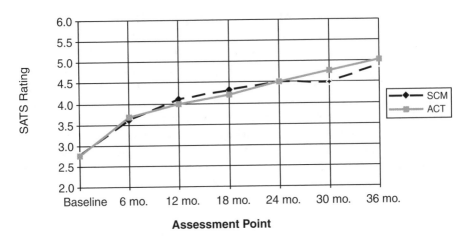

Note: For SATS ratings: 2=Engagement, 3=Early Persuasion, 4=Late Persuasion
5 = Early Active Treatment, 6=Late Active Treatment

## Panel 2

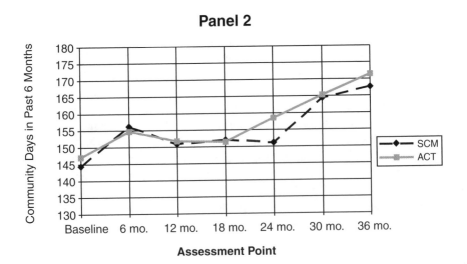

*Figure 1*. ACT and SCM group means over time for SATS Ratings (Panel 1) and Community days (Panel 2) in the NH dual disorders study (N0203).

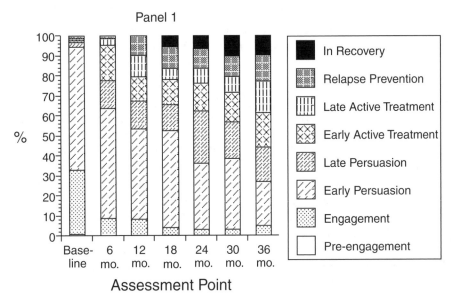

Panel 1

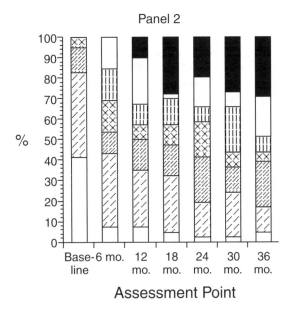

Panel 2

*Figure 2.* Longitudinal progress through the stages of substance abuse treatment for persons with schizophrenia (Panel 1; *N*=94) and the bipolar disorder (Panel 2; N=41) in the NH dual disorder study.

with many of the problems common to urban settings in the United States. The programs, methods, and results of this study are presented elsewhere in greater detail (Bebout et al., 1997; Drake et al., 1993; Drake et al., 1997).

*Participants*

Initially, clients were assigned randomly to two multidisciplinary, integrated treatment teams within a single mental health center. Later, a non-equivalent comparison group was added to document the outcomes of usual care for homeless, dually diagnosed persons in the southeast DC area. Eligibility criteria included being homeless for at least two weeks out of the past 60 days and having diagnoses of both SMI and SUD. Of the 209 referrals who were screened for the integrated treatment (IT) condition, 158 met eligibility criteria and completed baseline interviews. An additional 90 individuals from similar settings were evaluated for the non-equivalent comparison group (standard treatment; ST); 59 met criteria and were enrolled in the study. The subjects were predominantly young, African-American, unmarried, and with high school or less education; the majority were women (due to deliberate over-sampling).

*Programs*

Clients in the IT group received mental health treatment, substance abuse counseling, and housing services through a single CMHC, which provided nearly all outpatient services and coordinated inpatient treatment as well. The two dual-disorder teams relied heavily on behavioral substance abuse treatment methods, although one team emphasized cognitive/behavioral approaches, and the other emphasized social network approaches. Clients in the ST group received services through multiple agencies in the existing housing, substance abuse, self-help, and community mental health systems in DC. Although many of the ST subjects entered housing arrangements that required involvement in self-help programs, little integration among mental health, substance abuse, and housing services was available. Thus, in terms of research design, the key difference between the two groups (IT vs. ST) was the level of integration of services.

*Measures*

Prior to study entry, co-occurring diagnoses of SMI and SUD were established using the SCID. At study entry and at 6, 12, and 18 months after entry, subjects received a one-hour structured interview. The research interview included the following measures from the substance use and housing domains: The Alcohol

Dependence Scale (Horn et al., 1984) to assess the extent of the alcohol dependence syndrome, the ASI to assess seven areas of functioning related to substance abuse, and the Personal History Form (PHF) (Barrow et al., 1985) to assess housing history and status. The research interview also contained items relating to demographic information and clinical history, objective and subjective quality of life, and current psychiatric symptoms. Each follow-up interview included assessment of services used during the prior 60 days. Other data included clinical ratings, agency service use and housing data, and urine toxicology screens.

*Group equivalence and attrition*

The IT and ST groups were similar demographically at intake, and they were equivalent in their history of homelessness and in substance use disorder diagnoses. The IT group had a higher proportion of persons with schizophrenia, whereas the ST group had a higher proportion with major depression. In the 60 days prior to study entry, IT subjects spent more time in institutional settings (hospitals), while ST subjects spent more time homeless. Subjects in the ST group showed a trend toward having a higher rate of attrition from the study: 12 of 59 in ST (20.3%) vs. 18 of 158 in IT (11.4%). Compared to subjects who completed the study, dropouts were more likely to be Caucasian, better educated, previously married, recently homeless, and less severely drug dependent. Dropouts from both groups were similar and did not differentially bias the outcome analyses.

*Process analysis*

The Treatment Services Interview (McLellan et al., 1992) was used to record self-reports of services received during the 60 days prior to each assessment. At each follow-up, the two groups reported similar amounts of total services, of substance abuse services, and of housing support services. Among the 22 individual service categories, the IT group reported more professional substance abuse counseling and mental health counseling than the ST group; the ST group reported more self-help services.

*Substance abuse and housing outcomes*

Substance use outcomes were determined by researchers' consensus ratings on the AUS, DUS, and SATS. Participants with alcohol use disorder at baseline in the IT group improved more on the AUS than similar subjects in the ST

145

group, whereas those with drug use disorder at baseline improved similarly on the DUS in both groups. Figure 3 (Panel 1) shows that improvements on the AUS for the IT group were in the clinically meaningful range, with the average subject dropping from the abuse/dependence range (=3) to the non-problem-

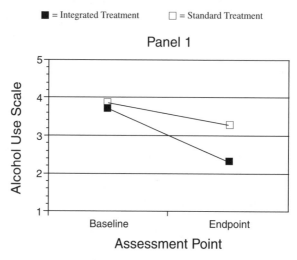

■ = Integrated Treatment          □ = Standard Treatment

Note: AUS Ratings: 1=Abstinence, 2=Non-problematic use, 3=Abuse 4=Dependence, 5=Severe dependence

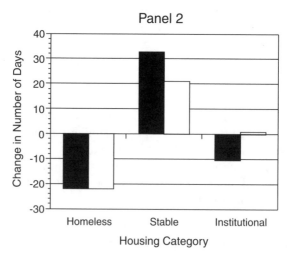

*Figure 3.* Baseline-to-endpoint changes in alcohol use (Panel 1) and in housing status (Panel 2) in the DC dual disorder study. AUS Ratings (Panel 1) are for persons whose primary substance of abuse at study entry was alcohol (*N*=103). Change in housing categories (Panel 2) is for the 60-day period prior to assessment (*N*=187).

atic use range (< 3), while the average subject in the ST group remained in the abuse range. The IT group also made more progress toward recovery from substance abuse, as SATS ratings at end-point indicated that the average IT subject was in active treatment, whereas the average ST subject was still in the persuasion stage. Including additional covariates such as age, gender, psychiatric diagnosis, and history of psychiatric hospitalization in the statistical models did not change these results.

Housing data were combined into three categories, as the reported number of days in: (1) homeless settings, (2) institutions, or (3) stable housing during the 60 days prior to assessment. Figure 3 (Panel 2) shows that the IT and ST groups had equivalent reductions in the mean number of days in homeless settings. With regard to stable and institutional housing, significant group-by-time interactions indicated that days in stable housing increased more in the IT group than in the ST group, and days in institutional settings decreased for IT subjects, but remained stable for ST subjects.

## Discussion

The positive findings regarding substance abuse outcome in these studies are in marked contrast to longitudinal studies of substance abuse in the traditional service system (Drake, Mueser, Clark & Wallach, 1996). Yet our results are quite consistent with recent studies of outpatient programs that provide long-term, integrated substance abuse and mental health treatment for patients with dual disorders (Detrick & Stiepock, 1992; Drake et al. 1993; Durrell et al., 1993; Godley et al., 1994; Meisler et al., 1997). When substance abuse is understood as a chronic, relapsing condition; when integrated mental health and substance abuse treatment is provided; and when treatment models incorporate outreach to engage clients and a stage-wise approach to substance abuse treatment; then many persons with dual disorders make steady progress toward recovery from substance abuse.

Both studies also showed that integrated dual disorders treatment improves the housing outcome. There was a reduction in psychiatric hospitalization in the NH Study for both case management conditions, consistent with earlier studies of ACT (Burns & Santos, 1995). In the DC Study, both hospitalization and homelessness decreased for the IT group. Prior studies of homeless adults with mental illness generally found that intensive case management, increased access to housing, and supports related to housing lead to decreased time homeless and increased time in stable housing (Caton et al., 1993; Center for Mental Health Services, 1994; Lipton et al., 1988; Morse et al., 1992; Wasylenki et al.,

1993). These same studies also indicated that substance abuse is a central factor in housing crises and returns to homelessness (Caton et al., 1993; Center for Mental Health Services, 1994). The results from the DC Study support these findings in two ways. First, integrated dual diagnosis treatment that includes housing services reduces homelessness and increases community tenure. Second, analyses of the housing data indicate that substance abuse is the most powerful predictor of failure to attain stable community housing (Bebout et al., 1997).

In both studies, differences in substance abuse and housing outcomes due to variations in the models of integrated treatment were few. Numerous factors in the NH Study led to a convergence of the ACT and SCM conditions, thereby precluding strong group effects but supporting the effectiveness of integrated dual diagnosis treatment in general. In the DC study, the two treatment models within the IT condition differed more conceptually than practically, and their overall effectiveness was substantial and somewhat greater than that for standard services (ST condition). These findings suggest that it is the general features of integrated treatment, such as, assertive outreach, long-term perspective, stagewise approach, team organization, and substance abuse focus, that lead to successful treatment of dual disorders rather than the more specific features of any given model.

The costs and the cost-effectiveness of integrated dual disorders treatment have not been discussed in this paper, but must be taken into account in any comprehensive evaluation of mental health services. The conceptual, methodological, and empirical work in this area is growing, and as a result, policy decisions concerning integrated treatment for dual disorders will be better informed (Clark & Fox, 1993; Clark et al., 1994, submitted). The many methodological issues of design, measurement, and analysis, and their effect on inferential validity, are beyond the scope of this paper, although awareness of them is essential to critical analysis of reported research. Readers are referred to original reports of these and similar studies, and to sources on methodology (e.g., Hargreaves, Shumway, Hu & Cuffel, in press; McHugo et al., 1998) for discussion of these issues.

# Acknowledgements

This work was supported by U.S. Public Health Services grants MH-00839, MH-46072, and MH-47567 from the National Institute of Mental Health and AA-08341 and AA-08840 from the National Institutes on Alcohol Abuse and Alcoholism, by the New Hampshire Division of Mental Health, and by com-

148

munity mental health centers in New Hampshire and Washington, DC. The authors gratefully acknowledge the contributions to this work of Robin Clark, Gregory Teague, Theimann Ackerson, Richard Bebout, Maxine Harris, Haiyi Xie, Nancy Yovetich, Keith Miles, Lindy Fox, Joan Packard, Barbara Helmstetter, Pat McKenna, Susan Ricketts, Sara Koury, Bradley Dain, and Jeffrey Roach.

# References

Abram, K. M. & Teplin, L. A. (1991) Co-occurring disorders among mentally ill jail detainees: Implications for public policy. *American Psychologist*, **46**, 1036–1045.

Barrow, S. M., Hellman, F., Lovell, A. M., et al. (1985) *Personal History Form*. New York: New York State Psychiatric Institute.

Bartels, S. J. & Drake, R. E. (1996) Residential treatment for dual diagnosis. *Journal of Nervous & Mental Disease*, **184**, 379–381.

Bartels, S. J., Drake, R. E. & McHugo, G. J. (1992) Alcohol use, depression, and suicide in schizophrenia. *American Journal of Psychiatry*, **149**, 394–395.

Bebout, R., Drake, R. E., Xie, et al. (1997) Housing status among formerly homeless, dually-diagnosed adults in Washington, D.C. *Psychiatric Services*, **48**, 936–941.

Belcher, J. R. (1989) On becoming homeless: A study of chronically mentally ill persons. *Journal of Community Psychology*, **17**, 173–185.

Benda, B. B. & Datallo, P. (1988) Homelessness: Consequence of a crisis or a long-term process? *Hospital & Community Psychiatry*, **39**, 884–886.

Blankertz, L. E. & Cnaan, R. A. (1994) Assessing the impact of two residential programmes for dually diagnosed homeless individuals. *Social Services Review*, **68**, 536–560.

Burnam, M. A., Morton, S. C., McGlynn, E. A., et al. (1995) An experimental evaluation of residential and nonresidential treatment for dually diagnosed homeless adults. *Journal of Addictive Diseases*, **14**, 111–134.

Burns, B. J. & Santos, A. B. (1995) Assertive community treatment: An update of randomized trials. *Psychiatric Services*, **46**, 669–675.

Carey, K. B. (1996) Substance use reduction in the context of outpatient psychiatric treatment: A collaborative, motivational, harm reduction approach. *Community Mental Health Journal*, **32**, 111–134.

Caton, C. L. M., Wyatt, R. J., Felix, A., et al. (1993) Follow-up of chronically homeless mentally ill men. *American Journal of Psychiatry*, **150**, 1639–1642.

Center for Mental Health Services (1994) *Making a Difference: Interim status report of the McKinney Research Demonstration Program for Homeless Mentally Ill Adults*. Rockville, MD: Substance Abuse and Mental Health Services Administration, U.S. Department of Health and Human Services.

Clark, R. E. & Fox, T. S. (1993) A framework for evaluating the economic impact of case management. *Hospital & Community Psychiatry*, **44**, 469–473.

Clark, R. E., Ricketts, S. K. & McHugo, G. J. (1996) Measuring hospital use without claims: A comparison of patient and provider reports. *Health Services Research*, **31**, 153–169.

Clark, R. E., Teague, G. B., Ricketts, S. K., et al. (1994) Measuring resource use in economic evaluations: Determining the social costs of mental illness. *Journal of Mental Health Administration,* **21**, 32–41.

Clark, R. E., Teague, G. B., Ricketts, S. J., et al. (1998) Cost-effectiveness of assertive community treatment versus standard case management for persons with co-occurring severe mental illness and substance use disorders. *Health Services Research,* **33**, 1285–1308.

Cournos, F., Empfield, M., Horwath, E., et al. (1991) HIV seroprevalence among patients admitted to two psychiatric hospitals. *American Journal of Psychiatry,* **148**, 1225–1230.

Cuffel, B. J. (1996) Comorbid substance use disorder: Prevalence, patterns of use, and course. In *Dual Diagnosis of Major Mental Illness and Substance Disorder II: Research and Clinical Implications* (Eds. Drake, R. E. & Mueser, K. T.). San Francisco: Jossey-Bass.

Cuffel, B. J., Shumway, M., Chouljian, T. L. & MacDonald, T. (1994) A longitudinal study of substance use and community violence in schizophrenia. *Journal of Nervous & Mental Disease,* **182**, 704–708.

Daley, D. C., Moss, H. B. & Campbell, F. (1993) *Dual disorders: Counseling clients with chemical dependency & mental illness.* Center City, MN: Hazelden.

Detrick, A. & Stiepock, V. (1992) Treating persons with mental illness, substance abuse, and legal problems: The Rhode Island experience. In *Innovative Community Mental Health Programmes* (Ed. Stein, L. I.). San Francisco: Jossey-Bass.

Dickey, B. & Azeni, H. (1996) Persons with dual diagnoses of substance abuse and major mental illness. *American Journal of Public Health,* **86**, 973–977.

Dixon, L., McNary, S. & Lehman, A. (1995) Substance abuse and family relationships of persons with severe mental illness. *American Journal of Psychiatry,* **152**, 456–458.

Drake, R. E., Alterman, A. I. & Rosenberg, S. R. (1993) Detection of substance use disorders in severely mentally ill patients. *Community Mental Health Journal,* **29**, 175–192.

Drake, R. E., Bartels, S. J., Teague, G. B., et al. (1993) Treatment of substance abuse in severely mentally ill patients. *Journal of Nervous & Mental Disease,* **181**, 606–611.

Drake, R. E., Bebout, R. R., Quimby, E., et al. (1993) Process evaluation in the Washington, D.C., Dual Diagnosis Project. *Alcohol Treatment Quarterly,* **10**, 113–124.

Drake, R. E., McHugo, G. J., Clark, R. E., et al. (1998) Assertive community treatment for patients with co-occurring severe mental illness and substance use disorder: A clinical trial. *American Journal of Orthopsychiatry,* **68**, 201–215.

Drake, R. E., McHugo, G. J. & Noordsy, D. L. (1993) Treatment of alcoholism among schizophrenic outpatients: 4-year outcomes. *American Journal of Psychiatry,* **150**, 328–329.

Drake, R. E. & Mueser, K. T. (Eds.) (1996) *Dual Diagnosis of Major Mental Illness and Substance Disorder II: Research and Clinical Implications.* San Francisco: Jossey-Bass.

Drake, R. E., Mueser, K. T., Clark, R. E. & Wallach, M. A. (1996) The course, treatment, and outcome of substance disorder in persons with severe mental illness. *American Journal of Orthopsychiatry,* **66**, 42–51.

Drake, R. E., Mueser, K. T. & McHugo, G. J. (1995) Using clinician rating scales to assess substance use among persons with severe mental illness. In *Outcomes Assessment in Clinical Practice* (Eds. Sederer, L. I. & Dickey, B.), pp. 113–116. Baltimore: Williams and Wilkins.

Drake, R. E., Osher, F. C., Noordsy, D. L., et al. (1990) Diagnosis of alcohol use disorders in schizophrenia. *Schizophrenia Bulletin,* **16**, 57–67.

Drake, R. E., Teague, G. B. & Warren, R. S. (1990) New Hampshire's dual diagnosis program for people with severe mental illness and substance abuse. *Addiction Recovery,* **10**, 35–39.

Drake, R. E., & Wallach, M. A. (1989) Substance abuse among the chronic mentally ill. *Hospital & Community Psychiatry*, **40**, 1041–1046.

Drake, R. E., Yovetich, N., Bebout, R. R., et al. (1997) Integrated treatment for homeless, dually diagnosed adults. *The Journal of Nervous & Mental Disease*, **185**, 298–305.

Durell, J., Lechtenberg, B., Corse, S. & Frances, R. J. (1993) Intensive case management of persons with chronic mental illness who abuse substances. *Hospital & Community Psychiatry*, **44**, 415–416, 428.

Fischer, P. J. (1990) *Alcohol and Drug Abuse and Mental Health Problems among Homeless Persons: A Review of the Literature, 1980-1990.* Rockville, MD: National Institutes on Alcohol Abuse and Alcoholism.

Godley, S. H., Hoewing-Roberson, R. & Godley, M. D. (1994) *Final MISA Report.* Bloomington, IL: Lighthouse Institute.

Hargreaves, W. A., Shumway, W., Hu, T. W. & Cuffel, B. (1997) *Cost-Outcome Methods for Mental Health.* San Diego: Academic Press.

Haywood, T. W., Kravitz, H. M., Grossman, L. S., et al. (1995) Predicting the "revolving door" phenomenon among patients with schizophrenic, schizoaffective, and affective disorders. *American Journal of Psychiatry*, **152**, 856–861.

Hellerstein, D. J., Rosenthal, R. N. & Miner, C. R. (1995) A prospective study of integrated outpatient treatment for substance-abusing schizophrenic patients. *American Journal of Addictions*, **4**, 33–42.

Horn, J. L., Skinner, H. A., Wanberg, K. W. & Foster, F. M. (1984) *Alcohol Dependence Scale (ADS)* Toronto: Addiction Research Foundation of Ontario.

Lamb, H. R. & Lamb, D. M. (1990) Factors contributing to homelessness among the chronically and severely mentally ill. *Hospital & Community Psychiatry*, **41**, 301–305.

Lehman, A. F., & Dixon, L. (Eds.) (1995) *Double jeopardy: Chronic Mental Illness and Substance Abuse.* New York: Random Harwood Academic Publishers.

Linszen, D.H., Dingemans, P.M. & Lenior, M.E. (1994) Cannabis abuse and the course of recent-onset schizophrenic disorders. *Archives of General Psychiatry*, **51**, 273–279.

Lipton, F., Nutt, S. & Sabatini, A. (1988) Housing the homeless mentally ill: A longitudinal study of a treatment approach. *Hospital & Community Psychiatry*, **39**, 40–45.

McHugo, G. J., Drake, R. E., Burton, H. L. & Ackerson, T. M. (1995) A scale for assessing the stage of substance abuse treatment in persons with severe mental illness. *Journal of Nervous&Mental Disease*, **183**, 762–767.

McHugo, G. J., Hargreaves, W., Drake, R. E., et al. (1998) Methodological issues in ACT studies. *American Journal of Orthopsychiatry*, **68**, 246–260.

McLellan, A. T., Alterman, A. I., Cacciola, J., et al. (1992) A new measure of substance abuse treatment: Initial studies of the Treatment Services Review. *Journal of Nervous & Mental Disease*, **180**, 101–110.

McLellan, A. T., Luborsky, L., O'Brien, C. P. & Woody, G. E. (1980) An improved evaluation instrument for substance abuse patients: The Addiction Severity Index. *Journal of Nervous & Mental Disease*, **168**, 826–833.

Meisler, N., Blankertz, L., Santos, A. B. & McKay, C. (1997) Impact of assertive community treatment on homeless persons with co-occurring severe psychiatric and substance use disorders. *Community Mental Health Journal*, **33**, 113–122.

Miller, N. S. (Ed.) (1994) *Treating Coexisting Psychiatric and Addictive Disorders.* Center City, MN: Hezelden.

Minkoff, K. & Drake, R. E. (Eds.) (1991) *Dual Diagnosis of Major Mental Illness and Substance Use Disorder.* San Francisco: Jossey-Bass.

Morse, G., Calsyn, R., Allen, G., et al. (1992) Experimental comparison of the effects of

151

three treatment programmes for homeless mentally ill people. *Hospital & Community Psychiatry,* **43**, 1005–1010.

Mueser, K. T., Bellack, A. S. & Blanchard, J. J. (1992) Comorbidity of schizophrenia and substance abuse: Implications for treatment. *Journal of Consulting & Clinical Psychology,* **60**, 845–856.

Mueser, K. T., Drake, R. E., Clark, R. E., et al. (1995) *Evaluating Substance Abuse in Persons with Severe Mental Illness.* Cambridge, MA: Human Services Research Institute.

Osher, F. C. & Kofoed, L. L. (1989) Treatment of patients with psychiatric and psychoactive substance abuse disorders. *Hospital & Community Psychiatry,* **40**, 1025–1030.

Owen, R. R., Fischer, E. P., Booth, B. M. & Cuffel, B. J. (1996) Medication noncompliance and substance abuse among patients with schizohrenia. *Psychiatric Services,* **47**, 853–858.

Rahav, M., Rivera, J. J., Nuttbrock, L., et al. (1995) Characteristics and treatment of homeless, mentally ill, chemical-abusing men. *Journal of Psychoactive Drugs,* 265–289.

Regier, D. A., Farmer, M. E., Rae, D. S., et al. (1990) Comorbidity of mental disorders with alcohol and other drug abuse. *Journal of the American Medical Association,* **264**, 2511–2518.

Ridgely, M. S., Osher, F. C., Goldman, H. H. & Talbott, J. A. (1987) *Executive Summary: Chronic Mentally Ill Young Adults with Substance Abuse Problems: A review of Research, Treatment, and Training Issues.* Baltimore, MD: Mental Health Services Research Center, University of Maryland School of Medicine.

Shaner, A., Eckman, T. A., Wilkins, J. N., et al. (1995) Disability income, cocaine use, and repeated hospitalization among schizophrenic cocaine abusers. *New England Journal of Medicine,* **333**, 777–783.

Sobell, M. B., Maisto, S. A., Sobell, L. C., et al. (1980) Developing a prototype for evaluating alcohol treatment effectiveness. In *Evaluating Alcohol and Drug Abuse Treatment Effectiveness* (Eds. Sobell, L. C., Sobell, M. B. & Ward, E.), pp. 129–150. New York: Pergamon.

Solomon, J., Zimberg, S. & Shollar, E. (1993) *Dual Diagnosis: Evaluation, Treatment, Training, and Program Development.* New York: Plenum.

Spitzer, R. L., Williams, J. B. W., Gibbon, M. & First, B. B. (1988) *Structured Clinical Interview for DSM-III-R-Patient Version (SCID-P)* New York: Biometric Research Department, New York State Psychiatric Institute.

Swofford, C. D., Kasckow, J. W., Scheller-Gilkey, G. & Inderbitzin, L. B. (1996) Substance abuse: A powerful predictor of relapse in schizophrenia. *Schizophrenia Research,* **20**, 145–151.

Teague, G. B., Drake, R. E. & Ackerson, T. H. (1995) Evaluating use of continuous treatment teams for persons with mental illness and substance abuse. *Psychiatric Services,* **46**, 689–695.

Test, M. A. (1992) Training in community living. In *Handbook of Psychiatric Rehabilitation* (Ed. Liberman, R. P.), pp. 153-170. Boston: Allyn and Bacon.

Wasylenki, D. A., Goering, P. N., Lemire, D., et al. (1993) The hostel outreach program: Assertive case management for homeless mentally ill persons. *Hospital & Community Psychiatry,* **44**, 848–853.

# Community Mental Health Services

# Urbanicity and Schizophrenia

Hugh Freeman

Theories linking increased rates of mental illness to the crowding and resultant stress which are regarded as typical of cities have a long history (Torrey & Bowler, 1990). They were popular in the 19th century, with speculation, for instance, that such geographical disparities were consequent on "the stresses incident to active competition" (White, 1903). A general association has in fact been found between city life and poorer mental health, both in children (Rutter, 1981) – though not relating specifically to schizophrenia – and adults (Blazer et al., 1985). For instance, schizophrenic patients living in urban boarding homes demonstrated more serious psychopathology than those in rural ones (Davies, 1989), and in North American long-term follow-up studies, outcome was better in rural than in urban settings (McGlashan, 1989). Prevalence rates of schizophrenia reported from urban areas, both in Europe and the US, have generally been significantly higher than those of rural areas, though with some marked exceptions, such as the Istrian peninsula and isolated areas of Norway (Andersen, 1975) and Iceland (Helgason, 1964). In modern industrialized cities, the prevalence of schizophrenia and rates of first admission for it are said to be higher than average (Lewis et al., 1992).

Paradoxically, though, possibly the highest prevalence of schizophrenia ever measured (17.4 per thousand population) was reported from a thinly populated rural area of County Roscommon in the West of Ireland (Torrey, 1987), though there seems to be no evidence that this represented a higher-than-average incidence rate. What these anomalous rural areas may have as a common factor is a high proportion of unmarried males, living as farmers or rural laborers (Keatinge, 1987). Thornicroft et al. (1993) found that a rural area of the Veneto had twice the treated incidence and prevalence of urban South Verona, but offer no explanation for this. What is significant is that a strong association exists between excess prevalence of schizophrenia and some places with the opposite environmental characteristics to those of large cities. On the other hand, neurotic and personality disorders have generally been found to have a random distribution in cities (Giggs, 1980; Stefansson, 1984), though the findings about them from Mannheim, discussed below, were different.

Prevalence rates are likely to be influenced by factors such as migration, infectious disease, fertility and mortality, culture, and other social processes (Eaton, 1985). Cooper and Sartorius (1977), seeking an explanation for the emergence of schizophrenia as a major disorder in the 19th century, pointed out that large populations had accumulated then on a hitherto unprecedented scale, mainly through migration. As a result, cases of severe mental illness, which would previously have remained scattered in rural societies, became aggregated in such numbers that they represented a major public health problem. Furthermore, because of the demands of industrialization, many families became unable to manage psychotic relatives at home, where conditions were often very overcrowded, although this would have been possible in their previous agrarian settings. More recent relevant social processes include "deinstitutionalization," since there has been a widespread failure in Western countries to provide adequate community residences for schizophrenic patients leaving mental hospitals, so that they tend to drift into the poorest parts of cities, or even be resettled there by public services (Goldman, 1983).

However, from the point of view of etiological factors, data on incidence are more valuable than those on prevalence – if more difficult to determine. Henderson (1988) points out that the non-random distribution of the incidence of a disorder might be due to: (a) environmental factors having a direct effect; (b) the disorder or its promdromata influencing where people live; or (c) a third set of factors prior to both (a) and (b). All these possibilities need to be examined in relation to schizophrenia.

An international study of first-onset schizophrenia in both urban and rural catchment areas of twelve centers in both developing and developed countries (Varma et al., 1997) showed significant differences in illness variables between cases from the two types of environment. These differed in the type of onset of illness, the early manifestations and clinical diagnosis of schizophrenia, and the CATEGO classification. The Indian cases, and particularly the rural cohort there, differed strongly from those from industrialized countries. It was concluded that cultural factors, particularly urbanization, play a role in determining the onset, early manifestations, and typology of schizophrenia.

Explanations for geographical differences in the frequency of schizophrenia have, in many cases, made use of a pair of opposite tendencies – "social drift" and "social residue"; these are both varieties of the social selection hypothesis, and both represent forms of social segregation. "Social drift" is used to mean the migration of those affected by psychiatric morbidity to areas of a particular kind, where social demands on them may be less; it has been considered particularly relevant to schizophrenics, though alcoholics, drug addicts, people with marked personality disorders, and others with reduced social competence and affiliative bonds show the same tendency. Inner-city areas are the ones to which such affected individuals are most likely to migrate in Western countries, since these tend to contain both cheap, single-person accommodation and opportunities for casual but lowly paid work, whilst lacking any well-knit social structure which would make them feel unwelcome. At the same time, though, these environments are lacking in social support, which may operate as an adverse factor on mental health for some people. In many studies, the higher prevalence of schizophrenia in central city areas has been more marked in men than in women, which suggests that social influences affect the two sexes differently in this disorder, e.g., that men may be more likely to drift centrally.

On the basis of this view the reason for the onset of schizophrenia is not that those affected live in environmentally unfavorable areas, but that people with schizophrenia, like others who are socially marginal, become unable to live in better residential districts. This would result in them moving to the central parts of a city, where they experience few social or emotional demands. Thus, being resident in a poor environmental area is not an etiological factor in itself, but rather one associated with the development of the disorder. The "drift hypothesis" has been used to describe, firstly, movement down the socio-economic scale (intra- and inter-generational), and secondly, geographical movement to more deprived urban areas; both processes have been related to the presence of schizophrenia. Goldberg and Morrison's theory of inter-generational "social drift" (1963) was an hypothesis of great heuristic importance. However, it has been claimed (Dauncey et al., 1993) that this does not provide an adequate explanation for schizophrenics tending to be concentrated in central city areas, because the occupational classification they used is no longer appropriate, and because accurate data were missing at that time on the subjects' area of residence. These seem relatively small objections, though.

The reverse of the social drift process, but a similar hypothesis, is that of "social residue," i.e., that the mentally healthy migrate away from socially and environmentally undesirable areas, leaving the relatively incompetent behind (Freeman & Alpert, 1986). The result of this differential migration, in which those affected by morbidity of any kind fail to participate in a general movement to better environmental areas, is that levels of morbidity rise in the central areas and remain low in suburban or new communities. One example was in British new towns, in one of which a relatively low rate of serious psychiatric morbidity was reported, but misinterpreted, in the earlier years (Taylor & Chave, 1964); it was in fact a consequence of the processes by which their residents were selected. Another example, showing the opposite aspect of the process, is the dramatic population fall of the industrial city of Salford, beginning in 1928, which was the sharpest for any local authority in England (Freeman, 1984a); this resulted predominantly from the movement outwards of smaller family groups containing employed adults. Such a differential fall tends to leave behind those who are below average in social mobility, including the mentally and physically disabled, single-parent families, the elderly, etc; they have been described by Stromgren (1987) as a "residual population." As an example, Lei et al. (1974) found in a Californian city that the highest concentrations of mental retardation were in areas where the population had been longest established.

The "Breeder" or social causation hypothesis, on the other hand, assumed that environmental factors are either causative of schizophrenia or have to be present for a predisposed individual to become ill. Dunham (1965) stated that this hypothesis was dependent on a series of propositions:

1) Symbolic communication is essential for normal development, and lack of it leads to mental breakdown.

2) In an urban community, certain areas have a greater amount of disorganization than others.

3) Social disorganization is characterized by excessive mobility, ethnic conflict, breaks in communication, and lack of consensus.

4) Seclusiveness is a key trait in schizophrenia.

5) Persons who develop seclusive traits do so as a result of isolation or breaks in the communication process.

6) These conditions are found in certain areas identified as being disorganized.

These propositions were described by Dunham as "not completely substantiated," which very much understates the objections to them. He added that such etiological theories were "assumed to be adequate" and that the epidemiological evidence was then "often regarded as inferentially supportive of the original untested assumption." This is clearly very unsatisfactory from the scientific point of view.

Lewis et al. (1992) describe the social drift hypothesis as having been little challenged for 25 years, in spite of the evidence for it being weak. However, it had in fact been questioned by several workers. Lapouse et al. (1956) examined the movement of schizophrenic patients within a city over 20 years before the onset of psychotic illness, but found little evidence of downward drift, while a control group did not move significantly up the social scale, relative to them. Dunham (1969) stated that whereas the incidence of schizophrenia tended to be concentrated in central areas of Detroit in the 1930s, this was no longer so in the 1950s; the distribution of cases had become more dispersed. In Hamburg, Klusmann and Angermeyer (1987) found no concentration of first-admission schizophrenic patients in the central areas, though this was the case for readmissions. The difference between their findings and the original ones from Chicago was explained by the different historical development of the two cities, and by a trend towards greater environmental uniformity in urban areas. The Hamburg findings do in fact support the relevance of social drift for established cases of schizophrenia, but the data from Nottingham (Dauncey et al., 1993) are not confirmatory of the hypothesis in general.

Migration, however, is a difficult issue in relation to psychiatric morbidity, not least because there is evidence that both good and bad mental health may provoke a higher rate of mobility than the average, though for opposite reasons (Giggs, 1984). The two concepts of drift and residue make this dichotomy clear, and both may operate at the same time and place. The high prevalence of schizophrenia recorded both for inner city Salford (Freeman & Alpert, 1986) and for rural areas of the west of Ireland (Torrey, 1987) may well have resulted to a significant extent from migration: In both places, the population fell to half an earlier level over a period of about 50 years, though the Irish fall began much earlier. Since economic migration of this kind inevitably has a differential character, it will tend to alter levels of morbidity in the populations affected by it. Another factor which may have to be considered is that foreign immigrants tend to concentrate significantly in the central areas of large cities (Herbert & Johnston, 1976).

Evidence from a number of different places will now be examined, with the object of throwing further light on the possible etiological role of "urbanicity."

## Evidence from Swedish National Data

The hypothesis that the environment of cities can be directly related to a higher-than-average prevalence of schizophrenia has been proposed by Lewis et al. (1992). They claim that studies supporting the drift hypothesis have failed to take account of the nature of the population at risk – the single, mobile, young people who make up a greater proportion of urban populations than of others. To test it, they investigated the association between place of upbringing and the incidence of schizophrenia, using data from a cohort of 49,191 male Swedish conscripts, 21% of whom had been brought up in one of the three urban centers of Sweden. These data came from the Swedish National Register of Psychiatric Care, which recorded 83% of all admissions in 1973, but was closed in 1983. Incidence rates were calculated for a follow-up period of 14 years. Diagnoses of neurosis, personality disorder, and alcoholism, as well as cannabis use and reports of "feeling nervous" were commoner among those brought up in cities.

The incidence of schizophrenia was found to be 1.65 times higher among men brought up in cities than in those who had had a rural upbringing, despite adjustment for some other factors associated with city life but independent of the illness, such as use of cannabis, parental divorce, and family history of psychiatric disorder. The association of schizophrenia with urban life was also independent of family poverty, which in Sweden was commoner in rural areas.

To assess whether the effect of city upbringing was specific to schizophrenia, the strength of the association between urban upbringing and the development of the other psychoses was measured, and showed a similar though weaker trend. For schizophrenia, a strong linear trend was observed, with the highest rate in the cities, intermediate rates in large and small towns, and lowest rates in country areas. Since the *prevalence* of schizophrenia is only about 1.4 times higher in Swedish cities than in rural areas, genetic factors were considered very unlikely to explain this result. However, these findings did not distinguish between place of birth and place of upbringing. Furthermore, the relative risk from urban upbringing was very much less than the effects of lower intelligence, poor sociability, use of drugs, or a previous psychiatric diagnosis in adolescence.

Lewis et al. (1992) state that their study design eliminated the possibility that geographical drift could explain any observed association between city life and schizophrenia; in that case, undetermined environmental factors, believed to be present in cities, must be assumed to have increased the risk. They seem in fact to have returned to a modified version of the original "Breeder" hypothesis.

## Evidence from the United States

In the United States, Torrey and Bowler (1990) examined the geographical distribution of "insanity" and schizophrenia for 9 separate years between 1880 and 1963. The prevalence in Northeastern and Pacific Coast States was approximately three times that of those with a low rate (Southeastern and South Central); this difference was remarkably consistent over the 83 years, despite changes in diagnosis (insanity or schizophrenia) and in the categories recorded (hospitalized plus resident in the community, hospitalized only, first admissions only). These authors also compared urban/rural ratios (percentage of population living in towns of 2,500 people or more) in the different states with rates of insanity/schizophrenia, for 9 years between 1880 and 1963; they found high correlations between mental illness and urbanicity, i.e., residence in an urban area (as defined) for all years except 1963. Data on socio-economic status, ethnicity, and temperature for each state were also compared with first-admission rates and the resident hospitalization rate (1963) for schizophrenia. These rates correlated positively with socio-economic status as well as with urbanicity, but not with the other two factors. This positive correlation between higher socio-economic status and admission rates was unexpected, but since high regional correlations between urbanicity and socio-economic status were also found, there might have been a confounding effect between the two variables. As in Sweden, the per capita income of people living in American cities is higher than it is for those living in rural areas.

Since the variation in rates between states was greater than that for affective, substance abuse, anxiety/somatoform, or antisocial personality disorders (Burnam et al., 1987), diagnostic differences would have to be remarkably consistent over a very long period to provide the explanation for this geographical effect. Malzberg (1955) had noted "a general progressive increase in rates from the rural areas through the urban groupings," i.e., the larger the city, the higher the first-admission rate for schizophrenia, and Frumkin's (1954) study of first admissions to Ohio state mental hospitals reported that the urban rate was 1.9 times higher than the rural. The only American study that did not find a clear urban excess of schizophrenia was by Lemert (1948) in Michigan, where not only Detroit, but several rural counties had a high rate of admissions for schizophrenia.

Torrey and Bowler state that social drift is very unlikely to explain the state and regional differences in hospitalization rates for schizophrenia that they found over this very long period. From the sociological point of view, a study of mental illness in Arkansas (Stewart, 1953) had suggested that community pressure in rural areas made it more difficult to commit people to State hospitals, while the nuclear family was stronger there and more likely to have accommodation for a psychotic member. However, New York State hospital admission data for 1949-51 showed no difference in the duration of illness before admission for schizophrenics from rural and urban areas respectively (Malzberg, 1955), and the belief that bizarre people are more easily accepted by the community in rural areas remains unproven. Such social factors, though, would not affect comprehensive studies of prevalence rates which included both inpatient and community cases. Torrey and Bowler concluded that if a model of genetic predisposition combined with stress factors was to account for the geographical distribution of schizophrenia, it would be necessary to postulate either a selective migration of genetically predisposed individuals to both Northeastern and Pacific Coast States, and this was discarded as improbable, or else an urban stress factor that elicited the disease in genetically predisposed individuals in cities. That stress factor apparently remains unidentified.

The main methodological question raised by Torrey and Bowler's study is

161

their criterion for "urbanicity": The minimum population of 2,500 is little more than a large village, so that the conflation of all populated areas above that size – including the largest cities – might be concealing important differences between sub-groups with different orders of population. This has been a persistent, and still unresolved problem in all studies attempting to link psychiatric disorder with urban living.

## Evidence from Nagasaki

Turning to the incidence of schizophrenia, data have been published from three cities, of very varying characteristics. Firstly, an ecological study in Nagasaki by Ohta et al. (1992) examined the possible influence of social class. Characteristics of residents (employment status, occupational and academic career, household status, length of residence, housing tenure, and the proportion of young males in the population) were related statistically to the city's ecological structure. Contrary to some studies in Western cities, no significant differences in residents were observed between different areas, and no significant relationship between incidence rates of schizophrenia and social class. However, schizophrenic men tended to have lived in the central parts for a long time and to have relatively low socio-economic status, whereas incidence rates were low in the areas where residents could afford to own private dwellings. As in many other studies, the findings for women were not as consistent as those for men. Ohta et al. state that in Japan, differences in social class are not as marked as in Europe or the US, and the differences between residential areas not so clear. Japanese cities have not had long developmental backgrounds; since demolition and rebuilding have been frequent, areas containing poor housing have not had time to develop into residential districts with an established character.

This work seems to indicate that both the environmental characteristics of Japanese cities and the social structure of Japanese society are so different from those of Western cities that conclusions about the frequency of schizophrenia cannot reliably be extrapolated from the one setting to the other.

## Evidence from Camberwell

In Camberwell – an inner-city area of South London – all first-contact cases of schizophrenia recorded between 1965 and 1984 were compared with matched

162

non-psychotic patients, and investigated for place of birth and paternal occupation (Castle et al., 1993). Compared with controls, the schizophrenic cases were more likely to have been born in the socially deprived area and to have had fathers with manual, as opposed to non-manual occupations. The sample included the British-born children of Afro-Caribbean immigrants, but controlling for ethnicity did not alter the trends recorded. The results suggested, therefore, that individuals who develop schizophrenia are more likely than non-psychotic controls to have been born into socially deprived households. This would be associated with a greater risk of disadvantage both *in utero* and in early life. The favored explanation was that some environmental factor of etiological importance in schizophrenia is more likely to affect those born into households: (a) of lower socio-economic status and (b) in the inner city.

## Evidence from Chicago

In their classic study, Faris and Dunham (1939) found that first admissions for schizophrenia were concentrated in the city center, and that the rate became less in all directions towards the periphery. However, later findings in Detroit by Dunham (1965) did not confirm this finding, so that his view changed largely from a social causation to a social selection hypothesis. In later studies in Chicago, Levy and Rowitz (1973) found no clear-cut pattern for first admissions for schizophrenia; areas with high rates were scattered throughout the city. On the other hand, readmissions showed a marked excess in the poorer central areas, providing strong evidence for the "social drift" explanation. These authors speculated that Faris and Dunham's findings might have been contaminated by the lack of general hospital psychiatric beds at the time their research was done, so that most middle-class schizophrenics would not have appeared in the statistics – being treated either at home or in distant private hospitals. The absence of these cases from the data might thus have led to a misleading impression of a central excess of new cases.

## Evidence from Nottingham

In Nottingham, enumeration districts were statistically grouped into low-status and high-status clusters respectively; social deprivation emerged as mainly concentrated in the areas of post-1919 public housing and in some inner-city districts to privately rented housing. New cases of schizophrenia had been found

163

to be significantly more likely to come from low-status areas, in contrast to manic-depressive cases, which were evenly distributed over the two types of districts (Cooper et al., 1987). Dauncey et al. (1993) related the lifetime geographical mobility of a group of 67 patients suffering from schizophrenia to the ecological structure of the city: A skewed ecological distribution was found to begin early in the lives of the patients, and to be well established at least five years before initial contact with the psychiatric services.

The sample consisted of virtually all new cases of schizophrenia during 1978–1980. Most were male and presenting in the 15–34 age-range; 40% were either born outside the UK or had one or both parents born outside, but no particular migrant group predominated. The annual incidence rate in the most deprived area (0.18 per thousand) was three times that in the least deprived, so that the earlier findings on the same group of patients had persisted and could not be accounted for by the age-structure of the population. If there was a process of geographical "drift" affecting incidence, it would occur in the "prodromal" period before the first psychiatric contact, but in fact, five years before presentation, there was still a trend (non-significant) towards an excess of patients living in the most deprived areas, which contained only 18% of the at-risk population, but 33% of the patients – a statistically significant difference. The few patients who moved into the city in the five years before first presentation did not contribute to the skewed distribution. Of the 27 patients born in the central part of the catchment area, 23 originated in areas of social deprivation, this relationship being independent of ethnicity.

This study of a geographically defined and representative sample of patients making their first contact with psychiatric services was said to show that the incidence of schizophrenia correlated closely with levels of social and urban "deprivation"; most of the poor zones were central, but rates also remained high in the more scattered pockets of deprivation in peripheral areas. Though some degree of "drift" was likely, the base-line from which it took place was an already skewed pattern of residence, in that most cases originated in socially deprived areas. However, as in Hamburg, social drift could still be relevant to the distribution of established cases.

# Evidence from Salford

Salford, in the Greater Manchester conurbation is a very old industrial area with a highly developed network of psychiatric facilities. Since 1968, the community has had a population-based case register, linked with all specialist psychiatric agencies serving the population. For each patient, it records – on a cumulative basis – the total use of psychiatric services, including long-term follow-up.

Freeman and Alpert (1986a) found higher than expected prevalence rates of schizophrenia for 1974, compared with other industrialized countries (Babigian, 1985; Jablensky, 1986; Hafner & an der Heiden, 1986). These were most marked in the middle-aged, and a relationship was proposed with selective population movements, combined with the low mortality and frequently chronic course of the disorder. Data on out-patients, in-patients, visits by mental health professionals, depot injections, etc. were derived both from the case register and from inquiries to general practitioners (GPs). These prevalence figures were then analyzed in terms of distribution by electoral wards (Freeman & Alpert, 1986b); whilst in general this ecological method does not provide a satisfactory basis for epidemiological studies, it was felt to be useful in the case of Salford because both the social-class distribution of the population and characteristics of housing within its sub-areas were relatively homogeneous, compared with most cities. The data showed the city to be clearly divided on this basis into two separate zones – an inner one, in which all wards had a rate of schizophrenia above 5 per thousand general population, and an outer one in which all wards had a rate below that figure. Whilst the outer zone contained the three wards with the highest social-class level in the city, this separation was by no means clearly along such lines, since the same zone also included several wards of low socio-economic status. Thus, ecological analysis showed no direct relationship between prevalence of schizophrenia and social class, but the group of wards with higher rates were those closest to the center of the conurbation.

When the 1974 prevalence study was repeated for 1984, the point-prevalence rate of treated schizophrenia within this urban community had increased from 4.56 to 6.26 per 1000 adult population during the decade (Bamrah et al., 1992). In 1974, the peak period-prevalence rate was for those aged 45–54 years, but ten years later, the rates peaked for both sexes in the 55–64-year age group – much more sharply in women. This is in contrast to earlier studies, which showed peaks at younger ages (Shur, 1988), but the same as Torrey's (1987) finding in Roscommon. Thus, in some populations at least, the prevalence rate of schizophrenia is currently increasing, even if inception rates are average. In Salford, emphasis on reducing hospital stay had been compensated for by increased admission rates (mostly short-term) and greater support for patients living in the general community.

A number of factors might be responsible for such an increase in prevalence. In the first place, it seems likely that schizophrenic patients currently have a longer lifespan than previously, possibly owing to improved care. Since this rate mainly takes into account individuals with established illnesses, short-term influences would probably be social and environmental, rather than biological. The general population fell by 25% in the decade, though by 1982–84, some relative stability had occurred in this secular decline. The increase may therefore have reflected a continuing selective migration of healthy individuals out of the inner city. Whether or not this was the case, since the absolute numbers of schizophrenics present during 1974 and 1984 respectively fell substantially (from 624 to 557), selective in-migration of previously affected cases does not appear to have been a significant factor. People suffering from schizophrenia who are left behind in the inner city might be becoming progressively older and more chronic.

The "total" inception rate, i.e., of first contact with the case register, appeared to have decreased in the decade. This resulted from more patients maintaining contact with their professional careers than was previously the case, possibly because fewer were being discharged from follow-up or were defaulting. This greater continuity of care was made possible by the wide range of community services available, better co-ordination between them, and the precision with which cases were recorded. Both in-patient and out-patient facilities had improved, and there had been a major expansion in the community psychiatric nursing service, particularly within primary care, presumably improving liaison between psychiatrists and GPs. Although such systematic follow-up adds to the impression of chronicity of the sample, the case register had been fully operational for six years before the 1974 study, so that the results are unlikely to have been influenced by administrative factors.

This rise in prevalence appears to conflict with some recent findings which suggest that the frequency of schizophrenia is on the decline. However, such studies have dealt with first admissions or first contacts, and relate to populations which were different in character. In Salford, the population structure had altered considerably in the study period, with a sizeable reduction in overall numbers and a further increase in social deprivation and unemployment, thus enhancing its "inner-city" character that has long been – though for largely unexplained reasons – associated with high rates of schizophrenia. If the inception rate had in fact fallen, this would add emphasis to the effect of differential outward migration; any effect of the disease process on prevalence, related to the accumulation of chronic cases, would be attenuated in this way.

## Evidence from Mannheim

Hafner and Reimann (1970) determined the incidence of all psychiatric disorders for twenty areas within the city for 1965; significantly higher rates were found in socially disorganized areas, mainly in the center, with lowest rates on the periphery, particularly in villages with strong community activities. Similar data for the period 1974–1980 were examined by Weyerer and Hafner (1989), who found that the ecological distribution of disorders had remained very stable, in spite of large urban renewal programs in the inner city. Since 1965, the spatial concentration in the inner zone increased not only for schizophrenia, but also for neuroses and personality disorders – contrary to the findings of some other studies; however, there was no such concentration of affective psychoses. Alcoholism and other addictions were also strongly concentrated in the city center during both periods. Using the factor ecology method, Maylath et al. (1989) divided the 23 districts of Mannheim into five areas that were as homogeneous as possible for two principal components (segregation, density) In 1974–1980, all psychiatric disorders except affective psychoses and neurotic depression were found to be concentrated in areas that were centrally located and characterized by high population density, poor housing, low social status, and a high proportion of foreign residents.

Finally, Weyerer and Hafner (1992) examined whether the excess morbidity in the inner city in 1974–1980 could be explained by the high proportion of immigrants there. In fact, the high concentration in the inner zone was solely due to the German residents. This was a similar picture to the prevalence data for 1974–1977, which showed that the prevalence of all psychiatric disorders was about twice as high among the German population as among foreign residents, in the whole city. However, it contrasted with the findings of Giggs (1983) that in Nottingham, the incidence of schizophrenia among the foreign-born followed a classically zonal form, with the highest concentration in the central city. In Mannheim, the incidence of schizophrenia among the foreign-born in the inner zone (1.08) was little different from that in the outer zone (0.98), whereas for German residents, the figures were respectively 1.68 and 0.78, and those for the intermediate zone were midway between these rates. Weyerer & Hafner point out that if environmental conditions in the inner zone have an etiological effect in psychiatric disorders, "an explanation is needed of why they should only exert an effect on the German but not on the foreign residents." Between 1970 and 1978, a large proportion of the inner-city German residents moved out; whilst it is likely that these had a better health status than those who remained, there are no data to test this proposition. Unfortunately, the closure of the Mannheim psychiatric case register for political reasons prevented these trends being followed in more recent years.

# Evidence from Holland

Marcelis et al. (1998) recorded all births (*N*=42, 115) between 1942 and 1978 in Dutch municipalities and followed these up through the National Psychiatric Case Register for first admissions for psychosis between 1970 and 1992. Urban birth was associated with later schizophrenia, and less so with affective psychosis and other psychosis. Those born in the areas with the highest level of population density were twice as likely to develop schizophrenia. Also, associations were stronger for men, for individuals with an early age of onset, and in more recent birth cohorts. The data excluded psychiatric beds in general hospitals, which are nine percent of the total psychiatric beds.

The authors say it is possible that part of the effect could be due to differential immigration of parents carrying psychoses genes. An urban birth effect could not be distinguished completely from an urban residence effect, but the fact that effect sizes were smaller for effective psychosis than for schizophrenia may support an urban risk factor affecting vulnerable individuals around the time of birth – "if the high rates of disorder in urban environments were to be explained on the basis of high-risk groups experiencing more psychosocial stress around the time of illness onset, one would have expected a stronger effect of urban exposure on the rate of affective psychosis than on the rate of schizophrenia." However, as the authors point out, findings regarding affective psychosis cannot be generalized to all affective disorders.

The fact, that the effect of urbanicity was greatest in men and in younger age groups was thought by Marcelis et al. to be consistent with male sex and early onset both predicting poorer prognosis in schizophrenia. It is concluded that the urban risk factor represents a population-attributable fraction of 30% of schizophrenia.

# Season of Birth and Urban Residence

Dalen (1975) first reported from Sweden that excess of winter births among individuals with schizophrenia was somewhat higher in those born in urban areas. Among a group with high genetic risk in Denmark who developed schizophrenia, Machon et al. (1983) reported that in the urban births, significantly more cases were born in the winter. Takei et al. (1995), using data from England and Wales, reported that city birth was associated with a 19% increase among the autumn-born and a 21% increase among the winter-born. In Ireland, O'Callaghan et al. (1995) compared the place and season of birth of individuals with schizophrenia with those of the general population. Patients

168

who were urban-born were more likely than controls to be born in the winter, though this effect was much more pronounced for females. Van Os et al. (1996), using a Dutch national sample, found a significant association between urban and winter birth for broadly defined schizophrenia (both genders) and also for narrowly defined schizophrenia (females only). In France, Verdoux et al. (1997) found that individuals born in the most highly populated areas had a 20% increase in winter births, compared with those born in other areas. This effect was found equally for both genders.

Torrey et al. (1997) point out methodological limitations in all these studies, but the absence of contradictory findings gives much plausibility to a genuine association between the season of birth effect and urban residence. However, the cause of that effect itself remains largely unknown. Viral infections, particularly influenza, have often been proposed as the predisposing factor, yet women who actually had influenza during pregnancy did not produce offspring with an excess of schizophrenia (Crow & Done, 1992; Cannon et al., 1996). There is no evidence linking temperature or other weather effects to an increased risk of schizophrenia.

## Discussion

If there is an environmental factor, or group of factors, which is present more in cities than elsewhere and which has a direct positive effect on the incidence of schizophrenia, then theoretically, knowledge of what it might be could provide opportunities both for primary prevention and for offering treatment at earlier stages of illness.

Studies attempting to explain the uneven distribution of schizophrenia, both in different environments and among the social classes, have mostly focused more on individual than on environmental factors, though individual genetic predisposition can be linked to the process of social segregation (Eaton, 1980). Theories emphasizing that environmental influences relate to the experience of deprived inner city living – both psychological stressors and poor physical health-need not exclude the importance of biological factors, though. Similarly, hypotheses of a neurodevelopmental basis for schizophrenia (Murray et al., 1988; Castle & Murray, 1991), as well as the linking of maternal illness and birth trauma with schizophrenia (Knobloch & Pasamanick, 1961), are not incompatible with some environmental influence. Environmental risk factors might interact with developmental vulnerability for adult mental illness (Marcelis et al., 1998).

Jablensky (1988) pointed out the difficulty which arises from the lack of a clear-cut distinction between "social" and "non-social" (or biological) environmental factors. However, since the action of the latter is mediated by social circumstances, the two types are not mutually exclusive, but interact with one another. Non-social environmental factors connected with urban living include exposure to lead or other heavy metals, air-polluting gases, toxic waste sites, and industrial effluents, as well as birth complications and a higher rate of infectious diseases, especially where there are many persons per household and/or room (Torrey & Bowler, 1990). Hollingshead and Redlich (1958) reported an excess prevalence of schizophrenia in the socio-economic class V population of New Haven, many of whom were living in crowded tenements though housing conditions have since greatly improved in most Western countries. Damage to the central nervous system from head injuries, which are more common in cities, might also be a factor increasing the incidence of schizophrenia (Wilcox & Nasrallah, 1987).

Secondly, social environmental factors which are more common in cities include stressful life-events, which represent a risk factor for the development of many psychiatric disorders including schizophrenia (Brown & Birley, 1968; Brown & Prudo, 1981). These, however, might be more significant for affective disorders. Other urban factors that have been implicated include social isolation (Jaco, 1954), lack of control over the living environment – both isolation and overcrowding (Magaziner, 1988), and social over-stimulation, which can provoke psychotic breakdown in vulnerable individuals (Wing, 1989).

So far as crowding is concerned, though central city areas tend to contain more crowded accommodation than peripheral districts, any such influence on schizophrenia or other psychiatric disorders remains controversial. This is partly through frequent confusion between the concepts of density (number of persons resident per square unit of ground) and crowding (number of persons per living unit); a high rate of one does not necessarily indicate a similar rate of the other. Lawrence (1974) did not find evidence for any simple causal relationship between density and socio- or psycho-pathology. Galle et al. (1972) found that rooms per housing unit were an important predictor of admission to mental hospital, but this merely reflected the fact that people with more serious mental illness tended to live in single-room hotels, with many rooms per housing unit. Schweitzer and Su (1977), who examined data on persons per acre, structures per acre, persons per household, and persons per room in parts of Brooklyn, concluded that rates of household and family contact were significantly correlated with rates of mental hospital use. However, all of these studies are now rather old, none was specifically concerned with schizophrenia, separately from other disorders, and none provided evidence on incidence. Scientific interest in the subject has fallen off because of methodological difficulties, including the need for longitudinal rather than cross-sectional studies and the narrow range of densities in modem industrial cities (Freeman, 1984). In Western populations, there is now probably little difference between urban and rural populations in the degree of household crowding, which is largely governed by social class in both town and country.

As mentioned above, in the scientific study of these questions, the meaning of "urban" or even "city" also needs much clearer definition, because of the changes that have occurred worldwide since the 1950s. A fairly homogeneous community of 100.000 cannot be equated with a sprawling megalopolis of perhaps 15 million; settlements of the latter kind have been previously unknown in human history. Harpham (1992) points out that very little information is available on intra-urban differences in mental health, and that research on the social and economic characteristics of particular populations might be more productive than examination of their physical environments. The Japanese study by Ohta et al. (1992) seems to add weight to this view. Culturally, it would be wrong to extrapolate Western experience to cities of the world as a whole.

However, evidence from the US, reviewed above, indicates that – in that country at least – the relationship between schizophrenia and social class varies according to the size of the urban area. Kohn (1976) reported that the larger the city, the stronger the correlation between rates of schizophrenia and indices of lower social class, whereas this was not the case in small cities or suburban areas. Yet, in spite of the strong association between schizophrenia and a low social-class position, it has not so far been established that this is an etiological relationship. That a relationship of schizophrenia with lower social class was demonstrated only within large American cities would be at least partly explained by a double drift of individuals with schizophrenia – into the lowest socio-economic class and into a particular kind of urban area. No studies, though, have compared socio-economic status and prevalence rates in both rural and urban areas up to now. Hafner (1998) has pointed out that several studies of the early course of schizophrenia, before first contact with mental health services, have found a prodromal phase of several years' duration on average, in which there is an accumulation of negative and non-specific symptoms. Functional impairment, social disability, and adverse social consequences tend to emerge in the pre-psychotic phase and may convey a false impression of social disadvantage as an environmental factor of etiological importance.

Any lack of evidence for significant urban-rural differences in psychiatric morbidity may not mean that the hypothesis of additional social stress in cities is wrong, but rather that the usual urban-rural dichotomy does not represent it (Murphy, 1976). The reason suggested by Murphy is that each large rural or urban area is now too diverse to have the same impact from this point of view on all inhabitants. That point, however, was not made specifically about schizophrenia.

Though an association has been found between place of birth and the later development of schizophrenia, only the study of Astrup and Odegaard (1961) distinguished between place of birth and that of later upbringing. Their results indicated only a weak effect of birthplace among those who had moved since birth, so that the effect of a city upbringing was said to be more likely to be important than that of place of birth. This view has been contested by Marcelis et al. (1998).

If living in more urbanized areas is a risk factor for schizophrenia, then its prevalence might rise in developing nations that are currently undergoing rapid urbanization, though no firm evidence of such a change has yet been obtained. Similarly, if industrialization is also a major factor, one might expect prevalence to increase with modernization (Eaton, 1974), but in Taiwan, at a time when this process was occurring rapidly, Lin et al. (1969) found an actual *decrease* in schizophrenia over 15 years, despite an overall increase in psychiatric morbidity. It should not be assumed, though, that the full effects of urbanization are necessarily seen in the short term: An incubation period might extend over several generations, during which the environment continues to change, so that there could be a persisting cultural lag (Swedish Government, 1971). Henderson (1988) points out that urbanization, modernization, regional variation, and secular change have shared components, and that it is very difficult to identify clearly defined factors within them. However, unless this is done, attempting to establish independent effects for any of them must remain controversial. Similarly, Murphy (1976) emphasized that discovering the social causes of psychiatric disorder means not only developing case-finding methods for the dependent variables, but also locating those events in society which are genuinely antecedent to the disorders, and are therefore independent variables. The evidence discussed above indicates that the first of these tasks is being adequately accomplished for schizophrenia, but that the second remains much more difficult.

The question discussed here is part of the wider issue of the role of social factors in the etiology of schizophrenia. Jablensky (1986) concluded that there is only weak evidence for them having a direct effect of this kind: "Although social stress may be a trigger of the symptoms, schizophrenia does not have the characteristics of a stress reaction, or of a pattern of learned responses to threatening social situations." If that carefully supported view is accepted, then we would expect to see variations in prevalence between ecologically different areas for schizophrenia, but little difference in incidence. In the view of most investigators, the balance of evidence leads to that conclusion, in which case "urbanicity" would seem unlikely to survive as an independent variable in the etiology of schizophrenia.

Finally, if there has in fact been a secular fall in the incidence and/or sever-

172

ity of schizophrenia in the last 30 years or so – though this is by no means generally accepted (Jablensky, 1993; Harrison & Mason, 1993) – then this might have taken a differential form in terms of sex, age-group, social class, etc. Waddington & Youssef (1993) found that in a rural area of Ireland, the morbid risk for schizophrenia was 37% less in those born between 1940-69, compared with those born between 1920-39. However, the fall was much greater in females (-56%), compared with that in males (-19%). A similar differential fall was recorded on the Danish island of Bornholm, when the rates for 1935 were compared with those for 1983 (Stromgren, 1987). If these findings are supported, any relationship of schizophrenia to city living might have altered over time as a result of such changes, thus confounding even more an already highly complex question.

# Conclusion

The evidence from various situations that has been reviewed above does not lead clearly in any one direction. Dauncey et al. (1993) suggest that such data are best explained as combining elements of the two social processes of "Breeding" and "Drifting." In their view, the support these provide for a significant relationship between schizophrenia and a tendency for patients to originate in areas of urban deprivation points to a link between this disorder and an early environment of socio-economic deprivation. Similar findings have come from Camberwell (Castle et al., 1993). However, this need not be only the result of social influences, since the indices of deprivation involve a broad range of "non-social" variables, such as obstetric complications, low birth weight, and maternal viral infections (Jablensky, 1988). So far as immigration is concerned, Harrison et al. (1989) found that area of residence did not explain the higher rates of schizophrenia for Afro-Caribbeans in an urban setting, and in Mannheim, there was no evidence of an environmental effect on the foreign-born. Furthermore, selective migration (e.g., of those with some form of abnormal behavior) might result in a genetic risk which could act over several generations. It tends to be assumed that there is more deprivation in cities than elsewhere, but in many parts of the world, rural life is, on average, more deprived than that in cities – which is why so many people migrate to cities. The Dutch data of Marcelis et al. (1998) contain no information on social class, so that they might be affected by the "Ecological Fallcy" of assuming that schizophrenic individuals share the average characteristics of urban populations there.

The view that a factor of "urbanicity" – the precise nature of which so far remains unknown – could be a significant etiological influence in schizophrenia needs very careful appraisal. In the first place, it does not seem to take adequate account of the effects of migration, though that process is less relevant to incidence than to prevalence. For instance, because of the greater mobility in Swedish society since World War two, it is quite possible that social residue processes would have reduced the healthy population (in all senses) within that country's cities, correspondingly raising the proportion living there who have some form of morbidity. The young men in the sample of Lewis et al. who were born in cities may therefore have come disproportionately from families with either genetic or environmental handicaps – or both. Secondly, social class has not been fully separated from other influences: Lewis et al. (1992) refer to low socio-economic status as an "environmental" factor, which confuses the issue. Whilst "inner city" areas are nearly always characterized by a social-class composition that is skewed heavily towards the poorest groups, urban populations in many countries have a more favorable socio-economic level than rural populations, as indicated in American and Swedish studies, for instance. Cabot (1990) states that epidemiological studies of schizophrenia have focused so much on urban areas (and to some extent on middle-class patients) that, "We know very little about first contact rates ... among the rural poor of any country," though it is in precisely such areas that the high schizophrenic morbidity of Ireland, for instance, is suspected to be. Thirdly, the influence of schizophrenic suicides, particularly in the younger age-groups, deserves further examination; if these occurred at a differential rate in urban and rural rates respectively, prevalence rates could be affected. It is also likely that co-morbidity with alcohol and drug abuse, which continues to be an increasing problem in many countries, occurs at a higher rate in cities. Fourthly, the question of urban size remains neglected: Urbanicity can hardly be a common influence when the communities it describes can vary in size by a factor of 50.

City residence has a totally different meaning for those who live in a middle-class suburb, compared with those who live in a poor, working-class housing development. In one kind of area, the level of environmental stress is very low, while in the other it is very high. Yet they are all city residents. The view that maternal infection, particularly viral, is the key mechanism in an urban excess of schizophrenia is based on population rates of infection, which have an unknown relationship to rates in mothers of children who will develop schizophrenia. It is also subject to the Ecological Fallacy.

In Western countries, the old urban/rural dichotomy has largely broken down. Apart from fringe areas, most rural people live in similar housing, shop in the same supermarkets, and watch the same television programs as city people. The only big difference is the absence of high-rise flats in the country. With urban sprawl and the growth of what are described in America as "edge cities," it is often hard to say where the city ends and the country begins.

It may well be that when their effects have been fully explored, the two factors of migration and social class will provide much of the explanation for any urban excess. Nevertheless, Hammer (1978) offered a warning that "migration, social class and ethnic marginality are too gross as social variables and too complex as social phenomena to implicate any particular mechanism that would account for their association with psychopathology." She and some other authors, however, have identified adverse change in people's social networks as a possible common mechanism underlying these processes, and this hypothesis still remains to be fully examined. There are certainly associations between particular environments and particular characteristics of their populations, but this does not prove that the environment caused any of these characteristics.

# Acknowledgements

Some of this material previously appeared in a supplement to the *British Journal of Psychiatry* and is reproduced with permission.

# References

Andersen, T. *(1975)* Physical and mental illness in a Lapp and Norwegian population. *Acta Psychiatrica Scandinavica,* (suppl.), **263**, 47–56.

Astrup, C. & Odegard, O. (1961) Internal migration and mental illness in Norway. *Psychiatric Quarterly,* **34**, 116–130.

Babigian, H. M. *(1985)* Schizophrenia epidemiology. In *Comprehensive Textbook of Psychiatry IV.* (Eds. Kaplan, H. I. & Saddock, B. J.). Baltimore: Williams & Wilkins.

Bachrall, L. L. (1977) Deinstitutionalization of mental health services in rural areas. *Hospital Community Psychiatry,* **28**, 669–72.

Bamrah, J. S., Freeman, H. L. & Goldberg, D. P. (1991) Epidemiology of Schizophrenia in Salford, 1974-84: Changes in an urban community over ten years. *British Journal of Psychiatry,* **159**, 802–810.

Bardenstein, K. K. & McGlashan, T. H. (1990) Gender differences in affective, schizoaffective, and schizophrenic disorders. *Schizophrenia Research,* **3**, 159–172.

Bland, R. C. (1984) Long-term mental illness in Canada and epidemiological perspective on schizophrenia and affective disorders. *Canadian Journal of Psychiatry,* **29**, 242–246.

Blazer, D., George, L. K., Landerman, R., et al. *(1985)* Psychiatric disorders: A rural/urban comparison. *Archives of General Psychiatry,* **42**, 651–656.

Borga, P., Widerlöv, B., Cullberg, J. & Stefansson, C. G. (1991) Patterns of care among people with long-term functional psychosis in three different areas of Stockholm County. *Acta Psychiatrica Scandinavica,* **83**, 223–233.

Brown, G. W. & Birley, J. L. T. *(1968)* Crisis and life changes and the onset of schizophrenia. *Journal of Health & Social Behaviour*, **9**, 203–214.

Brown, G. W. & Prudo, R. *(1981)* Psychiatric disorder in a rural and an urban population. 1. Aetiology of depression. *Psychological Medicine*, **11**, 581–599.

Burnam, M. A., Hough, R. L., et al. (1987) *Archives of General Psychiatry*, **44**, 687–694.

Cabot, M. R. (1990) The incidence and prevalence of schizophrenia in the Republic of Ireland. *Sovial Psychiatry & Psychiatric Epidemiology*, **25**, 210–215.

Cannon, M., Cotter, D., Coffey, V. P., et al. (1996) Prenatal exposure to the *1957* influenza epidemic and adult schizophrenia: A follow-up study. *British Journal of Psychiatry*, **168**, 368–371.

Castle, D. & Murray, R. M. (1991) *The neurodevelopmental basis of sex differences in schizophrenia. Psychological Medicine*, **21**, 565–575.

Castle, D., Scott, K., Wessely, S. & Murray, R.M. (1993) Does social deprivation during gestation and early life predispose to later schizophrenia? *Social Psychiatry & Psychiatric Epidemiology*, **28**, 1–4.

Cooper, J. E. & Giggs, J. & Howat, J. (1987) Schizophrenia and the ecological structure of Nottingham. *British Journal of Psychiatry*, **151**, 627–633.

Crow, T. J., & Done, D. J. (1992) Prenatal exposure to influenza does not cause schizophrenia. *British Journal of Psychiatry*, **161**, 390–393.

Dalen, P. (1975) *Season of Birth: A Study of Schizophrenia and Other Mental Disorders.* New York: North Holland.

Danncey, K., Giggs, J., Baker, K. & Harrison, G. (1993) Schizophrenia in Nottingham: Lifelong residential of a cohort, *British Journal of Psychiatry*, **163**, 613–619.

Davies, M. A. (1989) Community adjustment of chronic schizophrenic patients in urban and rural settings. *Hospital and Community Psychiatry*, **8**, 824–830.

Dohrenwend, B. S. (1990) Socioeconornic status and psychiatric disorder – are the issues still compelling? *Social Psychiatry & Psychiatric Epidemiology* **25**, 41–47.

Dunham, H. W. (1965) *Community of Schizophrenia.* Detroit: Wayne State University Press.

Dunham, H. W. (1969) City core and suburban fringe distribution patterns of mental illness. In *Changing Perspectives in Mental Illness.* (Eds. Plog, S. C. & Edgerton, R. B.), pp. 337–363. New York: Holt, Reinhardt & Winston.

Eagles, J. M., Hunter, D. & McCance, G. (1988) Desline in the diagnosis of schizophrenia among first contacts with psychiatric services in north-east Scotland, 1969–1984. *British Journal of Psychiatry*, **152**, 793–798.

Eaton, W. W. (1980) A formal theory of selection for schizophrenia. *American Journal of Sociology*, **86**, 149–158.

Eaton, W. W. (1974) Residence, social class and schizophrema. *Journal of Health & Social Behavior*, **102**, 627–33.

Eaton, W. W. (1986) Epidemiology of schizophrenia. *Epidemiological Review*, **7**, 105–26.

Faris, R. E. L. & Dunham, H. W. (1939) *Mental Disorders in Urban Areas.* Chicago: University of Chicago Press.

Freeman, H. L. (1984) The scientific background. In *Mental Health and The Environment.* (Ed. Freeman, H. L.). London: Churchill Livingstone.

Freeman, H. L. & Alpert, M. (1986a) Prevalence of schizophrenia in an urban population. *British Journal of Psychiatry*, **149**, 603–611.

Freeman, H. L. & Alpert, M. (1986b) Prevalence of schizophrenia: geographical variations in an urban population. *British Journal of Clinical & Social Psychiatry*, **4**, 67–75.

Frumkin, R. M. (1954) Comparative rates of mental illnesses for urban and rural populations in Ohio. *Rural Sociology*, **19**, 70–72.

Galle, O., Gove, W. & MacPherson, J. (1972) Population density and pathology: What are the relationships for Man? *Science*, **176**, 23–30.

Giggs, J. A. (1980) Mental health and the environment. In *Environmental Medicine*. (Eds. Howe, G. M. & Loraine, J. A.). London: Heinemann Medical.

Giggs, J. A. (1983) Schizophrenia and ecological structure in Nottingham. In *Geographical Aspects of Health* (Eds. McGlashan, N. D. & Blunden, J. R.), pp. 197–222. London: Academic Press.

Giggs, J. A. (1984) Residential mobility and mental health. In *Mental Health and the Environment*. (Ed. Freeman, H. L.). London: Churchill Livingstone.

Giggs, J. A. & Cooper, J. E. (1986) Mental disorders and human ecological structure: A case study of schizophrenia and affective psychosis in Nottingham. *Cambria*, **13** (1), 151–180.

Goldberg, E. M. & Morrison, S. L. (1963) Schizophrenia and social class. *British Journal of Psychiatry*, **108**, 785–802.

Goldmann, H. H. (Ed.) (1983) International Perspectives in Deinstitutionalization. *International Journal of Mental Health*, **11**, 3–165.

Goodman, A. B., Segel, C., Craig, T. J. & Lin, S. P. (1983) The relationship between socioeconomic class and prevalence of schizophrenia, alcoholism, and affective disorders treated by inpatient care in a suburban area. *American Journal of Psychiatry*, **140**, 166–170.

Hafner, H. & an der Heiden, U. (1986) The contribution of European case registers to research on schizophrenia. *Schizophrenia Bulletin*, **12**, 26–51.

Hafner, H. & Reimann, H. (1970) Spatial distribution of mental disorders in Mannheim, 1965. In *Psychiatric Epidemiology*. (Eds. Hare, E. H. & Wing, J. K.). Oxford: Oxford University Press.

Hammer, M., Makiesky-Barron, S. & Gutwirth, L. (1978) Social networks and schizophrenia. *Schizophrenia Bulletin*, **4**, 522–545.

Hardt, R.H. (1959) The ecological distribution of patients admitted to mental hospitals from an urban area. *Psychiatric Quarterly*, **33**, 126–44.

Harpham, T. (1993) Urbanization and mental disorder. In *Principles of Social Psychiatry*. (Eds. Bhugra, D. & Leff, J.). Oxford: Blackwell.

Harrison, G., Holten, A., Neilson, D., et al. (1989) Severe mental disorders in Afro-Caribbean patients: Some social, demographic, and service factors. *Psychological Medicine*, **19**, 683–696.

Helgason, T. (1964) Epidemiology of mental disorders in Iceland. *Acta Psychiatrica Scandinavica, 173,* suppl. **40**, 1–258.

Herbert, D. T. & Johnston, R.J. (Eds.) *Social Areas in Cities*. Chichester: Wiley.

Hill, A. B. (1965) The environment and disease: Association or causation? *Journal of the Royal Society of Medicine*, **58**, 295–300.

Hollingshead, A. B. & Redlich, F. C. (1958) *Social Class & Mental Illness: A Community Study*. New York: Wiley.

Jablensky, A. (1986) Epidemiology of schizophrenia: A European perspective. *Schizophrenia Bulletin*, **12**, 52–73.

Jablensky, A. (1988) Schizophrenia and environment. In *Handbook of Social Psychiatry*. (Eds. Henderson, A. S. & Burrows, G. D.). Amsterdam: Elsevier.

Jablensky, A. (1993) The epidemiology of schizophrenia. *Current Opinion in Psychiatry*, **6**, 43–52.

Jaco, E. G. (1954) *The Social Epidemiology of Mental Disorders: A Psychiatric Study of Texas*. New York: Russell Sage Foundation.

177

Kaetinge, C. (1987) Schizophrenia in rural Ireland: A case of service overutilisation. *International Journal of Social Psychiatry*, **33**, 186–194.

Klusman, D. & Angermeyer, M. C. (1987) Urban ecology and psychiatric admission rates: results from a study in a city of Hamburg. In *From Social Class to Social Stress.*(Ed. Angermeyer, M. C.), pp. 16–45. Berlin: Springer-Verlag.

Knobloch, H. & Pasamanick, B. (1961) Genetics of mental disease. *American Journal of Orthopsychiatry*, **31**, 454–73.

Kohn, M. L. (1976) The interaction of social class and other factors in the etiology of schizophrenia. *American Journal of Psychiatry*, **133**, 177–180.

Lapouse, R., Monk, M. & Terris, M. (1956) The drift hypothesis in sociological differentials in schizophrenia. *American Journal of Public Health*, **46**, 978–986.

Lawrence, J. E. S. (1974) Science and sentiment: Overview of respect on crowding and human behaviour. *Psychological Bulletin*, **81**, 712–720.

Lei, T.J., Butle, E. W., Rowitz, L. & McCallister, R. J. (1974) An ecological study of agency labelled retardates. *American Journal of Mental Deficiency*, **79**, 22–1.

Lemert, E. M. (1948) An exploratory study of mental disorder in a rural problem area. *Rural Society*, **13**, 48–64.

Levy, L. & Rowitz, L. (1973) *The Ecology of Mental Disorder.* New York: Behavioral Publications.

Lewis, G., David, A., Andreasson, S. & Allenbeck, P. (1992) Schizophrenia and City Life. *Lancet*, **340**, 137–140.

Lin, Y. T., Rin, H., Yeh, E. K., et al. (1969) Mental disorders in Taiwan, fifteen years later. In *Mental Health Research in Asia and the Pacific*. (Eds. Caudill, W. & Lin, T. Y.). Honolulu: East-West Center Press.

Lindgren, B. (1990) The economic impact of illness. In *Costs of Illness and Benefits of Drug Treatment.* (Eds. Abshagen, U. & Münnich, F. E.). Munich: W. Zuckschwerdt Verlag.

Machon, R. A., Mednick, S. F. & Schulsinger, F. (1983) The interaction of seasonality, place of birth, genetic risk and subsequent schizophrenia in a high-risk sample. *British Journal of Psychiatry*, **143**, 383–388.

Magaziner, J. (1988) Living density and psychopathology: A re-examination of the negative model. *Psychological Medicine*, **18**, 419–431.

Malzberg, B. (1955) The distribution of mental diseases in New York State 1949-1951. *Psychiatric Quarterly*, **29** (suppl. 2), 209–238.

Marcelis, M., Navarro-Mateu, F., Murray, R., et al. (1998) Urbanization and psychosis: A study of 1942–1978 birth cohorts in The Netherlands. *Psychological Medicine*, **28**, 871–879.

Maylath, E., Weyerer, S. & Hafner, H. (1989) Spatial concentration of the incidence of treated psychiatric disorders in Mannheim. *Acta Psychiatrica Scandinavica*, **80**, 650–656.

McGlashan, T. H. (1989) A selective review of recent North American long-term follow-up studies of schizophrenia. *Schizophrenia Bulletin*, **14**, 515–542.

Murphy, J. E. (1976) Social causes: The independent variable. In *Further Explorations in Social Psychiatry*. (Eds. Kaplan, B. H., Wilson, R. N. & Leighton, A. H.). New York: Basic Books.

Murray, R. M., Lewis, S. W., Owen, M. J. & Foerster, A. (1988) The neurodevelopmental origins of dementia praecox. In *Schizophrenia: The Major Issues*. (Eds. Bebbington, P. & McGuffin, P.). London: Heinemann.

O'Callaghan, E., Sham, P., Takei, N., et al. (1991) Schizophrenia after prenatal exposure to 1957 As influenza epidemic. *Lancet*, **337**, 1248–1250.

O'Callaghan, E., Cotter, D., Colgan, K., et al. (1995) Confinement of winter birth excess in schizophrenia to the urban-born and its gender specificity. *British Journal of Psychiatry*, **166**, 51–54

Ohta, Y., Nakane, Y., Nishihara, J. & Takemoto, T. (1992) Ecological structure and incidence rates of schizophrenia in Nagasaki City. *Acta Psychiatrica Scandinavica*, **86**, 113–120.

Queen, S. A. (1940) The ecological study of mental disorder. *American Sociological Review*, **5**, 201–209.

Rutter, M. L. (1981) The city and the child. *American Journal of Orthopsychiatry*, **51**, 610–625.

Schroeder, C. W. (1942) Mental disorders in cities. *American Journal of Sociology*, **48**, 40–47.

Schweitzer, L. & Su, W. H. (1977) Population density and the rate of mental illness. *American Journal of Public Health*, **67**, 1165–1172.

Shur, E. (1988) The epidemiology of schizophrenia. *British Journal of Hospital Medicine*, **7**, 38–45.

Siverton, L. & Mednick, S. (1984) Class drift and schizophrenia. *Acta Psychiatrica Scandinavica*, **70**, 304–309.

Stefansson, C. G. (1984) Map analysis of psychiatric services. The application of a computerized psychiatric case register to geographical analysis. *Acta Psychiatrica Scandinavica*, **70**, 515–522.

Stewart, D. D. (1953) A note on mental illness in rural Arkansas. *Social Problems*, **1**, 57–60.

Stromgren, E. (1987) Changes in the incidence of schizophrenia? *British Journal of Psychiatry*, **150**, 1–7.

Takei, N., Sham, P. C., O'Callaghan, E., et al. (1995) Schizophrenia: increased risk associated with winter and city birth – a casecontrolled study in 12 regions within England and Wales. *Journal of Epidemiology and Community Health*, **49**, 106–109

Taylor, S. & Chave, S. W. P. (1964) *Mental Health Environment*, London: Longmans.

Thornicroft, G. (1991) Social deprivation and rates of treated mental disorder. *British Journal of Psychiatry*, **158**, 475–84.

Thornicroft, G., Bisoffi, G. de Salvia, D. & Tansella, M. (1993) Urban-rural differences in the associations between social deprivation and psychiatric service utilization in schizophrenia and all diagnoses: A case-register study in Northern Italy. *Psychological Medicine*, **23**, 487–496.

Torrey, E. F. (1987) Prevalence studies of schizophrenia. *British Journal of Psychiatry*, **150**, 598–608.

Torrey, E. F. & Bowler, A. (1991) Geographical distribution of insanity in America: evidence for an urban factor. *Schizophrenia Bulletin*, **16**, 591–604.

Torrey, E. F., Miller, J., Rawlings, R. & Yolken, R. H. (1997) Seasonality of births in schizophrenia and bipolar disorder: A review of the literature. *Schizophrenia Research*, **28**, 1–38.

Varma, V. K., Wig, N. N., Phookun, H. R., et al. (1997) First-onset schizophrenia in the community: Relationship of urbanization with onset, early manifestations and typology. *Acta Psychiatrica Scandinavica*, **96**, 431–438.

Van Os, J., Takei, N., Navarro-Mateu, F. & Murray, R. M. (1996) Season and place of birth in a sample of 22'361 patients with a diagnosis of schizophrenia. *European Psychiatry*, **11**, 428.

Verdoux, H., Takei, N., Cassou de Saint-Mathurin, R., et al. (1997) Seasonality of birth in Schizophrenia: The effect of regional population density. *Schizophrenia Research, 7*, 175–180.

Waddington, J. L. & Youssef, H. A. (1994) Evidence for a gender-specific decline in rate of occurrence of schizophrenia in rural Ireland over a fifty-year period. *British Journal of Psychiatry*, **164**, 171–176.

Weyerer, S. & Hafner, H. (1989) The stability of the ecological distribution of the incidence of treated mental disorders in the city of Mannheim. *Social Psychiatry & Psychiatric Epidemiology*, **24**, 57–62.

Weyerer, S. & Hafner, H. (1992) The high incidence of treated disorders in the inner city of Mannheim. *Social Psychiatry & Psychiatric Epidemiology*, **27**, 142–146.

White, W. A. (1903) The geographical distribution of insanity in the United States. *Journal of Nervous & Mental Disease*, **30**, 257–279.

Wilcox, J. A. & Nasrallah, H. A. (1987) Childhood head trauma and psychosis. *Psychiatry Research*, **21**, 303–307.

Wing, J. K. (1989) The concept of negative symptoms. *British Journal of Psychiatry*, **155**, 10–14.

# The Effectiveness of Case Management and Assertive Community Treatment for People with Severe Mental Disorders

Max Marshall and Austin Lockwood

## Introduction

In the 1960s, Western countries began to close large psychiatric hospitals and to care for severely mentally ill people in the community, but rising readmission rates soon suggested that this policy was failing a substantial number of patients (Rössler et al., 1992; Ellison et al.; 1974) It also became clear that community services were losing contact with patients and failing to meet their complex psychiatric and social needs (Melzer et al. 1991; Audit Commission, 1986). Case management and assertive community treatment (ACT) were developed to provide more effective community care to severely mentally ill patients. The two approaches share the same goals, to: (i) maintain contact with patients (Thornicroft, 1991), (ii) reduce the frequency and duration of hospital admissions (Rössler et al. 1995; Kanter, 1991), and (iii) improve clinical and social outcome (Holloway,1991). Nonetheless, despite these superficial similarities, there are fundamental differences between case management and ACT.

The key element of case management is the personal responsibility of the case manager for the "client." In the simplest form of case management ("brokerage"), each mentally ill person is assigned a "case manager" who is expected to: (i) assess that person's needs; (ii) develop a care plan; (iii) arrange for suitable care to be provided; (iv) monitor the quality of the care provided; and (v) maintain contact with the person (Holloway, 1991). The "brokerage" model has evolved into a number of more sophisticated models (Clinical Case Management, Intensive Case Management, and Strengths Case Management), each emphasizing the importance of the relationship between case manager and client (Rubin, 1992; Solomon, 1992).

181

By contrast, the essential element of ACT is team-work, the key relationship being between the ACT team and its clients, rather than between particular team members and particular clients. ACT teams are multi-disciplinary and often include psychiatrists. Team members work with different clients as required, and several members commonly work with the same client. Unlike most case management services, ACT teams (i) provide rather than "broker" interventions (preferably in patients' homes or places of work); (ii) practice "assertive outreach," (iii) emphasize medication compliance and (iv) offer emergency cover (Essock & Kontos, 1995; Olfson, 1990; Ellison et al. 1995). ACT teams invariably work with low staff patient ratios, whereas staff patient ratios vary in case management teams.

Case management is more popular than ACT: for example, a US survey of 323 case management teams found that only 10% regarded their team as practicing ACT (Ellison et al., 1995). In the UK case management (in the form of the Care Program Approach CPA) is mandatory for all patients with severe mental illness (Shepherd, 1990). However, despite the popularity of case management, a number of researchers have expressed doubts about its efficacy some have claimed that case management increases admission rates, whilst others have called for it to be replaced by ACT (Rossler et al. 1995; Franklin et al. 1987; Anon, 1995; Stein, 1992).

This review aims to evaluate the effectiveness of case management and ACT as strategies for caring for the severely mentally ill in the community. Two main comparisons were made: (i) case management versus standard community care; and (ii) ACT versus standard community care. The review did not cover studies in which ACT was used as an alternative to acute admission to hospital.

## Materials and Methods

*Inclusion criteria and search strategy*

The two reviewers independently searched: The Cochrane Schizophrenia Group's register of randomized controlled trials; EMBASE; MEDLINE; PsychLIT; and SCISEARCH. The search term was: ([case or care] and [management]) or (Assertive Community Treatment) or (PACT) or (ACT) or (TCL) or (Madison). Each reviewer read the abstracts of all publications detected, and selected studies where case management or ACT had been compared to a control treatment. The reviewers merged the studies they had detected to form a pool. Copies were obtained of all papers pertaining to the studies in the pool. In addition, any review articles that had been identified were obtained. The reference lists of all papers and review articles were scrutinized and reports of any additional trials were obtained. Finally details of unpublished trials were sought from authors.

The reviewers together evaluated the trials in the pool and decided which should be included in the ACT and case management comparisons. A quality rating was given for each trial, based on the three quality categories described in the Cochrane Collaboration Handbook (Sackett, 1994). Only trials in its category A or B were included in this review. Trials from the pool were selected for the ACT comparison if they were randomized controlled trials in which: (i) ACT was compared to standard community care; and (ii) subjects were mainly between the ages of 18–65 and suffering from severe mental disorder. Trials of ACT were defined as trials in which the intervention was described as "Assertive Community Treatment" or one of its synonyms. Trials were selected for the case management comparison if they were randomized controlled trials in which: (i) case management was compared to standard community care; and (ii) subjects were mainly between the ages of 18-65 and (iii) suffering from severe mental disorder. Trials of case management were defined as those in which the intervention was described as any variety of case management other than ACT. The reliability of the procedure for selecting trials was checked by asking an independent rater to repeat the classification exercise. Inter-rater agreement (between the independent rater and the reviewers) was 0.93 (Cohen's kappa) for inclusion in the case management comparison and 0.84 inclusion in the ACT comparison.

*Data extraction*

Data were extracted twice and cross-checked. Data were not included for outcomes where less than 50% of those assessed at base line were reassessed at follow-up. For categorical outcomes, for example "admitted" or "not admitted," a standard estimation of the "odds ratio" (OR) and its confidence interval (99%) was calculated. The number needed to treat statistically (NNT), was also calculated. Continuous data were only included if collected by a rating scale of established reliability and validity. The criterion for reliability and validity was that a description of the scale had been published in a peer-reviewed journal (because most scientific journals require that reliability and validity are demonstrated before publication). In addition, data from rating scales were excluded if (i) the scale failed to provide a single summary score (because testing of numerous sub-scores from the same rating scale is prone to Type 1 error); or (ii) they had been collected by the patient's case manager or therapist (because of the risk of rater bias). Finally, before inclusion, continu-

183

ous data were subject to a test of normality (standard deviation times 1.645 was less than the mean). The review did not report study findings that were based on the application of parametric tests to skewed data.

## Results

Of 58 studies in the pool, 10 were eligible for the case management comparison and 14 were eligible for the ACT comparison (see Tables 1 and 2 for details of studies). Two studies were included in both comparisons, as each had three arms (ACT, case management and control). The four main indices of outcome were (i) numbers maintaining contact with the psychiatric services; (ii) extent of psychiatric hospital admissions, (iii) improvement in clinical and social outcome and; (iv) costs in comparison to standard community care.

Subjects receiving case management (CM) or ACT were more likely to remain in contact with services than controls (for CM odds ratio = 0.69; 99% CI 0.50 – 0.96, n=1210; for ACT odds ratio = 0.63; 99% CI 0.41 – 0.96; n=951; see

*Table 1.* Case management versus standard community care: Details of included randomized controlled trials

| Trial | Design | Interventions |
|---|---|---|
| Curtis – New York 1992[19] | 145 control; 147 intervention; mean age=36; 59% female; 91% minority groups; 38% scz; mean previous admissions >1. Follow up: 35–52 months. | Control: Routine aftercare from Harlem Hospital Center (HHC). Case management "Intensive outreach case management" from multi-disciplinary team. Staff/patient about 1:35. |
| Ford – London 1995[20] | 38 control; 39 intervention; mean age=46; 53% female; 30% minority groups; 82% scz; 59.7% admitted last 2 years. Follow up: 18 months. | Control: Routine care from psychiatric services. Case management: intensive community support with a single accountable point of contact. Staff/patient about 1:10. |
| Franklin – Houston 1987[15] | 204 control; 213 intervention; mean age=49; 51% female; 24% minority groups; 56% schizophrenia; mean previous admissions 4. Follow up: 12 months. | Control: routine after care. Case management: brokerage form seven managers with graduate/ undergraduate degrees and mean 4.3 years experience. Staff/patient=1:30. |
| Macias – Utah 1994[21] | 20 control; 21 intervention; mean age not reported; 40% female; 0% minority groups; 46% scz; mean previous admissions not reported. Follow up: 18 months. | Control: psychosocial rehabilitation program. Case management: psychosocial rahbilitation and case management (Strengths model). Staff/patient=1:20. |

184

*Table 1 (continued)*

| Trial | Design | Interventions |
|-------|--------|---------------|
| Marshall – Oxford 1995[22] | 40 control; 40 intervention; mean age=48; 15% female; %minority not reported; 73.8% scz; 85% had >1mean previous admissions. Follow up: 7, 14 months. | Control: whatever care receiving at start of study. Case management: 3 case managers (one nurs) and a team leader (occupational therapist with extensive experience in case management. Staff/patient about 1:10. |
| Muijen – London 1994[23] | 41 control; 41 intervention; mean age=37; 44% female; 23.1% minority groups; 83% scz; mean previous admissions 5.7. Follow up: 6, 12, 18 months. | Control: care from CPNs. Case management: community support team of three CPNs and team leader. Staff/patient about 1:11. |
| Santiago – Arizona 1985[24] | 81 control; 78 intervention; majority under 35; 43% female; %minority not reported; 62% scz; 50% >5 mean previous admissions. Follow up: 6 and 12 months. | Control: routine care from psychiatric services. Case management: TNT – an intensive form of clinical case management. Staff/patient not clear. |
| Tyrer – London 1995[25] | 197 control; 196 intervention; mean age=44; 45% female; %minority groups not reported; 54% schizophrenia; mean number previous admissions not reported. Follow up: 18 months. | Control: routine care from psychiatric services. Case management: allocated a key worker under UK Care Programme Approach, responsible for maintaining fortnightly contact and monitoring). Staff/patient ration=not clear. |
| Quinlivan – California 1995[26] | 30 control; 30 ACT; 30 case management. Mean age about 37; 56% female; 18% minority; 67.8% scz; mean previous admissions not reported. Follow up: 2 years. | Control: public mental health system. Intervention 1 case management, staff/patient=1:40. Intervention 2: ACT, staff/patient=1:15. |
| Solomon – Philadelphia 1994[27] | 55 control; 43 intervention 1 (intencive case management); 42 intervention 2 (ACT). Mean age 35.4; % female 0; 64% minority; % scz not reported; mean previous admissions not reported. Follow up: 1&6 months. | Control: referral to local community mental health center (CMHC). Intervention 1: intensive case management from forensic case manager; staff/patient about 1:4. Intervention 2: ACT from team including 1.5 psychiatrist equivalents. Staff/patient about 1:10. |

185

*Table 2*. ACT versus standard community care: Included randomized controlled trials (for details of Quinlivan 1995 and Solomon 1994: see Table 1)

| Trial | Design | Interventions |
|---|---|---|
| Audini – London 1994[28] | 33 control; 33 intervention; mean age 37; 54% female; 26% minority; 30% scz; mean previous admissions not reported. Follow up: 4, 15 months. | Control: subjects who had previously received ACT received routine care from the psychiatric services. Intervention: subjects who had previously received ACT continued to do so. Staff/patient about 1:5 to 1:7. |
| Bond – Chicago 1 1990[29] | 43 control; 45 intervention; mean age not reported; 43% female; 36% minorities; 67% scz; mean previous admissions: 18. Follow up: 12 months. | Control: standard care from a drop-in centre. Intervention: ACT. Staff/patient about 1:10. |
| Bond – Indiana 1 1988[30] | 83 control; 84 intervention; mean age 34.5; 38% female; 34% minorities; 61% scz; mean previous admissions: 8.8. Follow up: 6 months. | Control: care from public mental health services including unspecified amount brokerage style case management. Intervention: Assertive Community Treatment. Staff/patient about 1:7. |
| Bush – Atlanta 1990[31] | 14 control; 14 intervention; median age = not reported; 43% female; 50% minorities; 86% scz; previous admissions: 2–18. Follow up: 12 months. | Control: low intensity case management from standard services. Case management: ACT based on Madison model. Staff/patient about 1:4. |
| De Cangas – Quebec 1994[32] | 60 control; 60 intervention. Mean age = not reported; (demographic data reported on completers only). Follow up: 6 months. | Control: routine in patient care followed by routine community care from hospital services. Intervention: "le case management affirmatif" (assertive case management). Staff/patient 1:20. |
| Godley – Illinois 1994[33] | 45 control; 52 intervention; mean age 34.3; 20.8% female; 18.8% minorities; 43.8% scz; mean previous admissions: about 2.9. Follow up: 12 months. | Control: routine care from the psychiatric services. Intervention: ACT modified for dual diagnosis.. Staff/patient about 1:15. |
| Hampton – Chicago 1992[34] | 83 control; 82 intervention; mean age 37.3; 23% female; 55.7% minorities; 42,1% scz; mean previous admissions: about 13. Follow up: 6 & 12 months. | Control: routine follow up care from the psychiatric services. Intervention: ACT. Staff/patient about 1:10. |

*Table 2 (continued)*

| Trial | Design | Interventions |
|---|---|---|
| Marx – Madison 1973[35] | 20 control; 21 intervention; mean age 29; 36.5% female; %minorities not reported; 80.4% scz; mean 3.5 admissions past 4 years. Follow up: 5 months. | Control: Aftercare from staff of rehabilitation unit. Intervention: Discharged to ACT. Staff/patient about 1:10. |
| Morse – St Louis 1992[36] | 64 control; 52 intervention; mean age 33.7; 42% female; 52.5% minorities; 30.1% scz; 75% at least one previous admission. Follow up: 12 months. | Control: routine care from outpatient psychiatric services. Intervention: ACT. Staff/patient 1:10. |
| Mulder – Missouri 1982[37] | 18 control; 18 intervention; mean age 30; 55.5% female; %minorities – not reported; 72.2% scz; mean previous admissions: 3.3. Follow up: not clear. | Control: routine care from the psychiatric services. Intervention: ACT. Staff/patient not clear. |
| Rosenheck – USA 1994[38] | 419 control, 454 intervention; mean age 47.6; 0% female; 20.2% minorities; 50.5% scz; mean previous admissions: not reported. Follow up: 24 months | Control: routine care from the psychiatric services. Intervention: ACT (although in one site the program was inadequately implemented). Staff/patient 1:7–1:15. |
| Test – Wisconsin 1991[39] | 47 control; 75 intervention; median age 23.1; 33% female; 4% minorities; 74% scz; mean previous admissions about 3.4. Follow up: 6, 12, 18, 24 months. | Control: routine care from Dane County psychiatric services, including some unspecified case management. Intervention: ACT. Staff/patient about 1:9. |

Figures 1 and 2). Thus, about seven extra patients remain in contact for every 100 receiving case management (number needed to treat = 14.3), whilst nine extra remain in contact for every 100 receiving ACT (number needed to treat = 11.6).

Subjects receiving case management were approximately twice as likely to be admitted to psychiatric hospital (OR 1.83; 99% CI 1.32 – 2.55; $n=1300$; see Figure 3) as subjects receiving standard care.

On the other hand, patients receiving ACT were considerably less likely to be admitted to hospital than subjects receiving standard care (OR 0.40; 99% CI 0.25 – 0.62; $n=596$; see Figure 4). The case management analysis showed heterogeneity for this outcome (Chi squared = 13.18, DF = 5), attributable to Macias-Utah. Exclusion of this study reduces the heterogeneity to insignificant levels (Chi squared = 2.41, DF = 4). The raw combined admission rates for experimental and control groups across trials were: ACT (treatment) 36.9%, ACT (control) 62.3%, CM (treatment) 30.7%, CM (control) 19.4%.

187

*Table 3.* Duration of hospital admissions (mean days per patient per month) in case management and ACT trials

| Trial | Duration index | | Duration control | | Significance |
|-------|---------------|--|------------------|--|--------------|
| *Case management trials* | | | | | |
| Marshall – Oxford 1995[22] | 1.0 | (2.1) | 1.5 | (4.4) | not clear |
| Muijen – London 1994[23] | 2.8 | (1.8) | 2.4 | (1.9) | not clear |
| Quinlivan – California 1995[26] | 2.8 | (4.6) | 5.5 | (8.8) | not clear |
| Tyrer – London 1995[25] | 1.4 | | 0.8 | | not clear |
| *ACT trials* | | | | | |
| Bond – Chicago[29] 1990 | 3.2 | | 5.3 | | $p<0.1$ using log-transformed scores) |
| Rosenheck – USA 1994[38] | 12.3 | | 18.9 | | $p<0.0001$ using log-transformed scores) |
| Quinlivan – California 1995[26] | 1.1 | (0.96) | 5.5 | (8.8) | not clear |
| Test – Wisconsin 1991[39] | 0.22 | | 1.8 | | $p<0.001$ using rank transformed scores) |

It was not clear whether case management experimental patients spent more time in hospital than controls. The data for mean days per month in hospital were positively skewed in all four studies reporting this outcome. The raw data are reported in Table 3, but the statistical significance of the differences between groups will remain unknown until there has been analysis of the original subject data. In contrast, ACT patients spent significantly less time in hospital than controls (see Table 3).

Data on clinical and social outcome were lacking, particularly in case management trials. The main reasons for this lack of data were: (i) use of dubious rating scales (as judged by lack of publication in a peer-reviewed journal); (ii) failure to report essential characteristics of the data, such as means and standard deviations; and (iii) incorrect analysis of data. For case management studies, some useful data existed for: (i) death; (ii) imprisonment; (iii) mental state; (iv) social functioning; and (v) quality of life. Overall, case management patients had a slightly higher mortality than control patients, but confidence intervals for the odds ratio were wide (OR 1.42; 99% CI 0.45 – 4.52; $n = 1049$). Concerning imprisonment, case management had no clear effect, but the power of the review was too low to detect important differences (OR 0.81; 99% CI 0.32 – 2.03; $n = 754$). Five outcome measurements based on data collected by standardized instruments (continuous data) were included in this review (see Table 4). On these measurements, there were no significant differences in favor of case management or standard care.

*Table 4.* Clinical and social outcome data collected by rating scales

| Trial | Variable | Index Score (SD) | Control Score (SD) |
|---|---|---|---|
| *Case management trials* | | | |
| Muijen – London 1994[23] | Mental State (Brief Psychiatric Rating Scale) | 45.7 (15) | 43 (12.5) |
| Muijen – London 1994[23] | Social Functioning (Global Adjustment Scale) | 41.8 (13.6) | 46.7 (14.6) |
| Muijen – London 1994[23] | Social Functioning (Social Adjustment Scale) | 4.3 (1.6) | 3.7 (1.5) |
| Marshall – Oxford 1995[22] | Social Functioning (REHAB) | 31.7 (29.3) | 40.8 (19.7) |
| Marshall – Oxford 1995[22] | Qualitiy of Life (Quality | 4.9 (1.0) | 4.9 (0.9) |
| *ACT trials* | | | |
| Audini – London 1994[28] | Mental State (Brief Psychiatric Rating Scale) | 41.4 (14) | 42.3 (12.4) |
| Audini – London 1994[28] | Social Functioning (Global Adjustment Scale) | 62 (22) | 62 (22) |
| Audini – London 1994[28] | Social Functioning (Social Adjustment Scale) | 3 (1.6) | 2.9 (1.0) |
| Morse – St Louis 1992[36] | Social Functioning | 2.9 (0.8) | 2.9 (0.7) |
| Audini – London 1994[28] | Satisfaction with Care (Client Satisfaction Questionaire) | 26.6 (4.5) | 22.9 (3.6) * |
| De Cangas – Quebec 1994[32] | High Expressed Emotion (five-minute speech sample) | 1.3 (0.5) | 1.7 (0.4) * |

For ACT studies, useful data existed for: (i) death; (ii) imprisonment; (iii) arrests; (iv) accommodation status; (v) employment; (vi) mental state; (vii) social functioning; (viii) patient satisfaction; and (ix) expressed emotion in relatives. ACT patients had a slightly lower mortality rate than controls (OR 0.6; 99% CI 0.13 – 2.73; $n = 667$), but confidence intervals were wide. Concerning imprisonment, the power of the review was too low to detect important differences (OR 1.02; 99% CI 0.52 – 1.97; $n = 591$). Patients receiving ACT were, however, significantly less likely to have been arrested than control subjects (OR 0.34; 99% CI 0.12 – 0.93; $n = 208$). ACT patients also had a significantly better accommodation outcome, being less likely to have been homeless (OR 0.23; 99% CI 0.08 – 0.64; $n = 374$) or to be not living independently (OR 0.29; 99% CI 0.14 – 0.61; $n = 251$). ACT patients also spent significantly more days in independent accommodation (Test-Wisconsin [39], analyzed using ranks) and significantly fewer days homeless (Morse-St. Louis [36], ana-

Table 5. Costs of care in case management and ACT trials.

| Trial | Cost type | Index group (SD) | Control group (SD) | % difference | Significance |
|---|---|---|---|---|---|
| *Case management trials* | | | | | |
| Franklin – Houston[15] | Hospital care | $137 | $120 | CM +14% | Unclear (no SD, no transformation) |
| Muijen – London[23] | Hospital care | £223 | £186 | CM +20% | Unclear (no SD, no transformation) |
| Ford – London[20] | Hospital care | (withheld until publication) | (withheld until publication) | – | |
| Quinlivan – California[26] | Hospital care | $221 (SE 66) | $378 (SE 108) | CM -42% | Unclear (no transformation) |
| Muijen – London[23] | All health care | £285 | £208 | CM +25% | Unclear (no SD, no transformation) |
| Ford – London[20] | All health care | (withheld until publication) | (withheld until publication) | – | |
| Quinlivan – California[26] | All health care | $251 | $405 | CM -38% | Unclear (no transformation) |
| Muijen – London[23] | All care | £285 (165) | £395 (269) | CM -28% | Unclear (no transformation) |
| Ford – London[20] | All care | (withheld until publication) | (withheld until publication) | – | |
| Marshall – Oxford[22] | All care | £249 | £272 | CM -8% | Not significant |
| *ACT Trials* | | | | | |
| Quinlivan – California[26] | Hospital care | $69.5 (SE 16.6) | $378 (SE 109) | ACT -82% | Unclear (no transformation) |
| Rosenheck – USA[38] | Hospital care | $977 | $1396 | ACT -30% | Unclear although log transformed |
| Bond Indiana[30] | Hospital care | $46.2 | $278 | ACT -83% | Unclear (no SD, no transformation) |
| Quinlivan – California[26] | All health care | $182 (SE 22.1) | $405 (SE 108) | ACT -55% | Unclear (no transformation) |
| Rosenheck – USA[38] | All health care | $1229 | $1489 | ACT -18% | Unclear although log transformed |
| Bond Indiana[30] | All health care | $230 | $455 | ACT -49% | Unclear (no SD, no transformation) |
| DeCangas – Quebec[32] | All care | $281 (139) | $488 (299) | ACT -42% | Costs normally distributed, p<0.05 |

lyzed after transformation). ACT patients were significantly less likely to be unemployed at the end of the study (OR 0.35; 99% CI 0.16 – 0.79; $n$ = 249). Six outcome measurements based on data collected by standardized instruments have been reported (see Table 4). There were no statistically significant differences between ACT patients and controls in mental state or social functioning, but ACT patients were significantly more satisfied and their relatives showed significantly lower levels of high expressed emotion.

Three aspects of cost were considered: (a) mean weekly costs of psychiatric hospital care; (b) mean weekly costs of all health care (including all medical care, all psychiatric care, and the costs of case management, but excluding accommodation other than hospital care); and (c) mean weekly costs of all care (including costs of accommodation). Five case management trials and four ACT trials provided useful data on costs, in comparison to control treatments (see Table 5). From case management trials, data were available on: (a) mean weekly costs of psychiatric hospital care (4 trials); (b) mean weekly costs of all health care (3 trials); (c) mean weekly costs of all care, including accommodation (3 trials). From ACT trials, data were available on: (a) mean weekly costs of psychiatric hospital care (3 studies); (b) mean weekly costs of all health care (3 studies); (c) mean weekly costs of all care (1 study). All the available data were positively skewed and cannot be definitively analyzed without the original patient data. A further complication, specific to cost studies, was that the data were in different currencies, and collected at different times and hence subject to variations in exchange rates. In terms of raw costs, it appeared that ACT was consistently superior to standard care, whereas case management was not (see Table 5), but this finding must be interpreted with caution.

## Discussion

In maintaining contact with patients, both case management and ACT were significantly better than standard care. This finding was consistent across all but one trial.

In terms of hospital admission, case management approximately doubled admissions relative to standard care, whilst ACT reduced admissions by about half. However three questions require discussion before attempting to interpret this finding. First, how far are any conclusions on admission rates affected by the heterogeneity amongst the case management studies on this variable? Second, how far did the intervention affect lengths of stay? Third, was there evidence of systematic differences between patients recruited to ACT and case management trials respectively?

191

In answer to the first question, the finding that case management increased admission rates is likely to be valid, despite the presence of heterogeneity, because the heterogeneity was attributable to one small study. This study used a pure form of "strengths" case management, and may be worthy of replication. In answer to the second question, the effect of ACT was to reduce length of stay, but the effect of case management was unclear. In answer to the third question, controls in ACT trials were three times more likely to be admitted to hospital than controls in case management trials (see results). This finding is due to ACT trials selectively recruiting subjects who had one or more previous admissions (13 out of 14 ACT trials used current admission or more that 2 previous admissions as an eligibility criteria as against 5 out of 10 case management trials, Chi square $p>0.001$, df = 2). It may therefore be concluded that ACT reduces admission rates in "revolving door" patients, whilst case management creates "revolving door" patients from those with previously low admission rates.

Neither case management nor ACT produced improvement in clinical outcome, but ACT showed notable advantages over standard care in social outcome. However, there are two reasons why case management might be somewhat more effective than the evidence suggests. First, all the trials had relatively short follow-up periods (no more than two years), so that it is conceivable that a gradual improvement in outcome was not detected. Second, it was necessary to exclude 17 outcome measurements from the case management comparison (seven because the rating scales in question were unpublished, eight because no means or standard deviations were presented or the data were incorrectly analyzed; data was collected by the case managers themselves and one because the follow-up rate was less than 50%). Better designed studies might have produced more evidence of effectiveness. Nonetheless, at present, the practice of case management cannot be justified on the grounds of improved clinical or social outcome for patients.

In terms of raw cost data, ACT was consistently superior to standard care, but case management was not. However, since these data were heavily skewed, a meta analysis of transformed individual subject data is required before definitive conclusions can be drawn. The quality of the cost data from the ACT trials was questionable. Mean weekly costs for all health care varied 7-fold between ACT trials, whilst hospital inpatient costs varied 14-fold. Such large variations suggest methodological discrepancies. By contrast, the data on cost of case management versus standard care was of good quality.

This review strongly supports assertive community treatment for people with severe mental disorder and a history of frequent admissions. However, it does not support the practice of case management, except in circumstances where a small increase in numbers remaining in contact with services is justified by a doubling of admission rates for all. This review has two implications for policy makers. The first is that "common sense" solutions, however popular and plausible, must be fully evaluated before their widespread implementation. The UK government, for example, made case management a stratutory obligation in 1991, in the form of the Care Program Approach. It is now difficult to tell how far rising admissions rates in the UK may be attributed to this policy, as further randomized controlled trials are not permitted. The second implication for policy makers is that they should promote ACT teams and as far as possible withdraw or modify existing case management services. UK policy makers should use the Care Program Approach to concentrate true Assertive Community Treatment on suitable patients, and should avoid the trend towards case management for all.

The demise of case management as a scientifically credible treatment leaves a gap that is not entirely filled by ACT. Researchers and commissioners should take up the challenge to develop alternatives that will provide cost-effective care without increasing admission rates.

## Acknowledgements

Austin Lockwood was supported by a grant from the Welcome Trust. This review was conducted with the support of the Cochrane Schizophrenia Group. The authors would like to acknowledge the assistance and support of Clive Adams, Rochelle Seifas, Alistair Gray and Rex Green.

This chapter is referring to two electronic reviews published on the Cochrane Library CD-Rom.

## References

Anon, A. (1995) Care-management: A disastrous mistake. *Lancet*, **345**, 399–401.
Audit Commission (1986) *Making a Reality of Community Care*. HMSO, London.
Beatty, W. W., Jocic, Z., Monson, N. & Staton, R. D. (1993) Memory and frontal lobe dysfunction in schizophrenia and schizoaffective disorder. *Journal of Nervous & Mental Disease*, **181**, 448–453.
Bellack, A. S., Mueser, K. T., Morrison, R. L., et al. (1990) Remediation of cognitive deficits in schizophrenia. *American Journal of Psychiatry*, **147**, 12, 1650–1655.
Berg, E. A. (1948) A simple objective technique for measuring flexibility in thinking. *Journal of General Psychology*, **39**, 15–22.
Brand, A., Hildebrandt, H. & Scheerer, E. (1996) Gedächtnisstörungen bei schizophrenen Erkrankungen. *Fortschritte der Neurologie & Psychiatrie*, **2** (64), 49–65.
Ellison, D., Rieker, P. & Marx, J. (1974) Organisational adaptation to community mental

health. In *Sociological Perspectives on Community Mental Health.* (Ed. Roman, P.). Davis Company, Philadelphia.

Ellison, M. L., Rogers, E. S., Sciarappa, K., et al. (1995) Characteristics of mental health case management: Results of a national survey. *Journal of Mental Health Administration,* **22,** 101–12.

Essock, S. M. & Kontos, N. (1995) Implementing assertive community treatment teams. *Psychiatric Services,* **46,** 679–83.

Franklin, J., Solovitz, B., Mason, M., et al. (1987) An evaluation of case management. *American Journal of Public Health,* **77,** 674–8.

Goldberg, T. E. & Weinberger, R. (1994) Schizophrenia, training paradigms, and the Wisconsin Card Sorting Test redux. *Schizophrenia Research,* **11,** 291–296.

Holloway, F. (1991) Case management for the mentally ill: Looking at the evidence. *International Journal of Social Psychiatry,* **37,** 2–13.

Kanter, J. S. (1991) Integrating case management and psychiatric hospitalisation. *Health & Social Work,* **16** (1), 34–42.

Melzer, D., Hale, S., Malik, S. J., et al. (1991) Community care for patients with schizophrenia one year after hospital discharge. *British Medical Journal,* **303,** 1023–6.

Olfson, M. (1990) Assertive community treatment: An evaluation of the experimental evidence. *Hospital & Community Psychiatry,* **41,** 634–41.

Rössler, W., Löffler, W., Fatkenheuer, B. & Riecher-Rössler, A. (1992) Does case management reduce the rehospitalization rate? *Acta Psychiatrica Scandinavica,* **86** (6), 445–449.

Rössler, W., Löffler, W., Fatkenheuer, B. & Riecher-Rössler, A. (1995) Case management for schizophrenic patients at risk for rehospitalization: A case control study. *European Archives for Psychiatry and Clinical Neurosciences,* **246,** 29–36.

Rubin, A. (1992) Is case management effective for people with serious mental illness? A research review. *Health & Social Work,* **17,** 138–50.

Sackett, D. L. (1994) *The Cochrane Collaboration Handbook.* Oxford, UK: The Cochrane Collaboration.

Shepherd, G. (1990) Case management. *Health Trends,* **22,** 59–61.

Solomon, P. (1992) The efficacy of case management services for severely mentally disabled clients. *Community Mental Health Journal,* **28,** 163–80.

Stein, L. I. (1992) On the abolishment of the case-manager. *Health Affairs,* **11,** 172–7.

Thornicroft, G. (1991) The concept of case management for long term mental illness. *International Review of Psychiatry,* **3,** 125–32.

# Comprehensive Care of the Schizophrenics – End of the Revolving-Door Psychiatry?

Wulf Rössler and Anita Riecher-Rössler

## Introduction

Recurrent hospital admissions have for a long time been at the focus of attention of both psychiatric epidemiology and mental health services research. In the field of psychiatric epidemiology rehospitalization, represents a reliable and easily assessed indicator for the course of severe mental disorders as in the case of schizophrenia. On the other hand, recurrent inpatient treatment can be looked at as a useful measure of the success or failure of community care. In this respect, the "revolving-door" phenomenon stands here for a negative connotation of psychiatry, referring to community care programs which fail to forestall rehospitalization. Revolving-door psychiatry has therefore become a synonym for ineffective and inadequate psychiatric care.

Assessing the real value of community care with respect to the risk of rehospitalization does, however, require a multidimensional view. One of the groups of patients particularly suited for the point of departure would be those with schizophrenic psychoses. Scarcely any other group of patients has been studied more extensively with respect to the life-long course of a disease. At the same time, schizophrenics have been at the center of psychiatric care reforms since its beginning, since the inhumane care these patients often received in asylums, revealed the urgent need for reform.

## The Course of Schizophrenic Psychoses

To review the course of schizophrenic psychoses adequately, prospective studies are needed of representative samples of first-onset, or at least first-admitted patients (Riecher-Rössler et al., 1995). The number of such studies has been rather limited.

One of the methodologically sound examples in the Buckinghampshire study by Shepherd et al. (1989) which examined 121 schizophrenic patients, 49 of whom were first-admitted patients from a defined catchment area, over a period of five years. These authors discovered that 55% of their cohort of first-admitted patients had to be rehospitalized during the follow-up period. In this time, the subjects spent approximately 8.5 months in hospital on average (first admission included), two of them spending nearly the whole period of five years there.

Another prospective epidemiological investigation is the WHO Disability-Study, which showed, for example, that in Mannheim, one of the study areas, the 70 first-admitted patients included and followed up over five years experienced on average nearly three admissions of approximately nine months' duration during the study period (first hospitalization included). Only 29% of these patients were not rehospitalized after their first admission (Biehl et al., 1986).

A further methodically sound study is the transcultural "Determinants of Outcome of severe Mental Disorders" study (Jablensky et al., 1992), also carried out by the WHO, which includes a larger study population than the two mentioned alone. Twelve centers in ten countries participated in this study, and all index patients of the various catchment areas were examined. First inpatient as well as outpatient contacts with various health and social services were registered, and it can be assumed that very few first registered patients were not included. In all, a representative population of 1379 patients was examined at the collaborating centers. During a two-year follow-up of 1078 patients, it was found that not one had to remain in hospital during the whole period of time. But 69% of all the cases had to be readmitted at some point during this time, with the various centers varying considerably in this respect.

In evaluating long-term treatment, psychiatric case registers have provided to be very helpful. They are reliable in assessing the treatment data of patients with severe mental disorders, and usually allow the analysis of longer time periods, than with epidemiological field studies. To investigate the rehospitalization rates of schizophrenics, Häfner et al. (1991) used the data of the Danish case register. 1169 patients were included who had been admitted for the first time in 1976 because of paranoid or schizophrenic psychosis. During a follow-up period of ten years, 70% of the patients had to be rehospitalized. Male patients had 3.7 and female patients 3.4 admissions on average during this period (index hospitalization included), amounting to an average rate of 486 days for the men and 354 days for the women respectively.

Although these studies have undoubtedly revealed a great risk for schizophrenics to be rehospitalized during the course of their illness, this risk seems to follow an uneven pattern over time. As has been shown in different studies (Engelhardt et al., 1992; Eaton et al., 1992), schizophrenic patients stand at high risk to be rehospitalized during the period of 2–4 years after the onset of their illness, whereas in the subsequent years, the severity of the illness often seems to subside, as indicated by a significant reduction of readmissions. Whilst there are different illness-related factors influencing the course of schizophrenia, such as age, gender, premorbid adjustment, or the social environment, it remains difficult to make a valid prognosis for individual cases.

Moreover, it is necessary to analyze to what extent rehospitalization is related to relapse resulting from the deterioration of the illness itself. It might be thought that the risk is more or less determined by variables other than the actual course of the disorder. But in a follow-up study over 13 years, Mason et al. (1986) analyzed this correlation in a group of 67 schizophrenic patients in Nottingham, showing that the patterns of rehospitalization and exacerbation of the illness showed a remarkable degree of resemblance in the course. Besides the known pattern of readmission during the years following the onset of schizophrenia, acute psychotic symptoms were displayed especially during the first years, with a continuous decline in the subsequent years. The dissimilarity between relapses and course of disease seem to lie in the fact that illness-related symptoms are present more frequently and over longer periods of time than is the case with rates and duration of readmission. Therefore, the criterion "rehospitalization" seems to underrate the extent of the progress of the illness, although reflecting its "natural" course.

# The Effect of the Mental Health Care System on the Course of Schizophrenic Psychoses

Various clarifications are needed in examining the effect of mental health care on both the course of schizophrenic illness and on rehospitalization risks. Questions associated with the effectiveness of the mental health care system need to be separated from inquiries into the effectiveness of individual treatment strategies (see Figure 1).

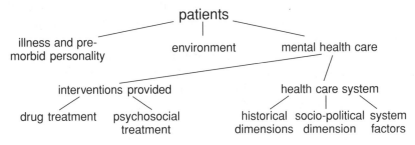

*Figure 1.* Risk factors influencing rehospitalization in schizophrenic patients

197

Analyzing whether and to what extent psychiatric treatment influences the course of schizophrenic illness, Hegarty et al. (1994) evaluated 320 studies conducted world-wide between 1895 and 1995, with a total population of 51,800 patients and 368 cohorts. After the mid-century, there were a remarkable number of patients whose improvement was significantly better, compared to those examined before the 1950s. While only 35% of the patients were rated in the category "improved" between 1895 and 1955, the percentage rose to 49% in the years 1956–1985. Hegarty et al. conclude that the reasons for this improved course lie in the development of therapeutic methods, especially the introduction of neuroleptics and psychosocial care. However, these two methods were not included in their metaanalysis. Wyatt (1994) confirmed their conjectures about neuroleptics by an evaluation of 22 follow-up studies, which demonstrated that early treatment favors a benign long-term course.

## Effectiveness of Psychopharmacological Treatment

The discovery of neuroleptic medication marked the beginning of an effective treatment of schizophrenics in the mid-1950s. To date, no alternative exists to treating the acute psychotic symptoms of schizophrenia with antipsychotic drugs. Moreover, neuroleptics are absolutely essential in the long-term treatment of schizophrenia, as the risk of relapse is substantially lowered thereby (e.g., Davis, 1975; Müller et al., 1977). At the same time, they provide the basis for rehabilitation, and this seems to be due to an increased tolerance towards emotional stress. However, even continuous pharmacological treatment still results in a monthly relapse rate of approx. 3.5%, as Weiden and Olfson (1995) concluded from a metaanalysis, compared to a relapse rate of approx. 11% in non-compliant patients. This poor compliance results mainly from the troublesome side-effects of conventional antipsychotic drugs. Nevertheless, our knowledge of when and under what circumstances drug maintenance therapy might be discontinued is insufficient. As Weiden and Olfson pointed out, on average 8.4% of patients per month suffer a relapse after medication has been stopped with medical approval. For many patients, a lower dosage is recommendable as an alternative and is comparable to standard treatment in relapse prevention, with significantly reduced adverse effects (Schooler, 1991). A second alternative is interval drug therapy which, however, has not fulfilled its expectations up to now (Gaebel, 1995a).

# Effectiveness of Psychosocial Treatment

In addition to psychopharmacological treatment, a variety of different psychosocial treatment approaches have been developed. Besides a range of diversified programs aimed at training social skills (e.g., Liberman, 1982, 1987), psychosocial program for family members also need to be incorporated in a comprehensive care approach.

As a result of modern community care, an enormous psychological and financial burden has been imposed upon relatives of the patient. In the light of this knowledge, a series of family programs have been developed, each setting different priorities (Goldstein et al., 1978; Leff et al., 1982, 1985; Falloon et al., 1982, 1985; Hogarty et al., 1986). Despite some differences, these programs share a set of common features in giving support to families to cope with the illness (Strachan, 1986). These programs have effectively reduced the relapse rate, when combined with antipsychotic drug treatment.

# Effectiveness of the Mental Health Care System

When looking at institutional care, various dimensions in the development of mental health care have to be considered:

- The historical dimension,
- The socio-political influence on the provision of mental health services, and finally,
- System factors, i.e., coordination of the various care sectors, in particular outpatient and inpatient care.

*The historical dimension*

During the nineteenth century, the psychiatric profession had a favorable belief in its treatment strategies, although no effective pharmacological treatment was available at that time. Isolation of the mentally ill in institutions that were located outside communities seemed to be a suitable method to shield the patients from the pathogenic influences of their social environment. However, it was eventually realized that successful treatment was not frequent. The numbers of inpatients in institutions that were initially meant for "curable" cases rose continuously. Griesinger (1872) commented on this development that: "In mental institutions there is nothing more difficult than a continuous and efficient discharge of the mentally ill, and a certain number of them always will remain there for years even when they were thought of as incurable."

Both geographical isolation and growing neglect by the local authorities and by the public led to a deterioration of the premises and trained personnel, which finally prevented adequate long-term care. Public awareness of the mental hospitals remained insignificant for decades in Germany. It was only in the 1960s and 70s that the deplorable condition of the mental hospitals began to attract public notice, thus initiating reforms. These reforms acknowledged that severe mental illness by no means has to result in the chronicity so often associated with it as a result of observing long-term patients in the former mental institutions. The custodial practices of these institutions deprived many of the patients of their basic social skills, so that most of them no longer had the desire to leave hospital (Wing, 1976).

The beginnings of the reforms were characterized by creating living accommodation outside a mental hospital for long-term patients. In socio-psychiatric reforms, readmission of former long-term patients was commonly considered a defeat, which had to be avoided under any circumstances. However, hospital care now represents only one aspect of diversified community care systems and services, which promote the long-term reintegration of chronically ill and disabled patients. This is also demonstrated by the fact that today, patients stay in hospital for a considerably shorter time than before. Whereas in the past prolonged, if not life-long hospitalization was common, patients admitted to a mental hospital at present in Germany stay there for 62 days only on average (Rössler and Salize, 1996).

*The socio-political dimension*

Although many experts tend to think that the mental health care reforms were the result of some dedicated politicians, by and large, they were determined more by the general social and health care reforms of the period. In the case of Germany, the reduction of surplus beds in the state mental hospitals coincided with the Hospital Finance Act which granted subsidies for investment and maintenance for building for acute care hospital only, thereby producing a sharp reduction in the bed for all medical disciplines (Zumpe, 1978).

Due to the present discussion of costs in the health care system, the number of psychiatric hospital beds is likely to be further reduced. In contrast, no additional outpatient and rehabilitative services have been developed so far. Persisting and striking discrimination against the chronically mentally ill and handicapped still continue and health care services do not easily allow for their social reintegration. Services seem to be adapted mainly to the needs of the physi-

200

cally disabled, in terms of funding, rehabilitation, and institutional structures, not taking into account the specific needs of the chronic mentally ill (Rössler et al., 1995).

Since chronically mentally ill and impaired persons often do not meet the requirements for social insurance benefits, a financial scheme has been established for these persons, resulting rehabilitation being financed by the social welfare system. However, the consequence of such a scheme is that the private financial resources of the patient have to be exhausted to the point of poverty in order to receive the required services.

Such a system, as applied in Germany, does not prevent the unnecessary hospitalization of patients who do not qualify for rehabilitation funds in outpatient care. At present, comprehensive care programs providing integrated medical, psychiatric, and psychosocial services can only be provided for inpatient care and do not meet the needs of chronically ill schizophrenic patients. Due to the significantly *improved* service supply of the mental hospitals in Germany, implemented by the Personnel Act, there is a strong tendency to hospitalize patients in sufficient outpatient services are not available.

*The influence of system factors*

Influenced by such socio-political developments, mental health services research has studied how the various care sectors are inter-related. One of the crucial questions is to what extend the provision of outpatient care influences inpatient care and, particularly, whether sufficient outpatient care leads to reduced supply of inpatient care.

*Shortage of community-based care services*

It is not unusual for the decision makers to provide outpatient services only if the reductions can be achieved in other care services, mainly in inpatient care. Many experts also assume that "undoubtedly outpatient care reduces considerably the rate of unnecessary hospitalizations" "Deutscher Bundestag 1975). Empirical evidence for this, however, is not convincing. In some catchment areas, e.g., Mannheim, it became obvious that the implementation of comprehensive care systems generated complex system developments which exceeded by far the substitution of inpatient by outpatient care: For example, in the comprehensively equipped community care system in Mannheim, there was a 100% increase in treatment episodes between 1974 and 1980 in all sectors of care (see Figure 2).

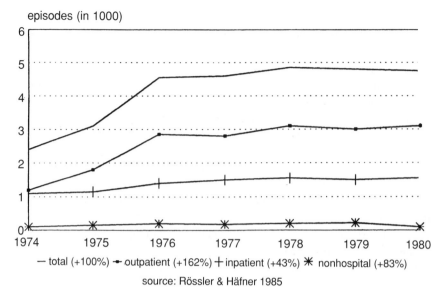

source: Rössler & Häfner 1985

*Figure 2.* Development of mental health service utilization in the city of Mannheim 1974–1980.

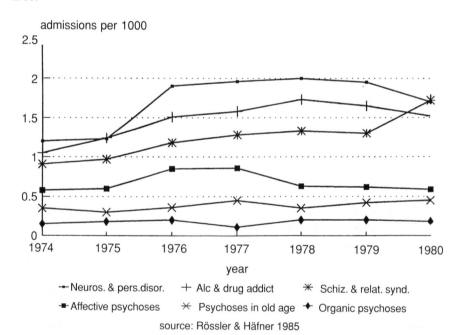

source: Rössler & Häfner 1985

*Figure 3.* Admission ratios for different diagnostic groups to inpatient treatment in Mannheim between 1974 and 1990.

Use of outpatient services increased by 162% and the admission rate in the mental hospitals of the Mannheim area increased by 43%. During this period, the hospitalization rate (see Figure 3) almost doubled for schizophrenic patients (Rössler and Häfner, 1985).

Thus, although a multitude of empirical data exists indicating effective treatment methods which reduce rehospitalization rates, various questions do remain: Not only can the effects in naturalistic settings, as in the Mannheim area, not be convincingly demonstrated, but opposite effects can also be observed. We have to deal with a certain "frictional loss" when putting into practice the results from controlled studies, so that efforts are being made, in terms of quality assurance, to minimize this loss. This does not, however, account for apparently opposite effects. Thus, we have to look elsewhere for an explanation. Health care systems are highly complex organizations, which are regulated by many different factors. Some of the more influential factors will be discussed below.

*The fragmentation of care*

Many professionals argue that increasingly fragmented and poorly co-ordinated services account for the "failure" of outpatient care in preventing rehospitalization. The implementation of such small-structured facilities and services raised hopes that the needs for care could be met with individually-tailored programs, comparable to a module system. However, its fragmentation resulted in a high rate of unmet needs for care, with occasional overprovision (BMJFFG, 1988). As a result, a new care approach has developed, particularly concerned with the co-ordination of the fragmented services. The co-ordination of services is linked with the concept of case management. In their original draft of the Community Support Program, the NIMH (1980) denoted this concept as the basis for co-ordinated and therefore need-related care. Whereas there are many English-language publications dealing with this subject (e.g., Renshaw, 1987; Holloway, 1991; Borland et al., 1989), evaluation research in the German-speaking countries is just at its beginning. In one of the few existing studies in Germany (Rössler et al., 1992, 1993, 1995), no significant effect of case management was found in the rehospitalization rate of the case managed chronic schizophrenic patient, compared to patients who did not receive case management, although the illness-related risk of rehospitalization was similar (see Figure 4).

There has been an increasing by critical attitude towards case management (Marshall et al., 1995; Marshall, 1996). Although most experts remain open-minded about its importance, there seems to be little evidence from controlled

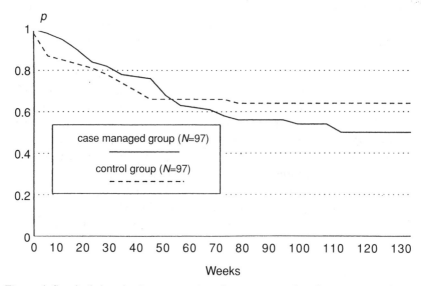

*Figure 4.* Survival time in the community of case-managed patients compared to control patients.

studies that case management is an effective tool in the prevention of rehospitalization. Some reviews demonstrate that shorter intervals between contacts can bring positive results or at least that the positive and negative results are more or less balanced then, whereas inclusion of management with longer intervals between contacts brings an increase in negative results, so that a large number of patients are still being rehospitalized in the long run (Rubin, 1992; Solomon, 1992).

## Distance to mental hospitals

Explaining the various factors influencing the utilization of health services, it must not be for forgotten that the use is also governed substantially by the users themselves. A number of studies demonstrated a reduction of hospitalization rates depending on the distance between place of residence and place of hospital. The inverse relationship between administrative prevalence and geographical distance was described by Edward Jarvis in 1852 and has gone down in literature as the "Jarvis Law." These findings were confirmed in a recent study by Meise et al. (1994). Analysis of all diagnostic groups showed that the hospitalization rate was reduced by more than 50% when the travel time amounted to 30–60 minutes (see Figure 5).

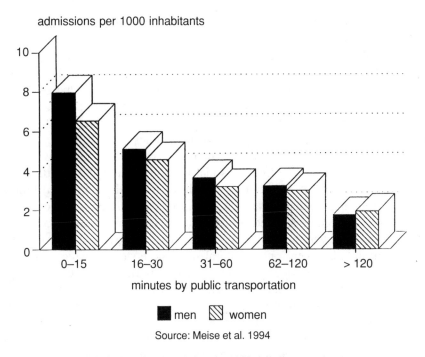

admissions per 1000 inhabitants

minutes by public transportation

■ men ⊠ women

Source: Meise et al. 1994

*Figure 5.* Hospital admissions by travel time in 1989 (all diagnoses).

A distinct variation was recognized between the various diagnostic groups (Meise et al., 1996). The sharpest reduction in utilization rate was found for patients with drug addiction, whereas those with affective psychoses had the lowest reduction. Schizophrenic patients ranged in the middle. Examining the different socio-demographic variables which are known to regulate the use of hospital care, it was found that the variable "distance to hospital" remained the most influential factor.

## Conclusions

Since the indicator "rehospitalization" is applied in many health care studies of schizophrenic patients, the studies presented here are only a small proportion of those which have dealt with this subject. Most epidemiological data show a relatively regular pattern of course of the illness, with a reduced need for treatment in the later stages. Even if the conclusion drawn from these course characteristics is that of an inherent course or autonomous nature of the illness, the question remains to what extent psychiatric and psychosocial factors might exert their influence on it.

The studies presented here give evidence of a significant reduction of the rehospitalization rate in this way, but the potential influence of these factors seems to be limited, insofar as the fundamental course of the illness does not alter. Proceedings next from the actual treatment provided to the level of services and institutions, a rather confusing picture emerges. Kluiter (1996) concludes from his review, which considered only studies with a randomized study design, that: "Community care arrangements are capable of reducing the need for inpatient treatment. The trouble is that we do not know to what degree."

In another review of 37 evaluation studies, an der Heiden (1986) found a reduced need for inpatient treatment due to outpatient care arrangements in 23, whereas 14 studies showed no correlation, or even an increased risk of readmission. However, most of these studies were not based on an experimental study design, but were rather naturalistic. These studies, which document the "natural" use of services, are characterized by much greater uncertainty with respect to the validity of their conclusions. Klinkenberg and Calsyn (1996) were therefore reserved in drawing conclusions from the research data of the past 20 years. With respect to the prevention of hospitalization these authors rate only one variable as having a positive effect – the extent of social support.

One aspect which has not been discussed in the work presented here is the effect of the social network of the affected persons on the risk of rehospitalization. Not only does this concern informal support by family members and friends, but also the extent to which professional helpers need to be added to the social network, and, whether or not the persons concerned perceive them as part of their social environment. These questions have not received sufficient attention so far in health care research. In a study of our own, not yet published, we analyzed this aspect and found a positive correlation between a reduced hospitalization rate of schizophrenics and the perceived number of professional helpers in their social network. This aspect has been discussed theoretically with respect to case management, indicating that in addition to pure co-ordination work, the relationship between affected persons and the providers of care is of fundamental importance for successful reduction of rehospitalization.

Along with other results, these findings indicate that in this complex subject, definite answers are not going to be available in the near future to the opening question – whether comprehensive care for the schizophrenics will lead to the end of "revolving-door" psychiatry. In any case, this can now mean that schizophrenic with life-long disability can live outside a hospital for the main part of their lives, with short interruptions only. For the benefit of our patients though, health services research should also direct its attention to other areas that have an impact on their situation for example, the life quality which they experience subjectively or the burden that, until now, has been carried by the families affected.

# References

Biehl, H., Maurer, K., Schubart, C., et al. (1986) Prediction of outcome and utilization of medical services in a prospective study of first onset schizophrenics. Results of a prospective 5-year follow-up study. *European Archives of Psychiatry & Neurological Sciences* **236**, 139–147.

BMJFFG (1988) *Empfehlungen der Expertenkommission der Bundesregierung zur Reform der Versorgung im psychiatrischen und psychotherapeutisch/psychosomatischen Bereich auf der Grundlage des Modellprogramms Psychiatrie.* BMJFFG, Bonn.

Deutscher Bundestag (1975) *Bericht über die Lage der Psychiatrie in der Bundesrepublik Deutschland – zur psychiatrischen und psychotherapeutischen/psychosomatischen Versorgung der Bevölkerung.* Bundestags-Drucksache 7/4200, Bonn.

Borland, A., McRae, J. & Lycan, C. (1989) Outcomes of five years of continuous intensive case management. *Hospital and Community Psychiatry,* **40**, 369–376.

Davis, J.M. (1975) Overview: Maintenance therapy in psychiatry. *Schizophrenia. American Journal of Psychiatry,* **132**, 1237–1245.

Eaton, W. W., Mortensen, P. B., Herrmann, H., et al. (1992) Long-term course of hospitalization for schizophrenia: Part I. Risk for hospitalization. *Schizophrenia Bulletin,* **18**, 217–228.

Falloon, I. R. H., Boyd, J. L., McGill, C.W., et al. (1982) Family management in the prevention of exacerbations of schizophrenia. *N Engl J Med,* **24** (306): 1437–1440.

Falloon, I. R. H., Boyd, J. L., McGill, C. W., et al. (1982) Family management in the prevention of morbidity of schizophrenia: Clinical outcome of a two-year longitudinal study. *Archives of General Psychiatry,* **42**, 887–896.

Gaebel, W. (1995a) Neuroleptische Intervalltherapie – eine Alternative zur Langzeitmedikation? In *Die Behandlung der Schizophrenien. State of the Art.* (Eds. Hinterhuber, H., Fleischhacker, W. W. & Meise, U.). Innsbruck, Wien: Verlag Integrative Psychiatrie.

Gaebel, W. (1995b) Qualitätssicherung diagnostischer und therapeutischer Massnahmen im psychiatrischen Krankenhaus. In *Qualitätssicherung im psychiatrischen Krankenhaus.* (Ed. Gaebel, W.), pp 87–108. Wien, New York: Springer-Verlag.

Goldstein, S. I., Rodnick, E. H., Evans, J. R., et al. (1978) Drug and family therapy in the aftercare treatment of acute schizophrenia. *Archives of General Psychiatry,* **35**, 169–177.

Griesinger, W. (1872) *Gesammelte Abhandlungen.* Berlin: Hirschwald.

Häfner, H., Maurer, K., Löffler, W., & Riecher-Rössler, A. (1991a) Schizophrenie und Lebensalter. *Nervenarzt,* **62**, 536–548.

Häfner, H., Riecher-Rössler, A., Maurer, K., et al. (1991b) Geschlechtsunterschiede bei schizophrenen Erkrankungen. *Fortschritte in Neurologie & Psychiatrie,* **59**, 343–360.

Hegarty, J. D., Baldessarini, R. J., Tohen, M., et al. (1994) One hundred years of schizophrenia: A meta-analysis of the outcome literature. *American Journal of Psychiatry,* **151**, 1409–1416.

an der Heiden, W. (1996) Können durch ausserstationäre Massnahmen stationäre Aufenthalte verhindert werden? *Gesundheitswesen*, **58**, Sonderheft, pp. 38–43.

Hogarty, G. E., Anderson, C. M., Reiss, D. J., et al. EPICS Schizophrenia Research Group (1986) Family psycho-education, social skills training and maintenance chemotherapy in the aftercare treatment of schizophrenia: I. One year effects of a controlled study on relapse and expressed emotion. *Archives of General Psychiatry*, **43**, 633–647.

Holloway, F. (1991) Case management for the mentally ill: Looking at the evidence. *The International Journal of Social Psychiatry*, **37**, 2–13.

Jablensky, A., Sartorius, N., Ernberg, G., et al. (1992) Schizophrenia: Manifestations, incidence and course in different cultures. A World Health Organization Ten-Country Study. *Psychological Medicine*, suppl. **20**, 1–97.

Klinkenberg, W. D. & Calsyn, R. J. (1996) Predictors of receipt of aftercare and recidivism among persons with severe mental illness: A review. *Psychiatric Services*, **47**, 5.

Kluiter, H. (1997) Inpatient treatment and care arrangements to replace or avoid it – searching for an evidence-based balance. *Current Opinion in Psychiatry*, **10**, 160–167.

Leff, J. P., Kuipers, L., Berkowitz, R., et al. (1982) A controlled trial of intervention in the families of schizophrenic patients. *British Journal of Psychiatry*, **141**, 121–134.

Leff, J. P., Kuipers, L., Berkowitz, R. & Sturgeon, D. (1985) A controlled trial of social intervention in the families of schizophrenic patients: Two year follow-up. *British Journal of Psychiatry*, **146**, 594–600.

Liberman, R. (1982) Assessment of social skills. *Schizophrenia Bulletin*, **8**, 63–83.

Liberman, R. (1987) *Current problems and strategies for the treatment of schizophrenia. Paper presented at the 140th Annual Meeting of the American Psychiatric Association* (May 12), Chicago/Illinois.

Marshall, M., Lookwood, A. & Gath, D. (1995) How effective is social services case management for people with long-term mental disorders? A randomised controlled trial. *Lancet*, **345**, 409–412.

Marshall, M. (1996) Case management: A dubious practice. Underevaluated and ineffective, but now government policy. *British Medical Journal*, **312**, 523–524.

Mason, P., Harrison, G., Glazebrook, C., et al. (1996) The Course of Schizophrenia Over 13 Years. A Report from the International Study on Schizophrenia (ISOS) Coordinated by the World Health Organization. *British Journal of Psychiatry*, 580–586.

Meise, U., Kemmler, G., Kurz, M. & Rössler, W. (1994) Zum Einfluss der Entfernung auf die psychiatrische Versorgung. *Neuropsychiatrie*, **8**, 31–32.

Meise, U., Kemmler, G., Kurz, M. & Rössler, W. (1996) Die Standortqualität als Grundlage psychiatrischer Versorgungsplanung. *Das Gesundheitswesen*, **58**, Sonderheft 1, 29–37.

Müller, P., Kind, J., Lohrengel, S., et al. (1977) Die neuroleptische Rezidivprophylaxe schizophrener Psychosen. *Nervenarzt*, **48**, 560–561.

NIMH (1980) *Toward a National Plan for the Chronically Mentally Ill. Department of Health and Human Services.* Rockville, MD, US.

Renshaw, J. (1987) Care planning and case management. *British Journal of Social Work*, **18**, 79–105.

Riecher-Rössler, A., Rössler, W. & Meise, U. (1995b) Der Verlauf schizophrener Psychosen – was wissen wir 100 Jahre nach Kraepelin? In *Die Behandlung der Schizophrenien*: State of the Art. (Eds. Hinterhuber H. & Fleischhacker, W.), pp 19–51. Innsbruck: VIP-Verlag Integrative Psychiatrie.

Rössler, W. & Häfner, H. (1985) Psychiatrische Versorgungsplanung. *Neuropsychiatrie*, **1**, 8–17.

Rössler, W., Fätkenheuer, B., Löffler, W. & Riecher-Rössler, A. (1992) Does case management reduce the rehospitalization rate? *Acta Psychiatrica Scandinavica*, 445–449.

Rössler, W., Fätkenheuer, B. & Löffler, W., (1993) *Soziale Rehabilitation Schizophrener – Modell Sozialpsychiatrischer Dienst*. Forum der Psychiatrie. Stuttgart: Enke Verlag.

Rössler, W., Löffler, W., Fätkenheuer, B. & Riecher-Rössler, A. (1995) Case management for schizophrenic patients at risk for rehospitalization – a case control study. *European Archives of Psychiatry and Clinical Neurosciences*, **246**, 29–36.

Rössler, W., Salize, H. J., Biechele, U. & Trunk, V. (1995) Sozialrechtliche und strukturelle Defizite der Versorgung chronisch psychisch Kranker und Behinderter. *Nervenarzt*, **66**, 802–810.

Rössler, W. & Salize, H. J. (1996) *Die psychiatrische Versorgung chronisch psychisch Kranker – Daten, Fakten, Analysen*. Band 77. Schriftenreihe des Bundesministeriums für Gesundheit. Baden-Baden: Nomos Verlagsgesellschaft.

Rubin, A. (1992) Is case management effective for people with serious mental illness? A research review. *Health & Social Work*, **17** (2),138–150.

Schooler, N. R. (1991) Maintenance medication for schizophrenia: Strategies for dose reduction. *Schizophrenia Bulletin*, **17**, 311–324.

Shephard, M., Wyatt, D., Falloon, I. & Smeeton, N. (1989) The natural history of schizophrenia: A five year follow-up study of outcome and prediction in a representative sample of schizophrenics. *Psychological Medicine*, suppl. **15**, 1–46.

von der Schulenburg, J. M. (1993) MPS-Studie. Mehr Klinikeinweisungen. *Deutsche Apotheker-Zeitung*, 29.11.1993.

Solomon, P. (1992) The efficiency of case management services for severely mentally disabled clients. *Community & Mental Health Journal*, **28** (3), 163–180.

Strachan, A. M. (1986) Family intervention for the rehabilitation of schizophrenia: Toward protection and coping. *Schizophrenia Bulletin*, **12** (4), 678–698.

Weiden, P. J. & Olfson, M. (1995) Cost of relapse in schizophrenia. *Schizophrenia Bulletin*, **21** (3), 419–429.

Wing, J. (1976) Eine praktische Grundlage für die Sozialtherapie bei Schizophrenie. In *Therapie, Rehabilitation und Prävention schizophrener Erkrankungen*. (Ed. Huber, G.). Stuttgart, New York: Schattauer.

Wiedemann, G. J., Thor-Wiedemann, S., Daxl, M., et al. (1994) Die Quadratur des Kreises: Universitäre Maximalversorgung mit Minimalaufwand. *Deutsches Ärzteblatt*, **91** (A), 2824–2829.

Wyatt, R. J. (1991) Neuroleptics and the natural course of schizophrenia. *Schizophrenia Bulletin*, **17**, 325–351.

Zumpe, V. (1978) Die Krankenhausgesetzgebung in der Bundesrepublik Deutschland und ihre Auswirkung auf psychiatrische Krankenhäuser. *Psychiatrische Praxis*, **5**, 1–13.

# Changes to the Hospital-Community Balance of Mental Health Care: Economic Evidence from Two UK Studies

Daniel Chisholm and Angela Hallam

## Introduction

Altering the balance of care between the psychiatric hospitals and the community is a key and often contentious component of mental health care policy in many countries. In the UK, it has been central government policy for many years. Since the early 1960s, policy documents such as *Better Services for the Mentally Ill* (Department of Health and Social Security, DHSS, 1975), financial mechanisms such as joint health and social services finance (DHSS, 1983), and numerous other affirmations of successive governments' commitment to community care, have encouraged the development of services to facilitate the closure of the large, old, and often remote psychiatric hospitals (DHSS, 1985; Department of Health, DH, 1989). Mental health policy in England is directed towards the closure of all long-stay hospitals by the year 2000 (DH, 1992).

Implementation of this policy has been slowed, however, by the apparent shortage of suitable community accommodation for people with long-term needs for care and support (Lelliott & Wing, 1994; Tyrer & Creed, 1995). The shortage of community beds has at least two potential consequences. First, it can cause the "silting up" of acute psychiatric inpatient beds, with people who do not need that intensity of treatment, denying other access to inpatient care or precipitating early discharge from inpatient facilities. Second, it may waste scarce resources by pushing up unnecessarily the costs of health care, especially hospital provision.

Achieving an appropriate balance of mental health care provision requires a matching of resources to identified and assessed needs. Complex organizational and financial arrangements between the multiplicity of agencies involved in the planning, funding, and delivery of mental health care, together with unidentified or unmet mental health needs in the population, create a wedge between need and service delivery or use. Analysis of these issues can be explored in relation to the hospital-community balance by measuring both the needs for and costs of provision within these two distinct care settings. The principal aim of this chapter is therefore to compare the costs of care for people with mental health problems who are resident in community versus hospital facilities, and to examine the cost implications of changes to the hospital community balance.

These issues are explored with reference to two large-scale studies in the UK: (1) a long-term follow-up study of hospital closure and reprovision in North London, and (2) a cross-sectional survey of mental health residential care across eight districts in England and Wales. Both studies have investigated a range of alternative accommodation options across a variety of providers (health, social services, voluntary organizations, and private agencies). They have also adopted similar methods for the assessment of use of resourcers by clients and of associated costs. All costs are expressed in pounds sterling but, due to the differential design and timing of the two evaluations, the base financial year is not consistent.

## Psychiatric Reprovision in North London

The relocation of psychiatric services in North London is being evaluated in an extensive program of research which started in 1985 and will continue until the autumn of 1998. In 1983, when the Regional Health Authority took the decision to close Friern and Claybury (two large Victorian psychiatric hospitals), it was agreed that the closure program would be monitored and evaluated. The Team for the Assessment of Psychiatric Services (TAPS) was set up to undertake a detailed assessment of patients before they left hospital, and to follow them up, one and five years after they moved to their community placements.

A cost-effectiveness evaluation has been closely integrated with the TAPS research from the beginning. This was carried out at the Personal Social Services Research Unit (University of Kent) until 1995 and subsequently from the Center for the Economics of Mental Health, Institute of Psychiatry. The evaluation is seeking to describe services used by the former inpatients of the two hospitals, to cost their use of those services, and to examine cost-outcome links. Detailed information about living circumstances, income, and use of services is collected for each study client, one and five years after leaving hospital. These data provide the basis for calculating costs, where individual unit costs are based upon the best estimates of long-run marginal opportunity

211

costs. The economic evaluation follows well-developed techniques of mainstream health economics.

The costs study sample includes 711 people who were formerly long-stay patients at Friern or Claybury Hospital (with at least one year's continuous inpatient stay) and who, if aged over 65, did not have a diagnosis of dementia. Several people fulfilled the study criteria more than once, however, so that the full costed sample comprises 751 service packages which were received during the first year in the study clients' community placements. For research purposes, it proved convenient to distinguish and describe annual cohorts of leavers from the two hospitals; ultimately, data were collected on all eight cohorts to leave Friern and the first five to move from Claybury.

*Costs of care one year after clients moved from hospital*

Figure 1 shows the comprehensive weekly costs of care for the former long-stay patients during the first year after the index discharge. Across all cohorts, this period spanned the time between 1985 and 1994, but costs are reported at the same financial year base (1995–1996). Costs include those absorbed by accommodation-related services, and the provision of all other service components that make up the clients' individual care packages. Accommodation costs account for 87% of the total costs of care (on average) and include the input of all staff on the payroll, direct running costs (such as heat, lighting, and provi-

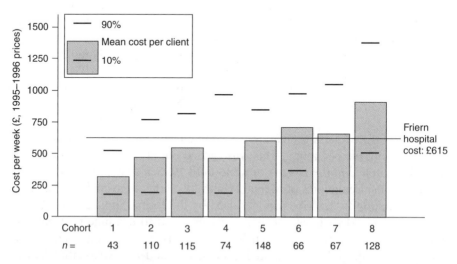

*Figure 1.* North London reprovision program: Hospital and community care costs by cohort.

sion), a capital cost for the building, and a contribution for the agency managing care.

The height of each bar shown in Figure 1 represents the mean lost of care for each successive cohort. As might be expected, there is a general trend for costs to increase as people with greater needs began to move out of hospital. It would be incorrect, however, to assume that all people in the earlier cohorts are less expensive to care for than all people in the later cohorts. To illustrate the *range* of costs of care, Figure 1 also shows smaller horizontal lines to indicate the 10th and 90th percentiles for each cohort. The trend of rising costs is still clear, but numbers of "low-cost" clients can be found among Cohort 7, almost the last group to leave hospital. Although the cost of supporting Cohort 8 members was generally high, even at Cohort 4, the community care packages received by 10% of the group cost more than £ 1000 per week (Beecham et al., 1997).

These findings make it clear for the majority of former long-stay patients, community care is not being provided cheaply. However, evidence on the outcome of patients recorded by the TAPS researchers indicates that the level of investment has been justified by the effects of relocation on the study clients. During the first year after the index discharge, their mental states had usually remained stable (with a significant decrease in negative symptoms). People appreciated the relative freedom of their community units and there was an increase in the number of people who were considered as friends by the study clients (Leff et al., 1996).

*Cost differences between Friern Hospital and community placements*

The reprovision program of long-stay hospital services from Friern and Claybury was well-planned and well-financed – two factors which have undoubtedly contributed to its success in terms of the outcome for clients. However, the relative "generosity" of the financial transfers from hospital (more ample than in many other regions of England) may have contributed to higher costs (Beecham & Lesage, 1997). Once costs data relating to all former long-stay patients had been collected and analyzed, it was important to discover how these costs compared with the cost of supporting the same people while they were living in hospital. Claybury residents were not included in the study after August 1990 (Cohort 5), but Friern patients were monitored until the hospital closed (March 1993). When considering hospital costs, therefore, only data pertaining to Friern and its former residents were used. For comparison with the costs of community-based care, the most appropriate year for the hospital costing is 1985–1986, because this was the year before the number of long-stay beds in the hospital began to decline under the Regional policy of reprovision. It is also the year that people in Cohort 1 moved from the hospital.

When inflated to 1995–1996 prices, the cost per patient per week in Friern Hospital was £ 615. This is a global picture: Since staffing in the acute wards would have been higher than this average, costs for the long-stay group would probably have been somewhat lower than this. The mean weekly cost in the community was £ 679 per week, when averaged over all long-stay patients from Friern *only*. We should be cautious, however, about making comparisons between such different models of care. For example, the size of the hospital population had already been reducing for 30 years, with associated cuts in direct running costs, overheads, and capital investment while community services are now still in their development phase.

Many people, particularly in the early cohorts, did not appear to need 24-hour nursing care: 14% of the full costed sample moved to domestic housing and live independently. A further 14% were accommodated in small group homes (staffed and unstaffed), adult foster care arrangements, or sheltered housing (Beecham et al., 1997). In general, it is the challenge that the later leavers present to planners, purchasers, and providers of services which is pushing up the average cost of care. Figure 2 shows the mean weekly cost for each cohort, when all earlier cohorts have been included in the calculation. Displaying the data in this way makes it easier to see that it was not until the costs of caring for Cohort 8 members were included that the mean cost *overall* of community care rose higher than the cost of the care provided in Friern Hospital.

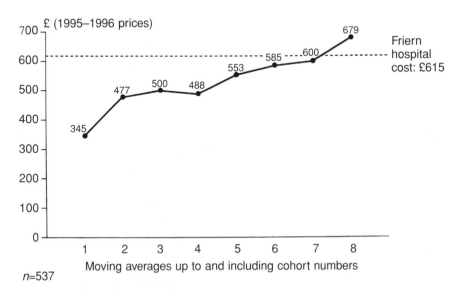

*Figure 2.* North London reprovision program: Total weekly costs of community care – moving averages for the eight cohorts of former Friern long-stay hospital residents.

214

In Cohort 8, 72 people were identified as presenting multiple problem behavior which would make community placement difficult. The senior nursing staff who had been responsible for their care while they were living in Friern felt that these people required the intensive levels of support which are only to be found in hospitals or hospital-like facilities. When asked to specify the problem behavior likely to impede community resettlement, aggressiveness, noncompliance with medication, and inappropriate sexual behavior were the most widely reported to TAPS researchers (Trieman & Leff, 1996a).

The three "receiving" district health authorities adopted very different means of providing for the people with special psychiatric needs. These were as follows:

1. A "special needs" ward and a rehabilitation ward, both in the psychiatric wing of a general hospital;
2. Three purpose-built houses in the grounds of a psychiatric hospital; and
3. A large house in a residential area, with close links to a general hospital.

The mean total cost of supporting people in the "special needs" group was £ 1095 per week (median £ 1237), 94% of which relates to accommodation costs (Hallam, 1996). The units were staffed almost entirely by qualified nurses, and the nurse-to-resident ratio was as high as 1.7 : 1 in two of the facilities. As might be expected, these two factors have a massive impact on cost. (Although the capital and initial costs were high – compared with other facilities – they represent less than 10% of the accommodation cost.)

Outcomes recorded for people in the "special needs" group differed from the remainder of the study sample. There was no overall change in their mental health after one year in these placements, and only minor gains in social and basic everyday living skills. The profile of severe behavioral problems was found to have changed over time, with one-third of the total problems subsiding and a similar number of new problems emerging. There was, however, a reduction in the frequency of aggressive behavior (Trieman & Leff, 1996b). This is an encouraging finding, given that violence was identified as the problem most likely to impede successful community placement.

*Long-term implications of community care*

The focus of the evaluation has now moved on to the longer-term implications of reproviding care in a community setting. Reporting on the first four cohorts of former long-stay patients, TAPS researchers found improvements in clients' mental state between one and five years, particularly in the reduction in neurotic symptoms such as tension, worry, and social unease; also in observed abnormalities of behavior, affect, and speech. Perhaps most importantly, there was a lessening of negative symptoms. Although the size of clients' social networks had not increased between one and five years, there was evidence that existing relationships had deepened (Leff et al., 1994).

Data on costs for the first five cohorts have been analyzed to date, and it has been possible to compare the service packages received by 211 people, one and five years after each person left hospital. At five years after discharge, as at one year, accommodation-related services dominate the costs of support. The majority of study clients continue to live in staffed facilities, where all or most of their health and social care needs are addressed by in-house staff. As shown in Table 1, the mean cost of accommodation was £ 536 per week (85% of the total cost of care). This is £ 45 per week higher than at the one-year interview point, a difference which is statistically significant ($p<0.05$: $t$-test for equality of means). It is possible that, in part, this reflects a service response to rising levels of physical need as residents grow older. Increasingly complex managing arrangements may also contribute to the rise in cost (Hallam et al., 1997).

Although services received independently of accommodation arrangements contribute little to total cost, they are vital elements of care packages, not least because of the evidence they provide of community integration. At present, we

*Table 1.* North London reprovision program: Service utilization after one and five years

| Service | One year | | Five years | |
|---|---|---|---|---|
| | % using | cost (£) | % using | cost (£) |
| Accommodation | 100 | 491 | 100 | 536 |
| Hospital inpatient | 26 | 14 | 16 | 22 |
| Hospital outpatient | 63 | 2 | 50 | 2 |
| Daycare –NHS | 44 | 18 | 32 | 30 * |
| – local authority | 33 | 11 | 14 | 13 |
| – vol organization | 29 | 9 | 13 | 10 |
| – social club | 10 | 1 | 13 | 2 |
| General practitioner | 96 | 2 | 61 | 2 * |
| Community nursing | 43 | 3 | 33 | 2 |
| Community psychiatry | 73 | 2 | 36 | 2 * |
| Community psychology | 33 | 2 | 28 | <1 * |
| Social work | 26 | 7 | 10 | <1 * |
| Education | 7 | 2 | 2 | <1 * |
| Sample size | 211 | | 211 | |

Costs are expressed in £ per week at 1995–1996 price levels, averaged across all people in the sample.
* indicates significant difference at $p<0.05$ ($t$-test for equality of means)

have data for 211 people at the two follow-up points. During the first year after their discharge from Friern or Claybury, ten services had been used by more than 25% of the study sample (apart from accommodation arrangements). Services were provided by a variety of agencies and organizations, in both the public and STET sectors. It is notable, however, that hospital services still provide a major source of support. At both the one- and five-year follow-up point, outpatient services were used by at least half the study sample and 16% had at least one inpatient admission. Almost all community and hospital-based services were used by fewer people in the fifth year after discharge than in the first. The weekly cost of services such as hospital inpatient care and NHS day care, however, were higher. This indicates that where services *were* being used, they were being used more intensively.

# The Mental Health Residential Care Study

This collaborative study between the Research Unit of the Royal College of Psychiatrists and the Center for the Economics of Mental Health, Institute of Psychiatry, set out to assess the needs and costs of residential care for people with mental health problems in a sample of eight areas of England and Wales. Eight services were selected from those expressing readiness to participate in the study (two inner city areas in London, two "suburban" areas, and four rural areas), which spanned a range of population sizes, population densities, and Jarman scores of social deprivation. Catchment populations ranged between 140,000 and 450,000, and the Jarman UPA8 indicators of deprivation levels ranged from 80 in the most rural area to 140 in one of the London areas (Jarman, 1983).

Data were collected for both facilities and their residents (Lelliott et al., 1996). The overriding criterion for inclusion of facilities was that they should have residents with functional mental illness as their principal client group (thereby excluding nursing homes for elderly people, facilities for people with learning disabilities and hostels for the homeless). An assessment was completed for all adult residents in these residential facilities; in facilities with a wider casemix, only those residents with mental health problems were assessed. In order to address issues of inappropriate placement, assessments were also completed for hospital in-patients who – over the course of the survey period (March to August 1994) – had had or reached more than a six-month stay (mainly residents on long-stay psychiatric wards), and for those inpatients with less than a six-month stay (largely occupying acute psychiatric wards) who were deemed by a charge nurse (and subsequently confirmed by a psychiatrist) to have had their discharge delayed. Data were collected on a total of 1951 residents and on 368 facilities, using specially-developed instruments – the Resident Profile and Facility Profile. There were a number of significant differences between localities, types of facility, and the public and private sectors (Lelliott et al., 1996).

The costs of hospital and community care were measured in the standard manner of health economics evaluations (Drummond et al., 1988). They were defined so as to include the costs of the facilities (revenue, capital, and overheads), nine commonly-used non-residential services, and residents' living expenses, including social security allowances (Chisholm et al., 1997). They were valued at levels which approximated as closely as possible to long-run marginal costs. Facility costs were calculated wherever possible from local accounts data, made available by managing agencies (NHS trusts, local authority social services departments, voluntary organizations, or private sector organizations); fees had to be used where accounts data were not made available (this was prevalent among privately managed facilities). It is important to emphasize that the costs are the *actual*, not necessarily the *ideal* costs of hospital or community-based care. The accommodation cost for each resident was calculated as the mean for the facility in which they lived.

*Analyses of cost differences*

Differences between hospital and community costs may reflect not only inherent differences between hospital and community settings in staffing levels and qualifications, but also differences in the characteristics of the people living in them. In particular, we hypothesized that hospital inpatients have clinical, behavioral, and other characteristics which require more specialist medical and nursing support than people living in community accommodation (Knapp et al., 1997). In these circumstances, cost comparisons between hospital and community which are based on today's cost levels should be adjusted for differences in patients or residents between them if the issue being addressed is the shifting balance between settings. That is, comparisons should be made on a like-with-like basis between the costs of accommodating people with the same characteristics (of severity, dependency, etc.) in the two settings. In the absence of randomization – which was never a possibility in this cross-sectional multi-area naturalistic design – standardization was attempted by using multivariate statistical analyses to examine the links between an individual's costs and their clinical and other characteristics. Standardized comparisons *between* hospital and community settings were made by using these estimated community sample equations to predict what the costs would be for people moving into community-based facilities from hospital.

*Comparing the costs of hospital and community care*

The mean and standard deviation costs of care for residents in hospital and community facilities are summarized in Table 2. The costs of hospital care are significantly greater than the costs of care in community accommodation in all eight areas surveyed. However, no adjustment has yet been made for any differences in residents' characteristics between settings.

Table 3 gives hospital-community comparisons, *after* standardization of resident characteristics. Two sets of findings – relating to different hypotheses – are shown. The first of these (marked "A" in Table 2) makes it apparent that in the two London areas and in three of the non-London areas, it would cost more to provide community care for people moving from hospital than it currently costs to support the community care sample ($p<0.05$: $t$-test for equality

*Table 2.* Mental health residential care study: The costs of hospital and community residential accommodation

| Area | Weekly cost (£, 1993/1994 prices) | | | | | | Significance of difference[1] |
|------|------|------|------|------|------|------|------|
| | Hospital | | | Community | | | |
| | mean | *sd* | *n* | mean | *sd* | *n* | |
| **Non-London areas** | | | | | | | |
| Area 1 | 571 | 92 | 26 | 261 | 117 | 62 | <.001 |
| Area 2 | 683 | 126 | 49 | 232 | 89 | 171 | <.001 |
| Area 3 | 619 | 88 | 36 | 258 | 108 | 123 | <.001 |
| Area 4 | 837 | 201 | 49 | 342 | 230 | 129 | <.001 |
| Area 7 | 707 | 186 | 30 | 478 | 271 | 128 | <.001 |
| Area 8 | 726 | 227 | 104 | 275 | 115 | 322 | <.001 |
| **All non-London areas** | 707 | 195 | 294 | 304 | 178 | 935 | <.001 |
| **London areas** | | | | | | | |
| Area 5 | 899 | 165 | 221 | 363 | 201 | 355 | <.001 |
| Area 6 | 871 | 121 | 31 | 447 | 206 | 68 | <.001 |
| **All London areas** | 894 | 160 | 252 | 376 | 204 | 423 | <.001 |

[1] $t$-test for equality of means, prededes by Levene's test of equality of variances (not reported)

of means). Consequently, a health authority or other agency in these areas which seeks to resettle the "average" hospital patient will have to find additional funding. In consequence, the savings of, for example, a dehospitalization program in these five areas would be exaggerated by today's observed average costs. In

219

the other three areas (labeled 1, 2, and 3), moving people from hospital to community residential accommodation would not represent a significant increase or decrease in the costs of their care. (In area 2, the result is marginal; $p=.061$). The available evidence thus provides strong but not universal support for the hypothesis that the cost of care in community residential facilities for people currently accommodated inappropriately in hospital will be higher than the cost of community residential care for people currently in the community.

The findings relevant to the testing of a further hypothesis – that the cost of care in community residential facilities for people currently accommodated in hospital will be lower than the cost of their current hospital care – are also summarized in Table 3 (marked "B"), and provide unequivocal support. The predicted cost of care in community residential facilities for people currently accommodated in hospital is significantly lower than the cost of their current hospital care in all eight areas. In each area, major savings could, therefore, be gained by shifting the balance from hospital to community care for those people covered by this study. The observed average weekly differences in cost be-

*Table 3.* Mental health residential care study: Observed and estimated costs

| Area | Predicted community cost for hospital residents | | Observed costs | | Tests of cost differences[1] | |
|---|---|---|---|---|---|---|
| | (Hyp A) | (Hyp B) | (Hyp A) | | (Hyp B) | |
| | mean | sd | mean | mean | p | p |
| **Non-London areas** | | | | | | |
| Area 1 | 284 | 57 | 261 | 571 | .104 | <.001 |
| Area 2 | 241 | 26 | 232 | 683 | .061 | <.001 |
| Area 3 | 263 | 44 | 258 | 619 | .610 | <.001 |
| Area 4 | 396 | 90 | 342 | 837 | .004 | <.001 |
| Area 7 | 643 | 248 | 478 | 707 | .007 | <.001 |
| Area 8 | 316 | 67 | 275 | 726 | <.001 | <.001 |
| **All non-London areas** | 382 | 114 | 304 | 707 | .001 | <.001 |
| **London areas** | | | | | | |
| Area 5 | 410 | 102 | 363 | 899 | <.001 | <.001 |
| Area 6 | 573 | 180 | 447 | 871 | .001 | <.001 |
| **All London areas** | 437 | 112 | 376 | 894 | <.001 | <.001 |

[1]$t$-test for equality of means

220

tween the two settings in London is £ 518 (= £ 894 – £ 376) and is partly due to the differences in the cost-raising characteristics of residents, equal on average to £ 61 (= £ 437 – £ 376), which is equivalent to 16% of the average London community care cost. However, most of the community-hospital difference in London is due to the fact that hospitals are intrinsically much more costly than community residential facilities, the average difference being £ 457 per resident week (equivalent to 122% of mean community cost). Outside London, the observed average weekly cost difference of £ 403 (= £ 707 – £ 304) is partly due to resident characteristics (£ 87 = £ 382 – £ 304), but again mainly due to the intrinsic difference between hospital and community settings. Again, considerable sums of money could apparently be saved if people inappropriatedly accommodated in hospital were to move to community residential facilities.

## Discussion

Changing the balance between hospital and community has been stimulated by a number of considerations, amongst which are cost and cost-effectiveness arguments. The evaluation of the Friern and Claybury reprovision program has demonstrated that gains can be achieved for long-stay residents across a number of outcome domains by providing community alternatives to hospital, and that these positive outcomes can be attained without a corresponding increase in expenditure (except for the last and most dependent hospital leavers).

Such shifts in the provision and location of services however, require for their implementation and success an adequate level of resources, particularly during the transitional phase a new community schemes are set up and developed. In the specific context of the North London reprovision program, such funding was made available, but more generally, intended changes to the balance of care have been slowed by the insufficient development of appropriate community residents. The results suggest that if inappropriately placed hospital inpatients were able to move to high-support hostels or other form of community accommodation for people with long- and short-term needs for care and support, leading to "bed-blocking" on acute inpatient facilities. The consequences of such a situation are not only clinically problematic, but also unsound economically. The residential care survey reported above included long-stay hospital patients as well as those with shorter admissions and community accommodation, even with seven-day-a-week, 24-hour nursing cover, there would be substantial savings on the costs of their care. The resources currently used to provide hospital inpatient treatment for this inappropriately placed group could be better used, *either* to provide better or more appropriate acute care for people with acute mental health needs *or* to be diverted to the community to fund new accommodation services.

The extent to which resources *can* be channeled towards these respective alternatives, however, is dependent on a number of inter-related issues surrounding the wider debate on long-stay hospital bed closures and acute bed requirements, including the rate at which bed closure programs have already been implemented, the presence of hypothecated and transitional funding to allow for the development of appropriate community accommodation, and the extent of unmet need.

There is certainly evidence to suggest that, particularly in the larger cities, there exists a large pool of unmet need for acute mental health services, including supported accommodation (Johnson et al., 1997). It is also apparent from the North London reprovision program that the relocation of psychiatric services has not eliminated the need for hospitals and the services they provide. There is a continuing need for the clinical and social support which can be obtained from inpatient, daypatient, and outpatient facilities. Put another way, the further reduction of inpatient beds should not be viewed as a simple panacea to achieve an appropriate balance of mental health care. Furthermore, it appears that caring for people with the most severe and complex sets of needs in the community may be *more* expensive than supporting them within the old institutions. In other words, community placement should not simply be viewed as a cheap substitute to inpatient care, but rather as a spectrum of provision that meets the diverse needs of people with mental health problems.

## Acknowledgements

The authors would like to acknowledge the other members of the research teams involved in the two economic studies reported here: 1) the North London Reprovision Program (Martin Knapp, Jennifer Beecham, Barry Baines, Andrew Fenyo and the Team for the Assessment of Psychiatric services). 2) The Mental Health Residential Care Study (Martin Knapp and Jack Astin at CEMH; Paul Lelliott and Bernard Audini at the Royal College of Psychiatrists' Research Unit).

# References

Beecham, J. K., Hallam, A. J., Knapp, M. R. J., et al. (1997) Costing care in the hospital and in the community. In *Community Care: Illusion or Reality?* (Ed. J. Leff). Chichester: John Wiley and Sons.

Beecham, J. K. & Lesage, A. (1997) Transferring lessons on transferring resources. Sante Mentale au Quebec, forthcoming.

Chisholm, D., Knapp, M. R. J., Astin, J., et al. (1997) The mental health residential care study. The costs of provision. *Journal of Mental Health*, **6**, 85–99.

Department of Health and Social Security (1975) *Better Services for the Mentally Ill.* HMSO, London.

Department of Health and Social Security (1983) *Care in the Community, HC(86)3, LAC(83)5.* HMSO, London.

Department of Health and Social Security (1985) *Mental illness: Policies for prevention, treatment, rehabilitation and care, Annex 1 to Government response to the Second Report from the Social Services Committee 1984-85, Cmnd 9624.* HMSO, London.

Department of Health (1989) *Caring for People: Community Care in the Next Decade and Beyond, Cm849.* HMSO, London.

Department of Health (1992) *The Health of the Nation, Cm1523.* HMSO, London.

Drummond, M. F., Stoddart, G. L. & Torrance, G. W. (1987) *Methods for the Economic Evaluation of Health Care Programmes.* Oxford Medical Publications, Oxford.

Hallam, A. J. (1996) Costs and outcomes for people with special psychiatric needs. *Mental Health Research Review*, **3**, Personal Social Services Research Unit, University of Kent at Canterbury.

Hallam, A. J., Beecham, J. K., Knapp, M. R. J. & Baines, B. (1997) Early indications of the long-term costs of psychiatric reprovision. *Mental Health Research Review*, **4**, Personal Social Services Research Unit, University of Kent at Canterbury.

Jarman, B. (1983) Identification of under-privileged areas. *British Medical Journal*, **286**, 1705–1709.

Johnson, S., Ramsey, R., Thornicroft, G., Brooks, E., et al. (Eds.) (1997) *London's Mental Health.* King's Fund, London.

Knapp, M. R. J., Chisholm, D., Astin, J., et al. (1997) The cost consequences of changing the hospital-community balance: The mental health residential care study. *Psychological Medicine*, **27**, 681–692.

Leff, J., Trieman, N. & Gooch, C. (1996) Prospective follow-up study of long-stay patients discharged from two psychiatric hospitals. *American Journal of Psychiatry*, **153**, 10, 1318–1324.

Leff, J., Thornicroft, G., Coxhead, N. & Crawford, C. (1994) A five-year follow-up of long-stay psychiatric patients discharged to the community. *British Journal of Psychiatry*, suppl., **25**, 13–17.

Lelliott, P., Audini, B., Knapp, M. R. J. & Chisholm, D. (1996) The mental health residential care study: Classification of facilities and description of residents. *British Journal of Psychiatry*, **169**, 139–147.

Lelliot, P. & Wing, J. (1994) National audit of new long-stay psychiatric patients: 2. Impact on services. *British Journal of Psychiatry*, **165**, 160–169.

Trieman, N. & Leff, J. (1996a) Difficult to place patients in a psychiatric hospital closure programme. *Psychological Medicine*, **26**, 765–774.

Trieman, N. & Leff, J. (1996b) The most difficult to place long-stay psychiatric inpatients: outcomes one year after relocation. *British Journal of Psychiatry*, **169**, 289–292.

Tyrer, P. & Creed, F. (Eds.) (1995) *Community Psychiatry in Action: Analyses and Prospects.* Cambridge: Cambridge University Press.

# Vocational Rehabilitation in Schizophrenia – New Findings in Outcome Prediction

H. Hoffmann, Z. Kupper and Barbara Kunz

## Introduction

A central issue in the rehabilitation of chronic schizophrenia patients is vocational reintegration. The majority of these patients need the environment of a sheltered workplace, whether this be in suitable enterprises within the special labor market, or in the form of "supported employment." In recent years in the United States, the model of supported employment has received widespread endorsement by its proponents, notably Bond et al. (1995, 1997) and Drake et al. (1995, 1996). Owing to the considerable differences between the socio-economic situation in the USA and that prevalent in Europe, the rate of vocational reintegration into the competitive labor market which is attributed to supported employment programs in the USA cannot be unrestrictedly compared to that achieved by participation in vocational reintegration programs in Europe, such as the $P^ASS$ – Program in Bern (for more detailed information, see Hoffmann, 1998). Even with the help of comprehensive integration programs, reintegration into the competitive labor market remains a very ambitious undertaking. The fact that these programs incur high costs and place substantial demands on human resources should oblige us to screen prospective participants carefully, not least in order to fulfil our responsibility towards the funding authorities. Even when stringent inclusion screening policies are applied, the rate of sustained reintegration into competitive employment lies at about 30% both in the USA and in German-speaking countries. Without pre-selection, the percentage would drop sharply, e.g., to the 5%–10% recorded in Bern (see Hoffmann, 1999).

Admission to a reintegration program is linked with feelings of hope and trust on the part of patients, their relatives and caregivers that the program will make vocational reintegration possible. If expectancies are not fulfilled, the disappointment is great, and some patients suffer severe crises when faced with failure. For all these reasons, we have been intensively investigating aspects of dynamics in rehabilitation and outcome prediction in vocational reintegration (Hoffmann & Kupper, 1996, 1997a & b, Hoffmann et al., 1998 a & b, Kupper & Hoffmann, 1995, 1996, 1998, Kupper, 1998). It appeared that very little has been published on outcome prediction in vocational rehabilitation in recent years. The most comprehensive overview is still to be found in the review article of Anthony and Jansen (1984). They postulated nine hypotheses, which are summarized in Table 1.

*Table 1.* Predictors of future work performance of the chronically mentally ill: Summary of the nine hypotheses of Anthony and Jansen (1984)

---

1. Psychiatric symptomatology is a poor predictor.
2. Diagnostic category is a poor predictor.
3. Intelligence, aptitude, and personality tests are a poor predictor.
4. A person's ability to function in one environment (e.g., a community setting) is not predictive of a person's ability to function in a different environment (e.g., a work setting).
5. There is little or no correlation between a person's symptomatology and functional skills.
6. The best clinical predictors are ratings of a person's work adjustment skills made in a workshop or sheltered job site.
7. The best demographic predictor is the person's prior employment history.
8. A significant predictor is a person's ability to "get along" or function socially with others.
9. The best paper-and-pencil test predictors are tests that measure a person's ego strength or self-concept in the role of worker.

---

Anthony and Jansen based their hypotheses on Anglo-American studies carried out between the late 1960s and early 1980s. With very few exceptions, however, all these studies exhibit distinct methodological shortcomings. Apart from that of Strauss and Carpenter (1972), all had diagnostically heterogeneous and poorly described populations. In some, the sample was not characterized at all (Green et al., 1968; Wilson et al., 1969) or simply described as "chronically psychotic patients" (Distefano & Pryer, 1970; Griffiths, 1974). None of the studies compared diagnostic discrete groups of patients with schizophrenia, affective, and non-psychotic disorders respectively. It was not until the early 1990s that two comparative studies were undertaken (Jacobs et al., 1992; Fabian, 1992). Both revealed that persons with schizophrenia had a poorer vocational outcome than those with other disorders.

On the other hand, it must not be forgotten that in the 1960s and early 1970s instruments for the reliable assessment of either social competence or psychopathology did not yet exist. It was only in 1974 that the concept of positive and negative symptoms was brought into discussion by Strauss et al. The "Prognostic Scale" developed by Strauss and Carpenter (1974), for example, contained only two items on social relationships, i.e., "frequency of social contacts" and "marital status," as well as three psychopathological items, viz., "flattened emotions," "presence of thought disorder, delusions or hallucinations"; and "presence of depression, hypomania or mania."

A further shortcoming of early rehabilitation research is that the samples were generally not very representative of the population that usually participates in vocational rehabilitation programs. Thus, for example, long-term hospitalized patients, who could draw little or no benefit from such programs, were often included in the samples.

The objective of the present study was to investigate Anthony and Jansen's nine hypotheses. As previously mentioned, the studies of Fabian and of Jacobs et al. indicated that schizophrenia patients have the poorest reintegration prognosis of all those suffering from chronic mental illness. Based on the findings of a previous study (Hoffmann & Kupper, 1997b), we hypothesized that in schizophrenia, psychopathology – and most particularly negative symptoms – have a decisive influence on prognosis. We therefore restricted our sample to chronic schizophrenia patients.

# Methods

*Background*
The $P^A SS$ -Program for vocational reintegration into competitive full-time employment developed at the University Psychiatric Services Bern has been described in detail elsewhere (Dauwalder & Hoffmann, 1992; Hoffmann & Kupper, 1997a). Patients attend a 5-phase program for a maximum of 18 months. Phase 1 is the assessment phase and lasts for two weeks, at the end of which, patients demonstrating less than 40–50% of ordinary work performance are excluded. Other exclusion criteria include a high level of manifest psychotic symptoms or insufficient motivation. Phase 2 takes place in a program-integrated workshop with a capacity for 15 participants. After approximately six months, during phases 3 and 4, the patients begin working on training jobs in local companies. Phase 5 is the aftercare phase. From the third phase onward, a mobile rehabilitation team supports not only the patients in their training jobs, but also their co-workers and supervisors. Other significant aspects of the program are the social skills training group, which meets twice weekly, and intervention in the relevant social environment, in the form of monthly systemic family therapy.

227

*Subjects*

To date, 69 patients have been enrolled in the program; 53 (77%) met DSM-III-R criteria for schizophrenia. Their average age was 27.7 years (SD 5.0). Sixteen participants were female (= 30%). Four patients were married, 7 separated, divorced or widowed, and the rest single. The mean duration of mental disorder was 5.0 years (SD 4.7,) during which time the patients had been admitted an average of 2.5 times (SD 2.1). Thirty-five (= 66%) had completed vocational training, 7 (= 13%) had failed to pass their final examination and only 11 (= 21%) were unskilled. The mean duration of unemployment before entering the program was 16.4 months (SD 14.5). On the Global Assessment of Functioning Scale (GAF), they scored an average of 43.3 points (SD 6.0), i.e., they were all seriously impaired in their social or occupational functioning.

*Measures*

For testing the nine hypotheses of Anthony and Jansen (1984), the following instruments were administered during the two weeks of the assessment phase as independent variables:

For testing hypotheses 1 and 5, the patient's symptomatology was assessed by the *Positive and Negative Syndrome Scale* (PANSS; Kay et al., 1992). The PANSS is a 30-item rating scale that constitutes three rationally derived categories: Positive symptoms, negative symptoms and general symptoms. All ratings were done by the first two authors, who were trained beforehand by rating videotapes of Kay et al.

For testing hypothesis 2, the remaining 16 non-schizophrenia participants of the $P^{A}SS$ – Program (10 patients with affective, and 6 with non-psychotic disorders) were not further allocated to subgroups. This small proportion of non-schizophrenia patients is attributable to the concept of the rehabilitation, which was designed primarily for patients with the diagnosis of schizophrenia. In all except two non-schizophrenia patients, the socio-demographic and work history data showed no significant differences from the schizophrenia sample. The mean age and consequently the duration of illness were significantly higher in the non-schizophrenia patients.

Since, to our knowledge, no comprehensive, useful instrument for testing vocational rehabilitation aptitude is available, we decided to dispense with aptitude tests in investigating hypothesis 3. To test intelligence, we used the German version of the *Wechsler Adult Intelligence Scale* (WAIS, Wechsler, 1964). As personality tests we selected the *Frankfurt Self-Concept Scales* (FSKN), constructed by Deusinger (1986), and the *IPC Scales* by Krampen (1981).

The FSKN distinguishes 10 different self-concepts, representing four dimensions of the self: The dimensions of competence and achievement, self-esteem, affects and sensibility, and a psychosocial dimension. The FSKN is a

228

self-report instrument comprising 78 items in a six-point Likert scale format, ranging from "fits very well" to "does not fit at all." Consistent with the studies of Deusinger, in our sample, all 10 scales were highly intercorrelated (Pearson's $r$ ranged from .44 to .81), and internal consistency was excellent (Cronbach's $\alpha = .95$). These results legitimized our using the sum score of the 10 scales as an overall measure of self-concepts.

The *IPC Scales* are a German instrument to measure perceived locus of control (LOC) as attributed to an internal (I) source, powerful others (P), or chance (C), and are a re-conceptualization of Rotter's *ROT-IE* (1966). The major differences from the *ROT-IE* are the three-dimensionality of the *IPC Scales*, and that each statistically independent scale consists of eight items in a six-point Likert scale format ranging from "completely wrong" to "absolutely correct." The items measure the degree to which a person perceives events in his life as being a consequence of his own acts, under the control of powerful others, or determined by chance.

The patient's functioning, as described in hypothesis 4, was assessed in an interview with the patient's closest relative by using the *Disability Assessment Schedule* (DAS-M, Jung et al., 1989). On grounds of the hypothesis, we decided to omit both items concerning the occupational role. All other items – including the overall assessment of social functioning – are listed in Table 2. For every item, intensity was rated on a 4-point scale and duration (i.e., whether manifest for more than half of the days of the previous month) was rated on a 2-point scale. The ratings were done by the two interviewers, who reached agreement on each item. The scores finally assigned were the sums of the scores for intensity and duration.

Our *Vocational Competence Scale*, the *Work Behavior Assessment Scale* (WBAS, Ciompi et al., 1977, 1979) and the sum score of the *Nurses' Observation Scale for Inpatient Evaluation* (NOSIE-30, Honigfeld, 1974; Honigfeld et al., 1986) were used to assess work adjustment skills made in a workshop or sheltered job site as posited in hypothesis 6.

Vocational competence was assessed weekly by two workshop supervisors in the $P^ASS$ – Program, using our specially constructed *Vocational Competence Scale*. This easy-to-handle eleven-point Likert scale format (ranging from "very poor" to "excellent") assesses the overall level of vocational competence, reflecting relevant work-related behavior such as performance, quality of work, and punctuality. This scale has been shown to correlate meaningfully (Pearson's $r = 0.70 - 0.94$) with a majority of the factors of the NOSIE-30 (Kupper, 1998).

The WBAS consists of fifteen 6-point scaled items, representing the three dimensions: "Work performance," "work attitudes" and "social relationships." The validity and reliability of all categories proved to be good to excellent (Dauwalder et al., 1978). The WBAS was introduced into our rehabilitation

229

unit in 1978 and has been in use for monthly work assessments since then. For this study, the ratings were made at the end of the assessment phase by consensus between two work supervisors. The z-transformed values of the 15 items were summarized to compose an overall score.

The NOSIE-30 is a short, widely-implemented scale with 30 items, representing 7 factors that can be grouped into sub-scores of positive and negative factors and a global score. The scores are easy to rate, and as an instrument, the NOSIE-30 is sensitive to changes in behavior in terms of both personal and social functioning and symptomatology. In a former study, we were able to demonstrate that the NOSIE-30 can also successfully be used in evaluating outpatients, as it allowed us to monitor outpatient dynamics in vocational rehabilitation more accurately than by using the *Vocational Competence Scale* (Hoffmann & Kupper, 1996). NOSIE-30 ratings were performed weekly in the vocational rehabilitation unit by the same two staff members, who reached consensus on the scores. At the training jobs, weekly ratings were done by the supervisors, who had been introduced to the rating procedures by rehabilitation staff members. Inter-rater reliability and consistency testing are reported in detail in Hoffmann et al. (1998a).

For testing hypothesis 7, we assessed each patient's prior employment history, including the level of education, total time of unemployment, employment rate since 20 years of age, and the rate for the previous two years.

The patient's ability to "get along" or function socially with others (hypothesis 8) was assessed with four variables from different instruments: (1) the "disorder of relating"-variable is the dimension of relating (including the items "emotional withdrawal" and "passive/apathetic social withdrawal") in the four-syndrome model of the PANSS proposed by Cuesta and Peralta (1995); (2) "social withdrawal" is an item of the DAS-M; (3) overall "social competence" was assessed weekly, analogous to "vocational competence," using an eleven-point Likert format scale (ranging from "very poor" to "excellent"). This scale assesses the overall level of relevant social behavior such as coping with negative feedback, conversational skills, and co-operating with co-workers and supervisors. It has also been shown to correlate in a meaningful way with subscales of the NOSIE-30, e.g., positively with "social interest," and negatively with "irritability" and "depression" (Kupper, 1998); and (4) "social relationships" is – as described above – one dimension of the WBAS.

Since the concept of ego strength has not found broad use in empirical research and self-concept generally is assessed without a focus on the role of worker, we approached hypothesis 9 by using the construct of locus of control. As perceived control reflects the person's generalized sense of confidence and experience of self as either a hopeful, causal agent in the world or as a despairing victim who is acted upon, the *IPC Scales* seem to be an appropriate measure to assess important aspects of a peron's self-concept, beliefs, and expectations (for further details see Hoffmann et al., 1998b).

To assess outcome prediction, the following three measures were chosen as dependent variables in all hypotheses but No. 5: (1) The mean of the weekly administered *Vocational Competence Scale* during the whole course of the program. At the training jobs, weekly ratings were performed by the supervisors who had been introduced to the rating procedure by rehabilitation staff members. (2) The mean of the monthly *Work Behavior Assessment Scale* (WBAS) during the whole course of the program; (3) As in previous studies, (Hoffmann & Kupper, 1997b; Hoffmann et al., 1998b), the patient's rehabilitation "outcome" was determined by the highest level he had reached in the 5-phase program: 1 = dropped out of the program after the assessment phase ($n = 14$); 2 = dropped out of the program in phase 2 ($n = 19$); 3 = dropped out from the training job in phase 3 or 4 ($n = 6$); 4 = obtained competitive full-time employment, but lost the job in phase 5 within the following six months ($n = 4$); 5 = obtained and maintained competitive employment for over six months ($n = 10$). The assessment of the person's "outcome" was carried out six months after the termination of the program.

We chose not only one but three dependent outcome measures, since each assesses a slightly different aspect of vocational rehabilitation. The first two assess vocational performance in the long-term course, whereby the first of these was administered at frequent intervals for the sake of expediency, the second was advantageous in that it was complemented by "work attitudes" and "social relationships" dimensions, and the third represented the goal of the vocational integration process that is influenced not only by patient-dependent factors but also by factors in the environment.

For testing hypothesis 5, the means of the *Nurses' Observation Scale for Inpatient Evaluation* (NOSIE-30), which were assessed weekly during the entire program, and the DAS-M overall assessment (administered in the assessment phase) were used to represent functional skills.

*Procedure:* Pearson's and Spearman's correlations, multiple backward and logistic regressions were computed by using SAS (1989) statistical software. Only those variables were put into a regression model that had correlated significantly ($p < .05$) with the dependent outcome measure.

# Results

The results of the correlational analyses presented in Table 2 (except the hypotheses 2 and 5) demonstrate that the three dependent outcome measures

*Table 2.* Correlations between the three dependent outcome measures and the administered measures of the nine hypotheses (excluding the hypotheses 2 and 5)

| Hypothesis | Measures | Vocational competence (weekly) | Work behavior assessment scale (WBAS, monthly) | Outcome |
|---|---|---|---|---|
| 1 | Positive symptoms (PANSS) | −.11 | −.11 | .07 |
| | Negative symptoms (PANSS) | −.50 **** | −.56 **** | −.38 ** |
| | General symptoms (PANSS) | −.39 ** | −.41 ** | −.16 |
| 3 | WAIS verbal | .22 | .25 T | .17 |
| | WAIS non-verbal | .41 ** | .39 ** | .37 ** |
| | Self-concept (FSKN sum score) | .23 | .18 | .31 * |
| | Internal locus of control (I) | .05 | .06 | .10 |
| | External locus of control: powerful others (P) | −.39 ** | −.38 ** | −.38 ** |
| | External locus of control: chance (C) | −.43 ** | −.41 ** | −.45 *** |
| 4 | Self-care (DAS-M) | −.43 ** | −.47 *** | −.34 * |
| | Spare-time activity (DAS-M) | −.37 ** | −.35 * | −.26 T |
| | Slowness (DAS-M) | −.33 * | −.36 * | −.08 |
| | Social withdrawal (DAS-M) | −.34 * | −.42 ** | −.11 |
| | Friction in interpersonal relationships (DAS-M) | 0.29 T | −.18 | −.25 |
| | Emergency or crisis behavior (DAS-M) | −.39 ** | −.50 *** | −.16 |
| | Participation in household (DAS-M) | −.39 ** | −.41 ** | −.13 |
| | Heterosexual role behavior (DAS-M) | −.47 ** | −.46 ** | −.36 * |
| | Interest in and demand for information (DAS-M) | −.34 * | −.47 *** | −.24 |
| | Overall assessment of social functioning (DAS-M) | −.36 * | −.48 *** | −.13 |
| 6 | Vocational competence (2 weeks) | .79 **** | .57 **** | .34 * |
| | Work behavior assessment scale (2 weeks) | .62 ** | .75 **** | .34 * |
| | NOSIE-30 global score | .46 *** | .55 **** | .10 |
| 7 | Unemployment | .08 | .14 | −.10 |
| | Employment rate since 20 years of age | −.01 | −.02 | −.12 |
| | Employment rate for the last 2 years | −.16 | −.09 | −.11 |
| | Education | .02 | −.09 | −.10 |

*Table 2 (continued)*

| Hypothesis | Measures | Vocational competence (weekly) | Work behavior assessment scale (WBAS, monthly) | Outcome |
|---|---|---|---|---|
| 8 | Disorder of relating (PANSS) | −.53 **** | −.48 *** | −.36 ** |
|  | Social withdrawal (DAS-M) | −.34 * | -.42 ** | −.11 |
|  | Social competence (2 weeks) | .45 ** | .52 *** | .16 |
|  | Social relationships (2 weeks) | .45 *** | .61 **** | .20 |
| 9 | Internal locus of control (I) | .05 | .06 | .10 |
|  | External locus of control: powerful others (P) | −.39 ** | −.38 ** | −.38 ** |
|  | External locus of control: chance (C) | −.43 ** | −.41 ** | −.45 *** |

T: $p < .1$; *: $p < .05$; **: $p < .01$; ***: $p < .001$; ****: $p = .0001$

differ only slightly in correlating with the independent measures. Only "outcome" shows a lower correlation than the two other dependent measures, with the variables of the hypotheses 4 and 8, representing different aspects of social functioning, and with hypothesis 6.

The correlations of positive symptoms, verbal intelligence measures, internal locus of control, friction in interpersonal relationships and all variables of hypothesis 7 with the outcome variables did not reach significance level. All other variables correlated significantly at least with one of the outcome measures, and were therefore used for the regression analyses.

Testing hypothesis 2, in which diagnosis is postulated as a poor predictor, revealed almost identical findings between schizophrenia ($n = 53$) and non-schizophrenia ($n = 16$) patients in all three outcome variables. The correlations between positive, negative, and general symptoms and the means of the NOSIE-30 global score and the DAS-M overall assessment (hypothesis 5) were all significant (with $r$ ranging from .38 to .66).

The results of regression analyses are summarized in Table 3. One major finding is that negative symptoms have high predictive value for vocational performance and outcome. Moreover, the variance of a patient's functional skills is explained to a considerable degree by schizophrenia symptoms. Thus, Anthony and Jansen's hypotheses 1 and 5 must be rejected for schizophrenia patients. By testing hypothesis 3, it became evident that the non-verbal part of the WAIS and the chance (C) dimension of locus of control (representing fatalism) predict vocational performance to about the same extent. The chance (C) dimension of locus of control (hypotheses 3 and 9) proved to be not only better than self-concept but the best predictor of outcome. Some social functioning

*Table 3*. Summary of the multiple backward and logistic regressions with the measures of the nine hypotheses (excluding the hypotheses 2 and 7)

| Hypothesis | Variables left | Vocational competence (weekly) | WBAS (monthly) | Outcome Association of predicted probabilities: concordant | discordant | tied | NOSIE global score | DAS-M overall assessment |
|---|---|---|---|---|---|---|---|---|
| | | Explained variance in the model: | | | | | Explained variance: | |
| 1 | Negative symptoms | 25% | 32% | 63.5% | 32.6% | 3.9%[1] | | |
| 3 | WAIS non-verbal | 17% | 15% | 64.3% | 32.1% | 3.6%[2] | | |
| | Self-concept (FSKN sum score) | | | 63.4% | 36.3% | 0.3%[3] | | |
| | External locus of control: chance (C) | 18% | 16% | 67.6% | 28.4% | 4.0%[4] | | |
| 4 | Self-care (DAS-M) | | | | | | | |
| | Heterosexual role behavior (DAS-M) | 24% | | | | | | |
| | Emergency or crisis behavior (DAS-M) | | | | | | | |
| | Participation in household (DAS-M) | | 29% | | | | | |
| | Self-care (DAS-M) | | | 49.7% | 24.5% | 25.7%[5] | | |
| 5 | Negative symptoms (PANSS) | | | | | | | |
| | General symptoms (PANSS) | | | | | | | |
| | Positive symptoms (PANSS) | | | | | | | |
| | Negative symptoms (PANSS) | | | | | | 51% | 33% |

Table 3 (continued)

| | | | | | | |
|---|---|---|---|---|---|---|
| 6 | Work behavior assessment scale (WBAS, 2 weeks) | 39% | | | | |
| | NOSIE-30 gobal score | | 40% | | | |
| | Vocational competence (2 weeks) | | | 59.1% | 32.0% | 9.0%[6] |
| | Vocational competence (2 weeks) | | | | | |
| 8 | Social competence (2 weeks) | 35% | 51% | | | |
| | Social relationships (2 weeks) | | | | | |
| | Disorder of relating (PANSS) | | | 59.5% | 29.6% | 10.9%[7] |
| 9 | External locus of control: chance (C) | 18% | 16% | 67.6% | 28.4% | 4.0%[4] |

[1] effect = 6.88, $df = 1$, $p < .01$ [2] effect = 9.67, $df = 1$, $p < .01$ [3] effect = 5.56, $df = 1$, $p < .05$ [4] effect = 12.11, $df = 1$, $p < .001$ [5] effect = 5.20, $df = 1$, $p < .05$ [6] effect = 7.11, $df = 1$, $p < .01$ [7] effect = 6.13, $df = 1$, $p < .05$

abilities (not assessed in a vocational environment) seem to have a certain predictive value on vocational performance and outcome – a finding that sharply contrasts with Anthony and Jansen's hypothesis 4. On the other hand, our findings that a person's work adjustment skills and ability to function socially with others are good predictors of future work performance are completely in line with Anthony and Jansen's hypotheses 6 and 8.

## Discussion

The findings of the present study confirm our assumption that the majority of Anthony and Jansen's hypotheses cannot withstand re-examination if newer, more sensitive instruments are administered and a sample of chronic schizophrenic outpatients, for whom a vocational rehabilitation program seems indicated, are chosen, instead of a heterogeneous sample of the chronically mentally ill.

A crucial problem in vocational outcome research is that no consensus prevails concerning the definition of outcome. The term "outcome," therefore, means different things across studies and each investigator conceptualizes and measures a different notion of it. Consequently, a cross-comparison of results in studies that have implemented different measures is difficult. This, of course, holds equally true for the independent measures. To minimize this difficulty, in our study we administered various instruments that assess different aspects of the same variable, e.g., outcome, social functioning, or social relations. These yielded consistent results throughout.

One caveat is that we investigated a selected population of fairly stabilized schizophrenia outpatients who exhibited only few positive symptoms such as delusions and hallucinations. These patients were motivated to become socially and vocationally reintegrated, and attained a minimum work performance comparable to 40–50% of ordinary work performance. They are not representative of the entirety of the chronic schizophrenic outpatient population, but rather of those who are possible candidates for a rehabilitation program for vocational reintegration into competitive employment. Therefore, this study may be considered a useful contribution to a more precise circumscription of the population that could best profit from a comprehensive vocational integration or supported employment program. Furthermore, it demonstrates that research with more homogeneous, well-defined samples clarifies some contradictory results arising from broadly-defined, samples of the chronically mentally ill.

*Hypothesis 1:* Our findings correspond with those of Pogue-Geile and Harrow (1985), Massel et al. (1990), Solinski et al. (1992), Lysaker & Bell (1995),

Anthony et al. (1995), and Hoffmann & Kupper (1997b), all of whom found a significant negative correlation between work performance and negative symptoms. It is notable that Anthony et al. (1995) found a moderate relationship between symptomatology, as assessed by the BPRS and work skills, and a stronger relationship between negative symptoms and work skills. Nonetheless, it seems that they subsequently attempted to moderate their original position on this relationship by stating that "symptoms should not be considered a proxy measure for vocational functioning among persons with severe mental illness." On the other hand, it has since become evident that negative symptoms are the typical and enduring characteristic feature in the long-term course of schizophrenia (Pogue-Geile & Harrow, 1985; Fenton & McGlashan, 1994), and that prominent negative symptoms are accompanied by a distinctly unfavorable course of the disease (Andreasen, 1985; Crow, 1985; Carpenter et al., 1988).

*Hypothesis 2:* The potential predictive value of the diagnostic category is still a controversial subject in the literature. Primarily earlier studies, but also those by Mowbray et al. (1995) and Reker et al. (1996) as well as our findings, attribute no predictive value to diagnosis. In contrast, Strauss & Carpenter (1972), Bell et al. (1990), Fabian (1992), Jacobs et al. (1992), and Beiser et al. (1994) have all verified a significantly poorer vocational outcome for schizophrenia patients. This conflict of findings becomes even more evident in the study of Anthony et al. (1995), where a poorer outcome in schizophrenia patients was reported, although no significant difference in work skills among the diagnostic subgroups was found. A possible explanation for these divergent findings may be the different criteria applied for the selection of the samples. The greater the need for vocational rehabilitation as a consequence of the individual's disability, and the less representative the sample is for the whole population of a disorder, the more minor the role that diagnosis plays.

*Hypothesis 3:* The WAIS was used in various studies on schizophrenia to control for signs of general cognitive impairment (Dickerson et al., 1991; Corrigan, 1994; Brekke et al., 1997; Iverson et al., 1998; Kupper & Hoffmann, 1998). If one does not focus on the results of its subtests, this is a rather global measure of neurocognitive functioning that only leads to equally global conclusions such as "smarter patients function better than duller patients" (Green, 1996). Therefore, in several studies the WAIS has been supplemented or replaced by more specific instruments (cf. review of Green, 1996). In one of these studies it was demonstrated that cognitive impairments such as thought disorder, deficits in information processing, and poor concept formation can discriminate patients who improve in the course of a vocational rehabilitation program from those who do not (Lysaker et al., 1995), which substantiates our finding. Thus, not only intelligence, but also more specific cognitive impairments may have predictive value for vocational competence and outcome in schizophrenia patients.

It is notable that both personality tests proved to be good-to-excellent predictors of vocational outcome. These findings underline Strauss's statement (1989) that the long-term course and outcome of schizophrenia are determined by the interaction between the disorder and the person, and also Eugen Bleuler's notion (1911) that deterioration and improvement in the long-term course of schizophrenia often depend on the patient's self.

The finding that persons suffering from a chronic disease report a significantly higher external locus of control has been replicated several times (Strickland, 1978; Wallston & Wallston, 1981 & 1982), as has the relationship of external locus of control with generally poor adjustment (Krause & Stryker, 1984; Flemming & Spooner, 1985; Layton, 1985). Numerous studies have also reported schizophrenia patients to score more external on locus of control than other diagnostic groups (Seeman & Evans, 1962; Harrow & Ferrante, 1969; Cash & Stack, 1973; Varkey & Sathyavathi, 1984; Goodman et al., 1994). Therefore, it is not surprising that fatalism is also a good predictor of vocational performance and outcome in chronic schizophrenia patients. Wehmeyer (1994) reached, albeit in a different context, the same conclusion: "Individuals who have more internal orientations are probably more likely to obtain competitive employment, whereas individuals with more external orientations may be more likely to be in more sheltered environments or unemployed."

*Hypothesis 4:* Our findings are in line with those of Tessler and Manderscheid (1982) and Arns and Linney (1995), who both found that functional skills in non-vocational environments have a strong positive relationship to the level of vocational independence in the chronically mentally ill. In a multivariate regression analysis, Mowbray et al. (1995) also attested predictive value for work status to functional skills. These congruent findings would indicate the rejection of Anthony and Jansen's hypothesis.

*Hypothesis 5:* In a recently published study we demonstrated that schizophrenia outpatients' behavior (assessed by the NOSIE-30) can be predicted by the PANSS dimensions "conceptual disorganization" and "disorder of relating" (Hoffmann et al., 1998a), results which are corroborated by the present findings. Furthermore, relationships between psychopathology and social competence have been revealed in several studies (Jackson et al., 1989a & b; Bellack et al., 1990; Mueser et al., 1990; Solinski et al., 1992; Hoffmann & Kupper, 1997b). All these studies reported significant correlations between social competence and negative symptoms, but not with positive symptoms (see also Halford & Hayes, 1995). An explanation of these findings may be that some scales for rating negative symptoms include items which relate to social functioning. Thus, the apparent ability of negative symptom scores to predict poor

238

social functioning may in some cases partly reflect a conceptual overlap between ratings on scales for negative symptoms and those used to rate social competence (see also Barnes & Liddle, 1990). Therefore, whether the deficits in social competence are the sequelae of, or synonymous with negative symptoms cannot be determined (Jackson et al. 1989a); and the question of whether negative symptoms are a manifestation of social impairment or *vice versa* is still unanswered (Bellack et al., 1990).

*Hypothesis 6:* That a person's behavior in a workshop or sheltered job site has a high predictive value for future work competence and behavior is not surprising, since important aspects of successful work behavior are assessed with these instruments by well trained and experienced supervisors. Furthermore, dependent and independent instruments are partly identical. Therefore, the most robust regression is the one on "outcome." An earlier study (Hoffmann & Kupper, 1997b) also yielded work performance in the program's workshop as a significant predictor of "outcome," but negative symptoms and social competence proved to be the better predictors, both cross-sectionally and in the long-term course. Thus, the conclusion may be drawn that the ratings of a person's work adjustment skills acquired in a workshop or sheltered job site constitute very good, but not the best clinical predictors. Nevertheless, as work adjustment skills are relatively easy to assess and usable across all diagnoses, they should continue to be essential components of every work-related assessment.

*Hypothesis 7:* Our findings that the level of education is a poor outcome predictor are not only in line with those of Anthony & Jansen (1984) but also those of Gmür (1987), who restricted his sample to schizophrenia patients. On the other hand, our results indicating that a person's prior employment history is a poor predictor of outcome are inconsistent with the literature (see overview in Weis, 1990). Buell and Anthony (1973), for example, reported that employment history accounts for 53% of the variance in the post-hospitalization employment rate. A possible explanation for the present findings may be the quite rigorous eligibility criteria for the $P^ASS$ – Program, which may discourage patients with a poor work history from applying. It is of particular interest that in a sample where this obviously strong predictor of outcome is no longer of central importance due to the screening procedure, other, more subtle factors become prominent.

*Hypothesis 8* is the only hypothesis with which we can fully agree. This concurrence is founded upon the results of the studies on social skills training (Wallace et al., 1992; Bellack & Mueser, 1993) and on the present findings, where it is remarkable that the "disorder of relating" dimension is as predictive of outcome as is vocational competence. These findings are supported by those of an earlier study (Hoffmann & Kupper, 1997b), where we showed that disorder of relating and social competence, as assessed by the *Role Play Test*, have major impact on outcome as postulated by Anthony & Jansen (1984) and in the studies of Strauss and Carpenter (1977) and Ciompi et al. (1979).

*Hypothesis 9:* Our findings substantiate the results of a recently completed study on resignation, where fatalism proved to be the best predictor of poor vocational outcome together with other relevant factors such as locus of control by powerful others, outcome expectations, negative symptoms, and depressed-resigned coping (Hoffmann et al., 1998b). We reported that individuals who tend to believe that they exercise little or no control in a specific situation are inclined to generalize this belief and will, when experiencing a situation of real uncontrollability, be quicker to react helplessly and give up. The interaction between the individual's behavior and the disorder appears to be not linear but circular, and may lead to reciprocal escalation and stagnation in a vicious circle. The patient seems to develop negative behavioral motivation, to lose self-confidence, become demoralized, and finally give up believing in a successful outcome. In time, such interaction patterns may become increasingly stable, and as a consequence, the disorder becomes chronic, which itself precludes frequent active, change-oriented coping behavior. Once the role of being a chronic patient is adopted as a mode of coping, the individual allows others to take control and gives up expectations for the future. The belief in future achievements is crucial to successful rehabilitation outcome. With this in mind, it may be hypothesized that the *IPC Scales* are an excellent paper-and-pencil test for predicting vocational reintegration.

*Table 4.* Predictors of the vocational reintegration of schizophrenia outpatients for whom a vocational rehabilitation program seems indicated

1. Negative symptoms are good predictors, but positive symptoms are not.
2. It remains unclear to what extent diagnosis has predictive value.
3. Intelligence and personality tests have predictive value.
4. A person's social functioning abilities in non-vocational environments and spheres of life are predictive of a person's ability to function in a work setting.
5. There is a significant correlation between a person's symptoms and functional skills.
6. Ratings of a person's work adjustment skills made in a workshop or sheltered job site are good clinical predictors.
7. A person's level of education and prior employment history are poor predictors.
8. A significant predictor is a person's ability to "get along" or function socially with others.
9. An excellent paper-and-pencil test predictor is a test that measures a person's locus of control.

Based on our findings and the above discussion, we have reformulated Anthony and Jansen's hypotheses for schizophrenia patients. These are presented in Table 4.

Although we have demonstrated in the present study that negative symptoms have important predictive value in a sample of chronic schizophrenia outpatients, and that psychopathological parameters are more instrumental in the prediction of work performance than was previously assumed, psychopathology alone does not account for outcome, but should be viewed as one important factor among several. In order to obtain a comprehensive appraisal of vocational capacity in schizophrenia patients, the eligibility assessment of every vocational rehabilitation program should combine measures of psychopathology with other predictive measures. These would ideally include cognitive impairment, vocational and social competence in a workshop setting, social functioning in non-vocational environments and personality tests sensitive to fatalistic beliefs, since these have at least the same predictive value for poor outcome as do negative symptoms.

The reformulated hypotheses, based on the findings of the present study, make no claim to universal validity. Further studies are needed to substantiate them, and not only with samples of chronic schizophrenia outpatients for whom vocational reintegration seems to be indicated. However, our results find substantial support in other recent studies and provide evidence that Anthony and Jansen's hypotheses should be used only with great caution when predicting vocational capacity and outcome.

## Acknowledgements

This research was supported by the Swiss National Science Foundation, Grant 3200-028795.

## References

Andreasen, N. (1985) Positive and negative schizophrenia: Definition and reliability. *Archives of General Psychiatry*, **39**, 784–788.

Anthony, W. A. & Jansen, M. A. (1984) Predicting the vocational capacity of the chronically mentally ill. Research and policy implications. *American Psychologist*, **39**, 537–544.

Anthony, W. A., Rogers, E. S., Cohen, M. & Davies, R. R. (1995) Relationships between psychiatric symtomatology, work skills, and future vocational performance. *Psychiatric Services*, **46**, 353–358.

Arns, P. G. & Linney, J. A. (1995) Relating functional skills of severely mentally ill clients to subjective and societal benefits. *Psychiatric Services,* **46**, 260–265.

Barnes, T. R. E. & Liddle, P. F. (1990) Evidence for the validity of negative symptoms. In *Schizophrenia: Positive and Negative Symptoms and Syndromes* (Ed. Andreasen, N. C.), pp. 43–72. Basel: Karger.

Beiser, M., Bean, G., Erickson, D., et al. (1994) Biological and psychological predictors of job performance following a first episode psychosis. *American Journal of Psychiatry,* **151**, 857–863.

Bell, V., Blumenthal, St., Neumann, N.-U., et al. (1990) Integration und Reintegration ersteingewiesener psychiatrischer Patienten. *Psychiatrische Praxis,* **17**, 144–149.

Bellack, A. S., Morrison, R. L., Wixted, J. T. & Mueser, K. T. (1990) An analysis of social competence in schizophrenia. *British Journal of Psychiatry,* **156**, 809–818.

Bellack, A. S. & Mueser, K. T. (1993) Psychosocial treatment for schizophrenia. *Schizophrenia Bulletin,* **19**, 317–336.

Bleuler, E. (1911) *Dementia Praecox or the Group of Schizophrenias.* New York: Universities Press.

Bond, G. R., Dietzen, L. L., McGrew, J. H. & Miller, L. D. (1995) Accelerating entry into supported employment for persons with severe psychiatric disabilities. *Rehabilitation Psychology,* **40**, 75–93.

Bond, G. R., Drake, R. E., Mueser, K. T. & Becker, D. R. (1997) An update on supported employment for people with severe mental illness. *Psychiatric Services,* **48**, 335–346.

Brekke, J. S., Raine, A., Ansel, M., et al. (1997) Neuropsychological and psychophysiological correlates of psychosocial functioning in schizophrenia. *Schizophrenia Bulletin,* **23**, 19–28.

Buell, G. & Anthony, W. (1973) Demographic characteristics as predictors of recidivism, and post-hospital employment. *Journal of Consulting & Clinical Psychology,* **20**, 361–365.

Carpenter, W. T., Heinrichs, D. W. & Wagman, A. M. (1988) Deficit and nondeficit forms of schizophrenia. *American Journal of Psychiatry,* **145**, 578–583.

Cash, T. F. & Stack, J. J. (1973) Locus of control among schizophrenics and other hospitalized psychiatric patients. *Genetic Psychology Monographs,* **87**, 105–122.

Ciompi, L., Ague, C. & Dauwalder, J. P. (1977) Ein Forschungsprogramm zur Rehabilitation psychisch Kranker. I. Konzepte und methodologische Probleme. *Nervenarzt,* **48**, 12–18.

Ciompi, L., Dauwalder, H. P. & Ague, C. (1979) Ein Forschungsprogramm zur Rehabilitation psychisch Kranker. III. Längsschnittuntersuchungen zum Rehabilitationserfolg und zur Prognostik. *Nervenarzt,* **50**, 366–378.

Corrigan, P.W. (1994) Social cue perception and intelligence in schizophrenia. *Schizophrenia Research,* **13**, 73–79.

Crow, T. J. (1985) The two-syndrome concept: Origins and current status. *Psychological Bulletin,* **11**, 471–486.

Cuesta, M. J. & Peralta, V. (1995) Psychopathological dimensions in schizophrenia. *Schizophrenia Bulletin,* **21**, 473–482.

Dauwalder, H. P., Ciompi, L. & Ague, C. (1978) Prognostische Indikatoren, Mediatorensystem und Kontingenzmanagement in der Rehabilitation psychisch Kranker. In *Verhaltenstherapie in der psychosozialen Versorgung* (Eds. Deutsche Gesellschaft für Verhaltenstherapie e.V.), pp. 196–207. Mitteilungen der DGVT, Sonderheft II.

Dauwalder, H. P. & Hoffmann, H. (1992) Chronic psychoses and rehabilitation – an ecological perspective. *Psychopathology,* **25**, 139–146.

Deusinger, I. (1986) *Die Frankfurter Selbstkonzeptskalen.* Göttingen: Hogrefe.

Dickerson, F. B., Ringel, N. B. & Boronow, J. J. (1991) Neuropsychological deficits in chronic schizophrenics. Relationship with symptoms and behavior. *Journal of Nervous & Mental Disease,* **179**, 744–749.

Distefano, M. K. & Pryer, M. W. (1970) Vocational evaluation and successful placement of psychiatric clients in a vocational rehabilitation program. *Americal Journal of Occupational Therapy,* **24**, 205–207.

Drake, R. E, Becker, D. R., Xie H. & Anthony W. A. (1995) Barriers in the brokered model of supported employment for persons with psychiatric disabilities. *Vocational Rehabilitation,* **5**, 141–149.

Drake, R. E., McHugo, G. J., Becker, D. R., et al. (1996) The New Hampshire study of supported employment for people with severe mental illness. *Journal of Consulting & Clinical Psychology,* **64**, 391–399.

Fabian, E. (1992) Longitudinal outcomes in supported employment: A survival analysis. *Rehabilitation Psychology,* **37**, 23–35.

Fenton, W. S. & McGlashan, T. H. (1994) Antecedents, symptom progression, and long-term outcome of the deficit syndrome in schizophrenia. *American Journal of Psychiatry,* **151**, 351–356.

Flemming, J. S. & Spooner, P. S. (1985) Five factor scales for I-E control and their relations to measures of adjustment. *Journal of Clinical Psychology,* **41**, 512–517.

Gmür, M. (1987) *Die Prognose der Schizophrenie unter sozialpsychiatrischer Behandlung. Langjährige Katamnese von Nachtklinik- und Klinikpatienten.* Stuttgart: Enke-Verlag.

Goodman, S. H., Cooley, E. L., Sewell, D. R. & Leavitt, N. (1994) Locus of control and self-esteem in depressed, low-income African-American women. *Journal of Community Mental Health,* **30**, 259–269.

Green, H. J., Miskimins, R. W. & Keil, E. C. (1968) Selection of psychiatric patients for vocational rehabilitation. *Rehabilitation Counseling Bulletin,* **11**, 297–302.

Green, M. F. (1996) What are the functional consequences of neurocognitive deficits in schizophrenia? *American Journal of Psychiatry,* **153**, 321–330.

Griffiths, R. D. P. (1974) Rehabilitation of chronic psychotic patients. *Psychological Medicine,* **4**, 316–325.

Halford, W. K. & Hayes, R. L. (1995) Social skills in schizophrenia: Assessing the relationship between social skills, psychopathology and community functioning. *Social & Psychiatric Epidemiology,* **30**, 14–19.

Harrow, M. & Ferrante, A. (1969) Locus of control in psychiatric patients. *Journal of Consulting & Clinical Psychology,* **33**, 582–589.

Hoffmann, H. (1999) Berufliche Integration in den allgemeinen Arbeitsmarkt – Ein realistisches Ziel für chronisch psychisch Kranke? *Psychiatrische Praxis,* **26**, 211–217.

Hoffmann, H. & Kupper, Z. (1996) Patient dynamics in early stages of vocational rehabilitation – A pilot study. *Comprehensive Psychiatry,* **37**, 216–221.

Hoffmann, H. & Kupper, Z. (1997a) PASS – Ein integratives Programm zur beruflichen Wiedereingliederung chronisch psychisch Kranker. In *Die Behandlung schizophrener Menschen – Integrative Therapiemodelle und ihre Wirksamkeit* (Eds. Dittmar, V., Klein, H. E. & Schön, D. S.), pp. 65–88. Regensburg: Roderer-Verlag.

Hoffmann, H. & Kupper, Z. (1997b) Relationships between social competence, psychopathology and work performance and their predictive value for vocational rehabilitation of schizophrenic outpatients. *Schizophrenia Research,* **23**, 69–79.

Hoffmann, H. & Kupper, Z. & Kunz, B. (1998a) Predicting schizophrenic outpatients' be-

243

havior by symptomatology and social skills. *Journal of Nervous & Mental Disease*, **186**, 214–222.

Hoffmann, H. & Kupper, Z. & Kunz, B. (1998b) The impact of "resignation" on rehabilitation outcome in schizophrenia – An exploratory study. *(submitted for publication)*.

Honigfeld, G. (1974) NOSIE-30: History and current status of its use in pharmacopsychiatric research. In *Psychological Measurements in Psychopharmacology* (Ed. Pichot, P.), pp. 238–263. Basel: Karger.

Honigfeld, G., Gillis, R. D. & Klett, C. J. (1986) Nurses' observation scale for inpatient evaluation. Skala zur Beobachtung stationärer Patienten durch das Pflegepersonal. In *Internationale Skalen für Psychiatrie* (Eds. Collegium Internationale Psychiatriae Scalarum). Weinheim: Beltz Test.

Iverson, G. L., Guirguis, M. & Green, P. (1998) Assessing intellectual functioning in persons with schizophrenia spectrum disorders using a seven subtest short form of the WAIS-R. *Schizophrenia Research*, **30**, 165–168.

Jackson, H. J., Minas, I. H., Burgess, P. M., et al. (1989a) Is social skills performance a correlate of schizophrenia subtypes? *Schizophrenia Research*, **2**, 301–309.

Jackson, H. J., Minas, I. H., Burgess, P. M., et al. (1989b) Negative symptoms and social skills performance in schizophrenia. *Schizophrenia Research*, **2**, 457–463.

Jacobs, H., Wissusik, D., Collier, R., et al. (1992) Correlations between psychiatric disabilities and vocational outcome. *Hospital and Community Psychiatry*, **43**, 365–369.

Jung, E., Krumm, B., Biehl, H., et al. (1989) DAS-M: Mannheimer Skala zur Einschätzung sozialer Behinderung. In *Internationale Skalen für Psychiatrie* (Eds. Collegium Internationale Psychiatriae Scalarum). Weinheim: Beltz Test.

Kay, S. R., Opler, L. A. & Fishbein, A. (1992) *Positive and Negative Syndrome Scale (PANSS) Rating Manual*. Toronto: Multihealth Systems.

Krampen, G. (1981) *IPC-Fragebogen zu Kontrollüberzeugungen*. Göttingen: Hofgrefe.

Krause, N. & Stryker, S. (1984) Stress and well-being: The buffering role and locus of control beliefs. *Social Science Medicine*, **18**, 783–790.

Kupper, Z. (1998) *Dynamische Modelle für chronische psychische Störungen*. Dissertation at the University of Fribourg *(submitted for publication)*.

Kupper, Z. & Hoffmann, H. (1995) The three months' crisis: Empirical investigation and simulation of the rehabilitation dynamics in chronic mental disorders. *Swiss Journal of Psychology*, **54**, 211–224.

Kupper, Z. & Hoffmann, H. (1996) Logical attractors: A Boolean approach to the dynamics of psychosis. In *Nonlinear Dynamics in Human Behavior. Studies of Nonlinear Phenomena in Life Sciences, Vol. 5*. (Eds. Sulis, W. & Combs, A.), pp. 296–318. Singapore: World Scientific Publishing.

Kupper, Z. & Hoffmann, H. (1998) The course of psychosocial rehabilitation: Patterns of response in a sample of schizophrenia patients *(submitted for publication)*.

Layton, C. (1985) The relationship between externality and general, non-psychotic psychiatric morbidity in normal males. *Perception and Motor Skills*, **61**, 746.

Lysaker, P. H. & Bell, M. D. (1995) Negative symptoms and vocational impairment in schizophrenia: Repeated measurements of work performance over six months. *Acta Psychiatrica Scandinavica*, **91**, 205–208.

Lysaker, P. H. & Bell, M. D. & Bioty, S. M. (1995) Cognitive deficits in schizophrenia. Prediction of symptom change for participators in work rehabilitation. *Journal of Nervous & Mental Disease*, **183**, 332–336.

Massel, H. K., Liberman, R. P., Mintz, J., et al. (1990) Evaluating the capacity to work of the mentally ill. *Psychiatry*, **53**, 31–43.

Mowbray, C. T., Bybee, D., Harris, S. N. & McCrohan, N. (1995) Predictors of work status and future work orientation in people with a psychiatric disability. *Psychiatric Rehabilitation Journal,* **19/2,** 17–28.

Mueser, K. T., Bellack, A. S., Morrison, R. L. & Wixted, J. T. (1990) Social competence in schizophrenia: Premorbid adjustment, social skill, and domains of functioning. *Journal of Psychiatric Research,* **24,** 51–63.

Pogue-Geile, M. F. & Harrow, M. (1985) Negative and positive symptoms in schizophrenia and depression: A follow-up. *Schizophrenia Bulletin,* **10,** 371–387.

Reker, Th., Eikelmann, B., Hagenbrock, M., et al. (1996) *Begleitende Hilfen im Arbeitsleben für psychisch Kranke und Behinderte.* Forschungsbericht 257, Sozialforschung. Bonn: Bundesministerium für Arbeit und Sozialordnung.

Rotter, J. B. (1966) Generalized expectancies for internal versus external control of reinforcement. *Psychological Monographs,* **80,** (1, Whole No. 609).

SAS Institute Inc. (1989) *SAS/STAT, User's Guide, Version 6, 4th edn.* Cary NC: SAS Institute Inc.

Seeman, M. & Evans, J. W. (1962) Alienation and learning in a hospital setting. *American Social Review,* **27,** 772–781.

Solinski, S., Jackson, H. J. & Bell, R. C. (1992) Prediction of employability in schizophrenic patients. *Schizophrenia Research,* **7,** 141–148.

Strauss, J. S. (1989). Subjective experiences of schizophrenia: Toward a new dynamic psychiatry. II. *Schizophrenia Bulletin,* **15,** 179–187.

Strauss, J. S. & Carpenter, W. T. (1972) The prediction of outcome in schizophrenia. Part I. Characteristics of outcome. *Archives of General Psychiatry,* **27,** 739–746.

Strauss, J. S. & Carpenter, W. T. (1974) The prediction of outcome in schizophrenia. Part II. Relationships between predictor and outcome variables. *Archives of General Psychiatry,* **31,** 37–42.

Strauss, J. S. & Carpenter, W. T. (1977) The prediction of outcome in schizophrenia. Part III. Five-year outcome and its predictors. *Archives of General Psychiatry,* **34,** 159–163.

Strauss, J. S. & Carpenter, W. T. & Bartko, J. J. (1974) The diagnosis and understanding of schizophrenia. Part III. Speculations on the process that underlies schizophrenic symptoms and signs. *Schizophrenia Bulletin,* **11,** 61–69.

Strickland, B. R. (1978) Internal-external expectancies and health-related behaviors. *Journal of Consulting & Clinical Psychology,* **46,** 1192–1211.

Tessler, R. C. & Manderscheid, R. W. (1982) Factors affecting adjustment to community living. *Hospital & Community Psychiatry,* **33,** 203–207.

Varkey, L. & Sathyavathi, K. (1984) Locus of control and other personality variables in psychotics. *Psychological Studies,* **29,** 83–87.

Wallace, C. J., Liberman, R. P., Mackain, S. J., et al. (1992) Effectiveness and replicability of modules for teaching social and instrumental skills to the severely mentally ill. *American Journal of Psychiatry,* **149,** 654–658.

Wallston, K. A. & Wallston, B. S. (1981) Health locus of control scales. In *Research with the Locus of Control Construct* (Ed. Lefcourt, H.), pp. 189–241, Volume 1, New York: Academic Press.

Wallston, K. A. & Wallston, B. S. (1982) Who is responsible for your health? The construct of health locus of control. In *Social Psychology of Health and Illness* (Eds. Sanders, G. & Suls, J.), pp. 65–95. Hillsdale: Lawrence Erlbaum.

Wechsler, D. (1964) *Die Messung der Intelligenz Erwachsener: Textband zum Hamburg-Wechsler-Intelligenztest für Erwachsene (HAWIE).* Bern: Huber.

Wehmeyer, M. L. (1994) Employment status and perceptions of control of adults with cognitive and developmental disabilities. *Research in Developmental Disabilities,* **15**, 119–131.

Weis, J. (1990) Die berufliche Wiedereingliederung psychisch Kranker – ein Literatur-überblick zur Erforschung und Evaluation der beruflichen Rehabilitation. *Psychiatrische Praxis*, **17**, 59–65.

Wilson, T. L., Berry, L. K. & Miskimins, W. R. (1969) An assessment of characteristics related to vocational success among restored psychiatric patients. *Vocational Guidance Quarterly*, **18**, 110–114.

# Author Index

Green, 49
Green, H.J. 226
Green, M.F. 88, 90, 91, 119, 237
Green, MF. 100
Griesinger, W. 199
Griffiths, R.D.P. 226
Grossmann, K.E. 21
Gruss, M. 19
Guenther, W. 6
Guthke, J. 89

Hafner, H. 165, 166, 171
Häfner, H. 7, 196
Hahlweg, K. 128
Hale, A. 34, 68, 70, 74
Halford, W.K. 238
Hallam, A. 210
Hallam, A.J. 215, 216
Hamers, J.H. 89
Hammer, M. 175
Hargreaves, W.A. 148
Harpham, T. 171
Harrison, G. 173
Harrow, M. 238
Haywood, T.W. 137
Heaton, R.K. 90, 91
Hecht, H. 128
Hegarty, J.P. 198
Helgason, T. 155
Hellerstein, D.J. 138
Hemsley, D.R. 14
Henn, F.A. 3, 7, 17
Herbert, D.F. 159
Heresco-Levy, U. 8
Heubrock, D. 93
Hodel, B. 121, 124, 127
Hofer, H. 63
Hoff, A.L. 55, 58
Hoffmann, H. 225, 226, 227, 230, 231,
    238, 239, 240
Hogarty, G.E. 199
Hollingshead, A.B. 170
Holloway, F. 181, 203
Honigfeld, G. 229
Horn, J.L. 145
Huang, W. 118

Iverson, G.L. 237

Jablensky, A. 12, 165, 169, 172, 173, 196
Jackson, H.J. 238, 239
Jaco, E.G. 170
Jacobs, H. 226, 237
Jacobs, H.E. 118
Janke, W. 128
Jarman, B. 217
Johnson, S. 222
Johnstone, E.C. 4
Jones, P. 13, 20, 21
Jung, E. 229

Kane, 61
Kanter, J.S. 181
Kapur, S. 62
Kay, S.R. 228
Keatinge, C. 155
Kemp, R. 133
Kern, R.S. 106
Killian, G.A. 51
Kim, J.S. 8
Klinkenberg, W.D. 206
Kluiter, H. 206
Klusmann, D. 158
Knapp, M.R.J. 218
Köhler, L. 20
Kohn, M.L. 171
Kopala, L.C. 62
Kornetsky, 51
Knobloch, H. 169
Krampen, G. 128
Krause, N. 238
Kröner, S. 15
Krystal, J.E. 39
Kunz, B. 225
Kupper, Z. 225, 226, 229, 230, 237

Lahti, A.C. 61
Lamb, H.R. 137
Lapouse, R. 158
Lawrence, J.E.S. 170
Layton, C. 238
Lee, M.A. 42, 54, 56, 58
Leff, J. 213, 216

# Subject Index